# THE CRIMEAN WAR

# THE CRIMEAN WAR

## *A Reappraisal*

Philip Warner

WORDSWORTH EDITIONS

## Acknowledgements

I would like to express my gratitude to Mrs Elizabeth de Clermont and to Mrs Georgina Mayne who very kindly lent me the letters of their ancestor, Captain Temple Godman; also to Mr James Ashley Nasmyth who very kindly lent me the letters of his ancestor, Captain G. A. Maude.





This edition published 2001
by Wordsworth Editions Limited
Cumberland House, Crib Street, Ware,
Hertfordshire SG12 9ET

ISBN 1 84022 247 6





Printed and bound in Great Britain
by Mackays of Chatham plc, Chatham, Kent.

# Contents

# Foreword

For just over a hundred years the Crimean War has been presented to the public as the classic model of military and medical blundering. Military inefficiency is felt to have been slightly redeemed by the glamour of the Charge of the Light Brigade, and medical chaos made acceptable by the subsequent achievements of Florence Nightingale. The facts that the Allies won a war against extremely tough opponents, that at the end of it the British Army had reached a very high pitch of efficiency, and that the campaign was one of extreme difficulty, are glossed over or completely ignored. Equally unbalanced is the criticism of the medical side. In the light of the knowledge of the day, and the absence of drugs which would have cured or alleviated disease, the second year of the Crimean War might well have been thought to be something of an achievement. But the saying 'Give a dog a bad name and hang it' applies as well to a campaign or general, as to anything else. Once the Crimean War had become the subject of highly emotional condemnation there was no checking the flood. Military writers themselves joined in the general denigration of all and sundry. This is not so surprising as it may seem, for military men who are unable to win glory (or be defeated) in present battles are much given to refighting the battles of the past, which they do with much greater success than those who were actually present. Equally full of martial spirit, strategic foresight and tactical ability are critics who have never heard a shot fired in war, never endured hunger, thirst, heat, or cold, and never commanded anyone, in war or peace, in their entire lives. There are of course many activities where the onlooker may see most of the game, where it is not necessary to be a performer in order to be a good reporter, and where a detached view may give a better perspective; warfare, however, is not one of them. At the moment of writing, the history of the First World War is being written about by many historians who were not born till long after it finished. They find its generals sadly lacking in the art of war and do not pause to consider that if every one of the nations involved fought the war in much the same way it is possible that that was because of the prevalent ideas on war and the situation at the time. Even those who criticized got on with it and fought. Times and attitudes had changed by the Second World War but this fact did not mean that the First World War could have been very different, nor the Crimean War, nor, for that matter, the Norman Conquest.

However, although there is too much condescending hindsight in military history, writers nowadays show increasing skill in tracing and collecting contemporary accounts. Fortunately publishers seem keen to publish—and the public to read—letters and diaries written on campaigns. Once this process starts, material turns up from all sorts of unexpected places. These letters and diaries, carefully treasured by the writers' families for purely sentimental reasons, now throw an entirely different light on many campaigns. There are, in fact, an astonishing number on the Crimea. The explanation is probably that this was the first overseas campaign when fairly large numbers of those involved were able to read and write; it was brief, intense, and far away, therefore romantic even if horrible—and the written material would have been kept rather than destroyed; the quantity was small enough to keep—although large in the aggregate —and was therefore not destroyed in someone's zealous spring-cleaning, as were so many letters from the trenches. There are probably other reasons for the survival of many Crimean records—that people put letters in lofts, did not change houses so frequently, did not live in flats, had more cupboards with drawers, and were not so deluged with reading material as today.

Reading contemporary accounts brings home the fact that of any battle or campaign there are at least four different versions. One is that of those who fought in it, two is of the generals who commanded in it, three is of those who reported on it at the time and made what they could of a mass of confused and often misleading information, and four is the version of those who had a theory about it and reported those facts which happened to fit the version they were trying to portray. Of all these sources the first and second are the ones which are given least credence because their authors are probably unskilled in literary matters. But for the historian they are the only source of value.

Information about battles prior to the Crimea was limited, but what is known scarcely suggests that they were more humane. The agonies of battles like Towton, Naseby, Blenheim, Austerlitz, to name but a few, were considerable. Medieval battles left most of the participants with painful holes and gashes from which recovery would be slow and the effects lasting. The badly wounded would be fortunate if someone finished them off swiftly, instead of merely robbing and mutilating them. Casualties from disease, starvation and exposure do not shock us because no one troubled to record their numbers, let alone the harrowing details. But when the Crimea came there was an entirely different situation. War correspondents, observers and even wives, were able to wander freely around the battlefield and record the astonishing fact that when wars came men died, were killed, were wounded and suffered. These points are more easily seen than the gains of a campaign and therefore were faithfully and dramatically recorded.

It would seem from their accounts that the Crimean War was the most mismanaged, brutal and futile campaign that has ever been fought. Yet probably the majority of battles fought before it had been worse and a number of those fought since have been as bad. But in most of those battles the men on the battlefield were accustomed to the horrors of war, and were hardened. They would not record details—these were no different from any other fight. Although leaving the record to the fighting men or letting correspondents roam freely does not give a true picture, in this book, by examining the contemporary accounts and weighing the incidents in the light of general conditions at the time, it is hoped to present a fair version of the events. This does not mean that the grimmer details will be omitted but it does mean that they will be seen in proportion to a harsh and tough age. For example, much is made of the lack of medical care available to men suffering from cholera in the Crimea but one doubts whether their plight was worse than those suffering from the same illness in Birmingham in 1849, and certainly they were better off than those dying of the same disease in Thailand in 1943. War is a grim business and suffering is endemic.

The plan of this book therefore is to describe the events of the war from the causes to the end, in chronological sequence, interpolating the account with contemporary views many of which have never before been published. Periodically an attempt will be made to put events in perspective. For example, it was doubtless ridiculous to appoint a man as old and sick as Lord Raglan to the post of commander-in-chief, but older and sicker men than he have held command successfully and many modern but more aged statesmen have apparently been quite capable of much more onerous assignments. Cardigan's entire behaviour, even when leading the famous charge, was clearly unbalanced, but if a nation once embarks on the madness of war it needs madmen to win it—or men who can become so unbalanced that their sense of self-preservation is entirely subordinated to showing no sign of fear in the most exacting circumstances. And if Cardigan was unbalanced he was not alone in military history. Any soldier in any army (or navy, or air force) will doubtless recall at least one officer who would have been capable of leading the Charge of the Light Brigade. Many of that type did not survive, and of those who did not much is recorded, for the men who had the dubious fortune to be present at the time were scarcely in the position to recommend the brave (and perhaps foolhardy) officer for a VC.

Soldiers' reminiscences when talking among themselves seldom dwell on heroic actions—these heart-stirring accounts are usually reserved for an audience of non-combatants. Soldiers tend to dwell on administrative chaos which usually occurs whether there is an enemy to be fought or not.

In the Crimea once one blunder had been made a number of others were bound to follow. It is interesting to isolate the blunders which caused other blunders because the first were possibly preventable but the second not. Any allotment of praise or blame should take this into account. Soldiers' reminiscences have this great virtue: they usually know where the initial mistake lay and rarely apportion blame for subsequent disasters which stem from it. And at least their views are first-hand.

# 1
# The Causes of the War

There are still memorials to the dead of the Crimean War in different parts of the United Kingdom. There is one, for example, in the middle of Carmarthen, on which the names of many hundred soldiers from the Royal Welsh Fusiliers are commemorated; there is another in London's Lower Regent Street to the Guards. Doubtless, like most soldiers in most wars, they had little idea of what they were fighting for. Sadly enough, in retrospect, we can understand the causes without really being able to justify the reasons.

The real causes were simple enough. Britain had an empire stretching round the world. One of its most valued parts was India. If any country threatened the line of communication through the Middle East that country must be checked.

Russia too had an empire, a huge sprawling land empire of some eight million square miles. Russia in fact was less a country than a conglomerate of countries and peoples. However, the looseness and backwardness of their territories did not stop the Russians from wishing to extend their influence.

France also had ambitions, and like the other countries was mesmerized by the importance of the Middle East.

Unfortunately there was considerable scope for ambitious countries in that area. Turkey, which had once ruled vast territories by a system in which terrorism alternated with neglect and inefficiency, was now feeble and in a state of general disorganization. Nevertheless she still maintained a ramshackle empire that contained some European countries. Twenty years before, Greece had wrested independence in a war that had attracted the attention and assistance of European powers. The danger from Turkey lay in her weakness which encouraged the ambitions and aroused the apprehensions of other powers. It was a curious situation with statesmen manoeuvring watchfully, doubting whether to make a move but only too ready to take alarm or react hastily to frustrate the ambitions of others. Such times are fraught with danger, for what one country thought was a justified precaution might well be interpreted by another as being an act of blatant aggression.

Had the Great Powers been blessed with far-seeing and prudent diplomats all might have been well. However, the Tsar Nicholas I had the sort of personality that goads others into precipitous action. His view of Turkey was expressed in the famous words, 'We have on our hands a very sick man', to which he added recommendations as to how the sick man's property should be disposed of. Turkey was not to be consulted. The Tsar hoped to win British approval by helping Britain to acquire Egypt but seemed unaware that Britain was not prepared to achieve this ambition at the cost of dismembering Turkey. This care for the preservation of Turkish integrity was ardently fostered by the British Ambassador to Turkey, Lord Stratford de Redcliffe, who felt that his country's interests would best be served by the preservation of Turkish territorial unity and the consequent frustration of Russian aims. His ardent espousal of the Turkish cause undoubtedly influenced Britain to concede less than it might otherwise have been disposed to do.

France's interest in the Middle East was as materialistic as everyone else's but the French were in a very strong position morally as the protectors of the Latin Church in the East. The 'Latin Church' was the Roman Catholic Church and the French had held this official position for just over one hundred years. Equally, however, the Russians considered themselves protectors of the Orthodox (Greek) Church. This protective attitude had a slightly hollow ring to the other powers, for the time of greatest need was now past and when the need had been there no one had shown much intention or ability to exercise protection. When the Turks had captured Constantinople (Byzantium) and adjoining lands in the fifteenth century they had brought the Moslem religion with them. The Turks had treated the Christian religion with such scanty respect that they had raised a formidable regular fighting force from circumcised Christian children. Constantinople had been an eastern Rome and the fate of its religious adherents had been extremely unpleasant. In subsequent centuries the lot of a Christian in Turkish-controlled territory had been difficult and dangerous, but it was only when

Turkey fell into decline that other powers found their consciences, and probably alertness to opportunity, aroused. However, quite apart from the statesmen of the Great Powers, whose attitude seldom seemed to stray far from the path of self-interest, there were Christians who were greatly concerned. Many of these wished to see the famous Holy Places in Palestine, and would make pilgrimages to do so. The Holy Places were cared for by priests of the Roman Catholic Church or the Greek Orthodox Church and there was constant friction as to what should be cared for by whom; the key to the main door to the Church of the Nativity in Bethlehem was felt by each side to be its own inalienable right. Eventually it was decided by French pressure and a compliant Pasha that the Roman Catholics should have this honour. The Greek Orthodox Church was disappointed but the main effect was on the Tsar of Russia who felt he had lost face. The dispute may in itself have been a trivial one but it is the effect of such reverses that cause otherwise intelligent men to make hasty decisions that may make thousands die in bloody and futile battles.

The Tsar has frequently been criticized for what appeared to be consistent stupidity and obstinacy. But there can be no doubt that he was sincere. In describing Turkey as 'the sick man of Europe' this was what he felt. Turkey was in decline and Turkey would soon disintegrate. Only a madman could ignore the fact that when Turkey broke up some vital strategic prizes would be available. The Tsar wished to ensure that Russia would gain as much as anybody else—and preferably more. He was in no way soothed by the fact that the French seemed to be gaining advantages without a break-up and that Britain was apparently happy to preserve the *status quo* for as long as possible. An added irritation was the personality of Lord Stratford de Redcliffe. He was a person of great gifts, wide influence, and an implacable determination to thwart the plans of the Tsar. The Russians had no doubts about the resolution of British diplomacy but were less sure of Britain's ability or desire to back it by the necessary force. There was much talk of universal peace in England in the mid-nineteenth century. The views of liberalism and retreat from imperial responsibility were freely expressed.

When the Great International Exhibition of 1851 was opened in Hyde Park it was thought by many to herald the dawn of an era of universal peace. Disputes might still occur but they would be settled by amiable discussion. Such views would be heard later, and mislead the Kaiser in 1914 and Hitler and Mussolini in 1939, and they were naturally enough interpreted by the Tsar as betokening a weakening of British drive. And as he must have been well aware of the sad state to which the British Army had been allowed to decline, his viewpoint can hardly be wondered at. As so often happens, the Tsar, feeling himself impeded and frustrated, began to wonder whether his rivals were mocking him. The situation seemed to call for a show of strength.

The decisive move which the Tsar subsequently made was probably not what he had intended in the first place. But his arch enemy Lord Stratford de Redcliffe was apparently at the point of retiring (he had actually resigned) and Colonel Rose (later to be a field marshal) was acting in his absence. Lord de Redcliffe was being prevailed upon to return but meanwhile the Tsar had decided that Prince Menschikov, who shared his views on the British Ambassador, should go to Turkey as a special envoy; it was hoped that the Prince's powerful personality would offset the evil influence of the English lord. Menschikov arrived in considerable style, accompanied by high-ranking Russian officers. This move on the part of the Russians, signifying as it did the intention and ability to follow words with force, cowed the Sultan. Colonel Rose knew the Turks were overawed and therefore suggested that the British fleet at Malta should sail towards the Dardanelles. This would perhaps have been asking for trouble, but the fact that the request had been made, and the Turks knew it, restored Turkish confidence. The French had in fact been prepared to move, which was considerably more than could be said for the British. Curiously enough, British action in restraining the French move had a positive effect on the situation; the Tsar realized that the Powers were not at the brink of war and the Russians were seen to be not so much belligerent as merely actively interested and wishing to show it. However, the Russian proposal to protect the Greek Orthodox Church, backed by a large Russian land and naval force, could well have been interpreted as being forceful. De Redcliffe was, of course, quite capable of dealing with the Russian proposal, and having secured his position with the Government, which was prepared to give him full support from the Army and Navy, encouraged the Sultan to state that the Russian proposals would infringe his sovereign rights but that he would ensure that if there were grievances on the part of his Christian subjects these would be investigated promptly, and rapidly redressed. The Turks were now espousing the very cause for which they had previously been attacked. Sometimes one can be too clever diplomatically. Menschikov was no fool, and was not prepared to look like one, so he broke off negotiations. De Redcliffe promptly called a conference of the French, German and Austrian representatives who felt that the Turkish reply was eminently suitable in the circumstances. Menschikov thought it over, and would have accepted a note rather than a treaty, but the Turks, confident of widespread support refused to agree (20 May 1853). Menschikov promptly returned to St Petersburg (present-day Leningrad) leaving the Turks to think it over, and perhaps change their minds.

During the next ten days the Crimean War could have been averted had the other powers shown any desire to use diplomatic approaches to reach a compromise. Nothing was done and the Russians quietly boiled with indignation until 31 May when they delivered a form of ultimatum to the Turks, stating that the Turks must agree or Russian troops would invade their territories. This forceful statement goaded the other powers into some diplomatic action. Britain, for her part, sent her fleet to Besika Bay near the mouth of the Dardanelles.

Nowadays, when much thought is given to interpreting the possible intentions of the Russians—and those of other countries too—it should surprise no one that the following month was unproductive. It was generally assumed that the Tsar, having been given a sharp warning, would abandon his ambitions and accept diplomatic defeat over Turkey. Even at the time it should have been realized that the Tsar and his generals were desperately in earnest. If Russia was ever to be an effective world power it had to have the freedom of the Black Sea, Bosphorus and Dardanelles. St Petersburg in the far north, and Vladivostok some seven thousand miles to the east could never be substitutes. It was not a new ambition and the Western powers should not have been surprised at what happened next—although they undoubtedly were.

The next Russian move had a semblance of legality, though no one could easily mistake its real purpose. In 1774 after a six years' war with Turkey the Russians had signed the Treaty of Kutchuk-Kainardji. This gave Russia valuable concessions and rights around the north of the Black Sea, and recognized her as the protector of the members of the Greek Orthodox Church in Turkey—a total of some fourteen million people. Among its provisions was one which stated that Russia had rights and interests in Moldavia and Wallachia (which are now part of Romania). These principalities lay north of the Danube and it was tacitly understood that the Russians could 'restore order' if necessary.

If wars can easily be caused by treaties being too rigid they can be caused even more easily by treaties being too loose. The Tsar knew perfectly well that he was entitled to take measures to stabilize Moldavia and Wallachia, and was equally aware that the right could be abused to further imperial ambitions. Consequently on 2 July 1853 Russian troops crossed the River Pruth and invaded Moldavia and Wallachia. They were, of course, taking appropriate precautions to preserve law and order, and this move could not in itself be deemed an act of war however embarrassing it might be to the Western powers. The Tsar, who had given the order personally, no doubt studied its effect to see the strength of the reaction.

It was not particularly strong. The British prime minister was Lord Aberdeen, a man of great integrity but a little too inclined to believe that the motives of others were as pure as his own; the Home Secretary was Lord Palmerston—whose view of the human nature of foreigners was diametrically opposed to that of Lord Aberdeen. The result was disharmony in the British policy-making, giving possible opponents the impression that Britain was in no mood to act, and that if she did it would not be effectively.

Equally aware of the vacillations at home was de Redcliffe, who was an expert on the Eastern mind, and a keen opponent of Russian ambitions in Turkey. He spared no effort to spur his country into positive action which might well be war. The Tsar somewhat under-rating both de Redcliffe and British resolve, felt that Britain was going through a pacifist phase and was unlikely to use force. He was in no way impressed with the French Emperor who, in fact, had a great deal to gain from a short successful war; it would divert attention from the arbitrary manner in which he had seized power, and would help to stabilize the country through a united effort.

Although the Russian occupation of Moldavia and Wallachia could be justified on treaty grounds the Turks did not see it that way and promptly declared war. The Russian response was to maintain an attitude of quiet dignity as long as it was possible. It was not possible for long, for elements of the Turkish Army moved up to the Danube and harassed the Russian outposts. There was one serious engagement in which the Russians were undoubtedly worsted. These incidents, for which the Turks can scarcely be blamed, made war inevitable, for they hardened the Russian resolve to achieve a victory and wipe off all these petty humiliations and reverses; they also made it impossible for Russia to withdraw. Equally, another event on a larger scale made it impossible for the Allies to accept the situation without betraying Turkey. That occasion was the destruction of the Turkish fleet at Sinope on 30 November 1853.

Since the declaration of war the Turks had been free to allow foreign warships through the Dardanelles for they were no longer bound by treaty obligations to the Russians. The Allied fleets were, in consequence, in the Sea of Marmora. The Russians, however, were dominant in the Black Sea where they had already scored a few minor successes against the Turks. This was not particularly difficult, for the Turkish Navy was notably inefficient. The Allies should of course have been in the Black Sea to police the area—they had clear instructions on this point—but were not. The Russians demonstrated on several occasions in front of Sinope, without stimulating the Allies into counter-action. Not surprisingly, the Russians decided to venture further. On 30 November they delivered a full-scale attack on Sinope where the Turkish fleet was anchored. The Turks fought with great gallantry but their entire fleet was destroyed by the Russians who gave no quarter—perhaps because they were not asked to do so. The entire Turkish fleet was destroyed, a mere four hundred out of four thousand surviving. It was a disaster for Turkey and a humiliation for British and French sea power.

Surprisingly enough this disastrous event did not goad the Allies into serious action. The stalemate continued until the following March. There was of course, little hope of avoiding a major conflict, but while the Tsar was making considerable efforts to gather an army the Allies produced no corresponding reaction. Finally in March 1854 the British foreign secretary, Lord Clarendon, sent a note supported by similar declarations from France and Austria, that unless the Russians evacuated or agreed to evacuate, Moldavia and Wallachia by 30 April 1854 their countries would be at war. However, they did not need to wait till April; by 19 March the Russians had declared they had no intention of complying. In consequence Britain and France declared war nine days later. They were not at this point formally in alliance but soon became so by a treaty signed on 11 April 1854. All this, although scarcely a rapid and satisfactory response to an honourable obligation, was at least progress; effectually however, it was purely a paper transaction. The Russians were on the Danube and ready to cross it, their fleet had destroyed Turkish sea power—such as it was. All that remained was for the Allies to deliver short, sharp punishment. The decision had been taken. Now was the time to implement it. As usual the Government turned to the Army and expected them to produce an impressive expeditionary force which would win a rapid but inexpensive victory.

# 2
# The Military Background

The British Army has a long experience of being asked to produce the impossible at short notice but the situation it was faced with in April 1854 exceeded all others in difficulty. The chief problem was not in overcoming the enemy but in confronting him with a force in any way related to Britain's potential, for since 1815 the Army had been run down and scandalously neglected. The brilliant armies that had won victories over Napoleon were now destroyed. The rot extended from top to bottom.

At the top there was a remarkably inefficient system of control. The Army was the responsibility of the Secretary of State for War and the Colonies, it being assumed that these two responsibilities were likely to go hand in hand. He was assisted by the Secretary-at-War, who conveyed the government's wishes to the Commander-in-Chief of the Army, a general whose headquarters was the Horse Guards.

Unfortunately this organization was completely divorced from that of the Master General of the Ordnance, who was not a soldier as might have been expected, but a Member of Parliament. He controlled the entire production of all forms of military equipment, including weapons, the supply of food to troops stationed at home and the engineers and artillery. This organization would have been sensible had it been properly linked to the Commander-in-Chief. It was efficient for engineers and artillery to come under the command of the department which could understand and supply their needs but not if it caused divided command at the top. Another peculiar department was the Commissariat which was responsible for feeding troops abroad, and which came under the Treasury—not an arrangement, one would feel, likely to be conducive to a good and varied diet. Another dependent organization was the Army Medical Board.

These arrangements reflected the concern of a democratic country, which had some experience and fear of autocrats, to safeguard itself from the danger of its armed forces being taken over in a *coup d'état*, and used against the will of the people.

In a period of continuous, or not too distant war, these arrangements could work reasonably satisfactorily. What they could not stand was the thirty-nine years of neglect and economy that had followed the Napoleonic campaigns. When later we read of the administrative chaos in medical arrangements, feeding, supply and transport, to name but a few, they become understandable if not excusable in the light of the decentralized higher command. Small wonder vital stores were left unloaded. Nobody in authority knew they were there or troubled to find out. Two essential and proved units had been abolished after the end of the Napoleonic Wars. They were the Waggon Train and the Staff Corps. Had they remained in existence the entire story of the Crimea would have been different. Both had been created in order to meet a vital need in the wars against the French. The Royal Waggon Train had ably conveyed supplies to wherever they were needed and served as an ambulance corps after battles. Fortescue states that the Waggon Train worked for sixty hours after the Battle of Waterloo. The Staff Corps was the nucleus of a staff college and studied the problems of the day. It would have saved endless time and agony in the Crimea.

The neglect and mismanagement of the Army between Waterloo and the beginning of the Crimean War is a remarkable, even if disgraceful, story. Yet in spite of its hardships and inefficiencies the Army managed to win a series of campaigns beginning with Ceylon in 1818 and continuing through wars in Burma, northern India, China, Afghanistan, South Africa and New Zealand to the First Sikh War which lasted from 1845 to 1849.

The process of rapid demobilization had begun very soon after the Battle of Waterloo. The country was in severe financial difficulty, money had depreciated during the previous twenty years, and there was a rapidly rising number of jobless and discontented citizens. In 1816 the Army had been reduced to 225,000 of whom 35,000 formed the army of occupation in France. Wellington had personally insisted that five troops of the Waggon Train should be kept to serve them. There were another 35,000 in Ireland and another 35,000 in India; the remainder—with the exception of the home garrison—were thinly spread trying to occupy the newly won territories. South Africa—to which the British had originally been invited by the Dutch who knew the French had overrun their homeland—was finally secured to the British Empire by an outright cash payment. However it would be many years before it ceased to be a drain on British resources and became an asset.

Three years later the Army had been reduced by half but even the most economy-conscious government could not convince itself that a figure of less than 120,000 was sufficient for the many tasks the Army was called upon to perform, which, until 1829, included that of serving as a home police force.

These numbers would have been considerably more appropriate had the soldiers been adequately fed, equipped, housed and cared for. But in no case was this so. Accommodation was overcrowded, unventilated, unsuitable and thoroughly unhealthy, yet there was vigorous opposition to the building of fresh barracks. Conditions were rarely better abroad than they were at home. A soldier was lucky if he had 300 cubic feet of air. Until 1827 soldiers slept in fours in wooden cribs but after that date they were the proud possessors of an iron bedstead each. The soldiers were, of course, extremely verminous and for that reason less efficient. Clothing was picturesque but unserviceable. In pattern and material it was cold in winter and oppressive in summer. Very little regard was paid to the temperature of the station at which the soldier was serving. In Canada, however, he was allowed to buy himself gloves—if he had the money. The soldier was at a considerable disadvantage in bad climates for he was expected to wear his uniform but nothing else in extremes of temperature. His civilian counterpart could muffle himself up with rags or discard clothing as he wished, but not so the soldier. Food was poor and monotonous. The daily ration was allegedly one pound of bread and three-quarters of a pound of beef a day but in practice the soldier was served with a beef broth of stringy meat, and potatoes. Sometimes he received a change in the form of salt pork but this was only issued because it was going 'off'. This spartan diet was served at 7.30 am and 12.30 pm. There was no provision for any food between 12.30 and the following day. Doubtless many soldiers acquired food, particularly vegetables, illegally, but the system which made this necessary was a rotten one.

There was virtually nothing in the way of amusement—though

the Guards occasionally played a brand of football. The ever-present temptation was drink, of which the strongest and most deadly varieties were the cheapest. Wholesome drinks like beer were put out of the soldier's reach by taxation whereas raw spirits were not only cheap but readily available because they were served in the regimental canteen run by profiteering civilian contractors. It was all too easy to set out to forget one's sorrows with a few drinks and to finish up in a brawl, and consequent severe punishment. Heavy drinking was not, of course, confined to the Army but characterized all levels of society.

The soldier was wretchedly paid and most of what he had went on drink; the officer, in spite of having purchased his commission, was by no means well off either. Commissions had originally been well worth the purchase money because the share out of captured goods gave a very fair return on the investment. But by the early nineteenth century they offered a very poor return for the investment because there were too many officers and too little to share. The return therefore came from pay, and was by no means satisfactory. In some regiments the constant changes of expensive uniform meant that a large private income was essential. To make matters even less efficient there was considerable jealousy and snobbery, which led to prejudice against the more experienced and efficient officers, many of whom had fought abroad.

Clearly, any army is scarcely likely to be effective without a first-class commander-in-chief. During the Napoleonic wars the Duke of Wellington had become a figure of legendary, but obviously well-deserved, respect. Unfortunately the very greatness of his reputation caused a fossilization in military thought; what was good enough for the Duke to beat Napoleon must be good for ever. When he died in 1852 there was little hesitation as to who should succeed him: it must be Lord Raglan. Although Raglan had had no experience of commanding troops in action he had been on the battlefield on several occasions and had, in fact, lost his right arm at Waterloo. He is said to have behaved with extraordinary and nonchalant bravery on that occasion for when the amputated arm was being taken away he suddenly asked for it to be brought back so that he could remove a ring from the finger. The episode may denote great courage, great concentration, or, possibly, an amazing degree of insensitivity. He had served on the Duke's Staff, been secretary to the Master General of the Ordnance, and Secretary-at-War for some twenty-five years. Subsequently he had become Master General of the Ordnance. This, plus a quiet but effective personality, should have made him an outstanding commander. But men must be judged by the events they control and although there have been many who have spoken highly of the qualities of Lord Raglan as a commander the sequence of the Crimean War hardly supports them. It seems that on more than one occasion he nearly resigned his military appointments as a protest against the economies being effected at the time; resignation is a weak form of protest which usually leaves a vacancy to be filled by a less-principled person, but to think of resigning and not do so but accept things as they are is not the mark of a great commander. To add to all this Raglan was now an elderly man—sixty-six is hardly an age for service on the battlefield. Menschikov was in fact a little older. Significantly, one of the most successful people was one of the youngest—Franz Todleben. In general the British Army in the Crimea was commanded by men who were far too old for active service. The Light Division was commanded by Sir George Brown* who had fought with distinction in the Peninsula—nearly half a century before, as had Sir de Lacy Evans, the Commander of the Second Division; Sir George Cathcart had also fought in the Napoleonic wars. The First Division was commanded by the Duke of Cambridge and the Third by Sir George England. All were therefore well past their first youth but the first three compensated for this by proved ability throughout their careers. The chief engineer, Sir John Burgoyne, was seventy-two, but his skill and experience of seige works and defences were irreplaceable. Other military figures of whom more would be heard later were Brigadier-General Airey, the quartermaster-general, with considerable operational influence, Brigadier Colin Campbell, who would win distinction at Balaclava, and General Scarlett who was the outstanding figure in the cavalry division (which was commanded by Lord Lucan and also contained the Earl of Cardigan). The naval contingent was commanded by Vice-Admiral Dundas, a capable but not very experienced sailor; second-in-command was Rear Admiral Sir Edmund Lyons, who subsequently enhanced an already distinguished reputation.

* He had strong views about hair: 'Where there's hair there's dirt, and where there's dirt there's disease!' but he was impressive at the Alma.

The French Army was commanded by Marshal St Arnaud. He appears to have been unpopular both with his own countrymen and with his allies. He died shortly after the Battle of the Alma and was succeeded by his second-in-command General Canrobert. Subsequently the French command passed to General Pélissier.

The British army which set out for the Crimea consisted of one cavalry and five infantry divisions, all of which were under strength, and also lacked essential transport and administrative services. Although the only physical standard required was that a man should be able 'to stand upright', years of strict parade-ground drill had made most of them steady, disciplined, and enduring in action. The soldiers' principal weapon was a Minié rifle. Although a muzzle-loader, like the Brown Bess which it had supplanted, it was a more penetrating and effective weapon. Unfortunately its possession was not limited to the British army; the French had them and so did the Russians. The French also had some breech-loaders. As will be seen later, in the description of the battlefield of the Alma, the Russians had a variety of weapons but few of them were very efficient.

Tactics were, of course, dictated by the range and fire of the weapons in all the armies, and as these did not vary significantly neither did the tactics. As a result, after a preliminary artillery duel the opposing forces moved so close to each other that every ball would find a target. Then, if there were no time to reload, it would be a matter of close quarters with the sword and bayonet. These tactics were practised on the parade ground and drill square and so modified that after a time the deployment of troops on the battlefield bore less relationship to the situation on the ground than what suited the drill book. Fieldcraft was rarely employed and there was undoubtedly much loss of life through its neglect; some regiments disdained to take cover, feeling that to do so would be bad for morale; others took the realistic view that once the regiment had scattered it would be almost impossible to get it back into formation again. Apart from drill the soldier in all armies spent much of his time maintaining his kit. Uniforms were designed for appearance rather than for practical use and the amount of cleaning and polishing was endless. This, of course, helped to keep the soldier out of mischief.

The harshest conditions of service were those endured by the Russians. The only exception was the Cossacks, who provided their own horses and arms and, as a skirmishing, foraging force, enjoyed considerable independence and a better standard of living than their fellows. The remainder were men who had not been adroit enough to avoid being called up for life. Astonishingly, they fought with courage, persistence and devotion in the extreme conditions of Sebastopol.

The Turks had more freedom than the Russians but their conditions and training were worse. As will be seen in Kars, they were not merely underpaid but simply unpaid. Nevertheless they too could fight like demons when given any good reason or a semblance of leadership.

The British Order of Battle was

FIRST DIVISION—*commanded by the Duke of Cambridge*

GUARDS BRIGADE (*Brig.-Gen. H. Bentinck*)
3rd Grenadiers
1st Coldstream
1st Scots Fusiliers

HIGHLAND BRIGADE (*Brig. Sir Colin Campbell*)
42nd Foot
79th Foot
93rd Foot
2 Fd Batteries

SECOND DIVISION—*commanded by Maj.-Gen. Sir de Lacy Evans*

1ST (RIGHT) BRIGADE (*Brig.-Gen. H. W. Adams*)
41st Foot
47th Foot
49th Foot

2ND (LEFT) BRIGADE (*Brig.-Gen. J. Pennefather*)
30th Foot
55th Foot
95th Foot
2 Fd Batteries

THIRD DIVISION—*commanded by Maj.-Gen. Sir Robert England*

1ST (RIGHT) BRIGADE (*Brig.-Gen. Sir J. Campbell*)
1st Foot
38th Foot
50th Foot

2ND (LEFT) BRIGADE (*Brig.-Sir W. Eyre*)
4th Foot
28th Foot
44th Foot
2 Fd Batteries

FOURTH DIVISION—*commanded by Maj.-Gen. Sir George Cathcart (killed at Inkerman)*

1ST (RIGHT) BRIGADE (*Brig. Torrens*)
20th Foot
21st Foot
57th Foot

2ND (LEFT) BRIGADE (*Brig. Goldie*)
46th Foot (2 Coys only)
63rd Foot
68th Foot
Div infantry, 1st Rifle Bde
2 Fd Batteries

LIGHT DIVISION—*commanded by Maj.-Gen. Sir George Brown*

1ST (RIGHT) BRIGADE (*Sir W. Codrington*)
7th Foot
23rd Foot
33rd Foot

2ND (LEFT) BRIGADE (*Brig.-Gen. G. Buller*)
19th Foot
77th Foot
88th Foot
Div Infantry, 2nd Rifle Brigade
1 Fd Battery 1 Troop horse artillery

CAVALRY DIVISION—*commanded by Lt.-Gen. Lord Lucan*

THE LIGHT BRIGADE (*Gen. the Earl of Cardigan*)
4th Light Dragoons
13th Light Dragoons
8th Hussars
11th Hussars
17th Lancers
1 Troop horse artillery

THE HEAVY BRIGADE (*Gen. the Hon. J. Scarlett*)
1st Dragoons (The Royals)
2nd Dragoons (The Scots Greys)
6th Dragoons (The Inniskillings)
4th Dragoon Guards
5th Dragoon Guards
1 Troop Divisional Horse artillery

The French divisions, four in number, were twice the size of the British, each having ten thousand men. The commanders were General Canrobert, General Bosquet, General Prince Louis Napoleon and General Forey. In addition they had eight and a half batteries of field artillery.

The Russian army was organized in three sectors under the commander-in-chief Prince Menschikov. The Right sector was commanded by General Kvetzinski, the Centre by General Gortschakoff, and the Left by General Kiriakoff.

# 3
# The Battle of the Alma

In warfare there are two main problems: one is the probable behaviour of the enemy, which is foreseeable and against which steps may be taken; the other is the behaviour of allies, which is utterly unpredictable as it does not have to conform to any set pattern.

The problem of allied co-operation began early in the Crimean campaign and continued throughout. A considerable factor was the fact that although the French were difficult allies they were extremely efficient, and won engagements both on the field and off it. They eventually outnumbered by nearly two to one the British force which, at the outset, only totalled twenty-six thousand. Marshal St Arnaud seemingly owed his position to the fact that he had backed Napoleon III in his *coup d'état.* His early career appears to have been erratic and wild. When appointed commander-in-chief he was already in very bad health, with attacks of severe pain, but this did not stop him trying to obtain control of the Turkish forces as a preliminary to becoming commander-in-chief of the entire Allied expeditionary force. Fortunately, Omar Pasha, the Turkish commander-in-chief, was a co-operative as well as able soldier; in consequence he was respected by Raglan and was not upset by—indeed got along very well with—Arnaud.

The war which now began took a predictable form in which strategy became an afterthought. It is easy to criticize from hindsight but the key to the miscalculations of the Crimean War was that nobody had any real idea of the appropriate strategy because nobody had any real idea of the enemy strength. The Russians had destroyed the Turkish fleet and their troops had made a cautious move which, if continued, would take them towards Constantinople. However, before they had done any harm on land the Turks had blocked their progress and with a few reinforcements could apparently do so indefinitely. Although Russian territory came close to the area, the probable battlefields were so far from the sources of supply—and the country in between was so difficult—that Russia would have immense difficulties in maintaining an offensive if the Turks put up a steady resistance. Because of the initial pattern of the war Allied troops were landed at Varna, in Bulgaria, on the western shores of the Black Sea, some three hundred miles from Sebastopol, which became the ultimate objective. To sit matters out at Varna however, and let time and weather bring the Russians to their knees was unthinkable, so a better and more spectacular strategy had to be devised. This was to attack the Crimean peninsula itself, notably the Russian naval base at Sebastopol. The latter was believed to be a formidable fortress but was of course no such thing, although, with the aid of time and a brilliant young engineer, it became one later. But it was thought—reasonably enough—that with possession of Sebastopol all Russian naval threats to Constantinople would be removed; and to make doubly sure that the Russian Navy would be suitably punished for its activities at Sinope other naval forces were sent to deal with the Russian Navy in the Baltic. If Sebastopol could be secured quickly the Allied forces could entertain themselves by watching the Russians—at a hideous disadvantage, with an enormously long line of communication—try to recapture it. If the Russians were prepared to stick obstinately at their task they might well exhaust themselves so much that they would be crippled militarily for years to come. It was an alluring thought but it did not turn out like that at all.

Disaster began from the very first days at Varna. The British force had embarked with no more preparation than a fortnight's camp at Chobham, Surrey, a place of desolate heathland that is still used as a training area; however this could hardly be accounted adequate preparation for a campaign in one of the most difficult areas in the West. However, individual regiments made their own preparation and practised with their arms. Had they not done so it would have been a sorry story but it did not, of course, compensate for the fact that there had been no adequate preparation for handling an army on the battlefield.

Some of the early arrivals, both British and French, landed and camped at Gallipoli; they were said (by an officer of the 55th, Hume) to have had a very hard time there. Others went to Scutari, where troops were reviewed by the Sultan of Turkey. They were paraded for inspection at 11 am and he arrived at 3 pm. Hume related:

> Varna was no paradise—a wretched place with very few shops. The French, as their usual custom was, had appropriated the best part of the town; they named the streets and established some cafés and shops where they sold champagne of sorts and excellent vermouth, which was described on the label as a 'cohite and a coholsome wine', a white and wholesome wine being meant.
>
> The heat in the camp was now rather trying. Upwards of 96° in our tents. Whenever there was a breeze, the dust was a caution.

Soon cholera broke out at Varna. Cholera is a waterborne infection and spreads with terrifying swiftness. A man may be alive and walking about, but dead, with his corpse being burnt, three or four hours later. Unfortunately for the army, corpses were not burnt at Varna and once water was contaminated the disease began to spread. However, not every case was fatal, nor did exposure invariably mean infection. Hume wrote:

> On 23 July we heard that the dreaded cholera had attacked the Light Division; there were several bad cases and some deaths. The Light and 1st Divisions suffered much, losing many men and some officers during the time they were encamped at Devna and Monastir. The 3rd Division near Varna and some of the cavalry regiments suffered a good deal. The 95th suffered severely, losing many men—I forget the exact number—at Yurksokova and Kosludshi. The 30th and 55th, although they were encamped close to the 95th, lost only a few men in Bulgaria from cholera—a proof, I think, that those regiments were acclimatized by being so long stationed at Gibraltar. . . . Everything was done by the officers to amuse the men: sports, cricket and racing were continually going on; early parades for drill, practising, entrenching, making gabions and fascines, and learning to use the new rifle kept everyone employed.

Gabions and fascines, which appear later in pictures of the Redan, were baskets of earth and bundles of sticks, which would stop rifle bullets. They were an essential part of the system of attack and defence as it had evolved at this period.

The new rifle was the Minié. It was a muzzle-loader but it had a rifle barrel with three grooves which would twist the bullet one inch in seventy-two inches. The bullet was seven-tenths of an inch in diameter and thus had great stopping power; furthermore it had a range of close on a thousand yards. It was not very accurate but this made little difference when it was firing at closely packed troops. As the Russians were accustomed to keep their men in close formation the effect of the Minié was greatly increased.

In spite of the casualties from disease and the inconvenience caused by lowering, but not fatal, complaints like diarrhoea, morale was high when the regiments embarked for the Crimean peninsula. They were, of course, taking the cholera with them and soon all the places they visited would be full of this and other fatal diseases. Hume described the scene:

> At noon the flotilla started. The smoke from countless steamers quite darkened the sky. During the day officers were to be seen marching up and down the decks with the kits that they were to land with strapped in various ways. As there was no transport, officers and men had to depend on what they carried themselves when they landed. This included three days ration of salt pork, biscuit and rum. I am afraid that some of the junior officers were much amused at seeing the old officers practising for the coming marches.

The trip took three days and the landings in Kalamita Bay, thirty-three miles north of Sebastopol, began on 14 September 1854. There was no opposition to the landing but it was, of course, observed. The Russian plan was to allow the force to land, then defeat it and drive the remnants into the sea. The scene as described by one of those there has a familiarity that most soldiers have experienced at least once.

> We were marched off into the unknown land about four miles. It was quite dark when we halted; rain came down in torrents. We were told to make ourselves comfortable for the night. What a night that was! I have spent many uncomfortable nights but that beat all for utter misery. Sleep was quite out of the question. Any one lying down got drenched. The only thing to be done was to walk up and down watching the attempts of the men to light fires from the weeds they collected off our bivouac ground. I have often wondered why a few enterprising Cossacks did not come and fire into our picquets. Of course we would have thought that the whole Russian Army was attacking us, and as the night was pitch dark, and we knew nothing of the country, no doubt we would have fired into the nearest regiment and they into us; but the night was evidently too bad for even a Cossack to be out. There were no alarms, and at last

daylight appeared, and very welcome it was to the drenched troops. Our first night in the Crimea decided the fate of many poor fellows who might otherwise have lived to meet the Russians. Cholera stuck to the army, and the night of the 14th September helped to spread the terrible disease.

However, conditions improved. Hume noted that the British troops were under strict orders not to loot, but to pay for everything; he had doubts about the French. He gave the strength of the armies at that stage as British: 26,000 infantry, 1,000 cavalry and 60 guns; French: 28,000 infantry, but no details of what proportion might be cavalry; Turks: 7,000 with 68 guns and no cavalry.

Five days later the armies set out at 6 am to march towards Sebastopol: 'The day was very hot with a blazing sun; the men suffered much from thirst. We marched about ten miles across a dry, treeless, uninteresting plain, not a drop of water to be got en route.' They were, of course, heading towards their first battle and considering the conditions since they had landed it was a miracle that they should be able to fight it at all, let alone win it.

The march towards the River Alma, where the first battle of the campaign was to take place, must have presented a picturesque though tragic spectacle. The advancing army approached on a front nearly four miles wide, and soon the three-mile-long column was straggling four or five miles to the rear. The day was warm and the troops were exhausted before they set out. The French and the Turks took the coastal side, the British marched inland.

Brackenbury's *Descriptive Sketches illustrating Mr William Simpson's Drawings of the Seat of War in the East*, published in 1855, described the scene as follows:

On the extreme right, with their right flank leaning on the sea, came the Turks, commanded by Suleiman Pasha, next to them the French, and on the left, and rather thrown back, the British. The Allied fleets accompanied and protected the right of the line and were in readiness, if necessary, to render services similar to those which had so admirable an effect to the events of the great action of the succeeding day. None who beheld will ever forget the magnificent spectacle presented by this first combined movement of the Allied forces. The line extended over many miles of country from the sea inland, and the ground over which the men had to pass was particularly favourable to the display of large masses of troops, consisting as it did of a considerable plain, broken at intervals by a series of low hills running at right angles to the sea. The September sun shone brightly on a forest of bayonets: and while the eye rested with delight on grand and imposing masses of colour, blended yet contrasted, the ear drank in a volume of sound in which the shrill notes of innumerable bugles, and the roll of countless drums, were now lost, now harmonized, in the multitudinous hum of the armed force on the march. As they crested one of the ridges we have just mentioned the first sight of the enemy greeted their longing eyes. On the other side of the intervening plain they discovered a large body of Russian Dragoons and Cossacks, supported by artillery posted on the hillside.

The appearance of the Allied Army on the march seems to have impressed many. Perhaps it contrasted sharply with their appearance earlier and later. Whatever the reason, much is made of the impressive appearance of the green and the gold, the bearskins and the plumes, the scarlet and the glitter. What is less in evidence is the information about forward patrols or scouts protecting the flanks; it seems that matters which had been routine in the Napoleonic wars had now been forgotten. As it happened, no disasters occurred as a result, but the neglect of general military principles led to near-disaster later. The Russians were using their cavalry very intelligently at this stage. Such skirmishers as Raglan had sent ahead of the Allied force were puzzled to know how to deal with the Cossacks, whether to take them on in minor battles and chance being overwhelmed by a larger force, or whether to keep close enough to the main body to make it impossible for the Russians to attack but at the same time invalidate their function as scouts.

However, this situation did not last long. By 20 September the expeditionary force had reached the Alma. On the opposite—that is the southern side of the river, Menschikov had drawn up the Russian Army. He knew that as yet Sebastopol had no proper defences and that here—on the slopes from the Alma—was the best place to repel the invader. In the event he lost the Battle of the Alma but came very close to winning the Battle of Sebastopol.

Raglan's appreciation of the place was as follows:

It crosses the great road about two-and-a-half miles from the sea, and is very strong by nature. The bold and almost precipitous range of heights, of 350 to 400 feet, that from the sea closely borders the left bank of the river, here ceases and formed their [the Russians'] left, and turning thence round a great amphitheatre or wide valley, terminated at a salient pinnacle, where their right rested, and whence the descent to the plain was more gradual. The front was about two miles in extent. Across the mouth of this great opening is a lower ridge at different heights, varying from 60 to 150 feet, parallel to the river, and at distances from it of 600 to 800 yards. The river itself is generally fordable for troops, but its banks are extremely rugged and in most parts steep; the willows along it had been cut down, in order to prevent them from affording cover to the attacking party, and in fact everything had been done to deprive an assailant of any species of shelter. In front of the position, on the right bank, at about 200 yards from the Alma, is the village of Bourliouk, and near it a timber bridge, which had been partly destroyed by the enemy. The high pinnacle and ridge before alluded to were the key of the position, and consequently there the greatest preparations had been made for the defence. Half-way down the height and across its front was a trench of the extent of some hundred yards, to afford cover against an advance up the even steep slope of the hill. On the right, and a little retired, was a powerful covered battery, armed with heavy guns, which flanked the whole of the right of the position. Artillery at the same time was posted at the points that best command the passage of the river and its approaches generally. On the slopes of these hills, forming a sort of table-land, were placed dense masses of the enemy's infantry, while on the heights above was his great reserve; the whole amounting it is supposed, to between 40,000 and 50,000 men.

This appreciation omits certain vital factors which—not surprisingly—were unknown to Lord Raglan. The front was rather broader than Raglan had estimated but it was also steeper and there were very few places where guns could advance. The river varied in depth, being fordable in some places but deep in others. The ground was high at two points—Telegraph Hill in the centre, which overlooked the main road, and Kourgané Hill to the right of the Russians and therefore facing the British. The front was, in fact, five-and-a-half miles long, and this was too much for Menschikov to cover. He decided that the area near to the sea was too steep to comprise any danger and therefore concentrated his entire infantry, a force of some thirty-three thousand, between the two hills. He placed his cavalry, 3,600 strong, on the right flank, put 20,000 troops facing the British and 13,000 against the French. Eighty-six guns were ranged on the British, thirty-six on the French. These dispositions have been criticized as being on too wide a front. He neglected to destroy a perfectly good road which led up from the village of Almatamack opposite the French position. He made insufficient fortifications, although what he did make produced a considerable blood bath later. These were the two earthworks, known as the Greater Redoubt and the Lesser Redoubt. The 'Greater Redoubt' was situated three hundred yards from the river on the lower slopes of Kourgané Hill. It was not a formidable obstacle, as it had no ditch and the embankment was only four feet high, but it contained twelve heavy guns. The 'Lesser Redoubt' was behind and to the right: it faced northeast and contained field guns.

Needless to say, Raglan and St Arnaud saw the situation differently. Raglan visualized a frontal assault; St Arnaud preferred a pincer movement in which the French would come in from the sea flank while Raglan turned the Russian right. Raglan, with his eye cocked to the Russian cavalry, and what it could do to a flanking movement, could not see his way to agreeing to the French plan. The compromise—as usually happens—was neither bold nor intelligent, for both sides decided to attack to their immediate front. The result was that the French saw too little of the battle and the British too much.

The battle, which had been decided upon at dawn, began with an artillery bombardment at 1.30 pm. At once a golden opportunity presented itself to either side, and was lost. The French advanced on the sea flank without opposition, climbed the cliffs without difficulty and advanced without finding the enemy. However their very success was disturbing for it was clear that they were now completely split off from the British contingent; if Menschikov could bring up the necessary reserves they could easily find themselves cut off and isolated from their allies. Menschikov did in fact bring up eight battalions from his reserve but, for reasons that were never disclosed, decided not to commit them. Although he robbed himself of a useful reserve for upwards of an hour the decision may not have been a bad one. Had the French been brought to battle they might have secured a swift victory; as it was they were not brought into the battle. If they had been it would have been impossible to have restrained them from the pursuit, and the campaign could well have been over within weeks.

Meanwhile the English force stood drawn up for battle, losing a man here and there from the Russian artillery. The position of the respective forces may be seen from the Appendix map. General Sir de Lacy Evans (2nd Division) was on the right of the English force, flanked by the French. The separation was at the village of Bourliouk. On his left was the Light Division under General Sir George Brown. In front of the Light Division lay Kourgané Hill with its formidable redoubts. There was no one on the left but behind was the 1st Division (the Duke of Cambridge) which was made up of Guards and Highlanders, and further back the Third Division. Well back and to the left was a cavalry force of a thousand under Lucan and Cardigan. There was a further reserve in the shape of the 4th Division but this was not committed.

Whatever tactics Evans had in mind were soon disrupted by Russian shells falling on Bourliouk and setting it on fire. He sent his brigade round, rather than through it, and as a result the left-hand brigade (Pennefather) became tangled with the Light Division. The Light Division soon had its hands full, for Codrington's brigade took heavy losses in crossing the river. It was impossible to re-form after the crossing so they went forward as they were, officers leading. With Codrington to the front, but with the others closely supporting him, the brigade charged up the slope to the Great Redoubt. The Russians were in great strength in front of the redoubt but this did not stop the British charge. Seeing the advance the Russians decided to save their guns rather than use them on the advancing brigade. The colours of the 23rd were placed on the breastwork and the men rallied round. To all intents and purposes the redoubt was won. All that was needed was adequate reinforcements to beat off the likely counter-attack. Reinforcements were indeed on the way and included the redoubtable Guards and Highlanders but, owing to some extraordinary—and never explained—reason, the order was given to retire. Mystified but superbly disciplined, Codrington's men began to retreat; Colonel Lacy Yea of the 7th Fusiliers could not, or would not, believe the impossible signal and proceeded to take on the entire Russian force unaided.

At this point Raglan decided to ride forward and see for himself what was going on. He avoided Bourliouk and advanced up the slope below Telegraph Hill. Here, unnoticed by anyone except the Russians, he had a vantage point behind the enemy lines from which he could clearly see what was happening. A few Russians observed the Allied Commander-in-Chief with some of his staff behind their lines but did not dream that he was almost on his own; in consequence they made no effort to capture him. Raglan, however, was blissfully unaware of his danger. Realizing that the position dominated the battlefield he sent for guns and men. They were not long coming and when they arrived astonished the British as much as the Russians. He had turned the Russian flank from the centre—a feat that can have been emulated rarely in military history. It gave encouragement to all the troops clinging to the shot-swept hillside, particularly to Lacy Yea and his fusiliers who were still doggedly battling with the nearest Russians.

Raglan was by now of course hopelessly out of touch with a battle in which rapid decisions were vital. Brigadier-General Airey, the quartermaster-general, was available to fill the breach. He lost no time in setting the 1st Division moving, led by the Guards Brigade.

The ground over which the advance took place was very rough, and partly broken up by houses and vineyards. An interesting contrast in styles then developed between the Scots Fusiliers and the Grenadiers. The former were in exemplary formation until they came to a stone wall facing their centre. They were ordered to 'break ranks and scale the wall' which they proceeded to do. At this point they could have paused and gone forward in perfect formation but were hurried before they had time to re-form. The Grenadiers were also given the order to advance but were delayed by their colonel who would not move until his formation was perfect. Subsequent events proved him right. The Scots Guards achieved their formation and went on, but the Coldstream Guards although in perfect formation, could not mount the very steep opposite bank of the stream in their sector. They therefore had to move downstream a little, after which they moved forward in perfect formation having gone through the exact procedure of a normal drill parade.

The confusion caused by the order to retire, and the refusal by some to obey it had caused a highly uncertain situation around the Great Redoubt. Apart from the Russian guns which were ranged on the redoubt from the hill behind there were several Russian regiments waiting their time to give battle. The disparity in numbers was 2,500 British to 12,000 Russians. As soon as their superiority had become apparent to the Russians they took advantage of it, and poured in vast numbers down the slope. Even before the fatal order to retire, there was extraordinary confusion, and the advancing Vladimir Regiment was mistaken for the French and not fired upon.

As the Light Division fell back, angry and bewildered, the Russian guns fired shot after shot in their general direction. The chief sufferers from this, however, were the Scots Fusiliers who were now advancing up the slope. Having taken a number of casualties from the Russian fire they then found themselves tangled up with the retreating Light Division, and also some Russians who were following up and bayoneting the wounded. They formed up and fired a volley but, before they could give as good account of themselves as they would have wished, they were ordered to return. The order, which was repeated several times, was probably meant for the Welsh Fusiliers. The Scots had no option but to obey and set off on the return journey. Inevitably they found themselves coming back to meet the Grenadiers and Coldstream. It was obvious to all that something had gone adrift with the orders so the Grenadiers, who were ahead, halted, and allowed the Scots Fusiliers to re-form. All three battalions were now in line. They were just in time to face the shock of the charge of the Vladimir Regiment which probably imagined it was on the point of winning the battle.

The eventual result was not however decided only by action here but also by Sir Colin Campbell with the Highland Brigade. For some time the Scots had awaited the order to advance and, when it came, pressed forward with the energy of men long held back. They were to the left of the Guards Brigade and some of their own soldiers were impeded—as the Guards were—by retreating members of the Light Division. Campbell's main concern however was the intentions of the Russian cavalry, but these showed little desire to move. When they finally advanced the precise orderly advance of the Guards Brigade was already pushing back the Russians; then in quick succession the Russians were hit first by the 42nd (the Black Watch) then by the 93rd (the Sutherlands) and then by the 79th (the Camerons). Unbelievably, three thousand Russian cavalry stood idly by and watched it happen, and four battalions of the Russian Oglutz Regiment made little response except to urge their comrades not to flee (before doing so themselves). The victory was clinched by Lucan's horse artillery which galloped up with six guns, giving the impression that there were plenty more where those came from, so briskly did they perform.

There was of course no doubt that the Russians were thoroughly defeated. The guns from the 2nd and 3rd Divisions had now come up to Raglan's vantage point and were choosing suitable targets in the close-packed Russian infantry. The French too were in a position to turn victory into rout. The reason they did not do so seems to have been unknown to anyone except St Arnaud for there is no doubt that the French regimental commanders were burning with rage and frustration at the inadequate part they had been allowed to take in the battle. It is said that when Raglan suggested that the French should pursue the Russians St Arnaud declined to give the order, with the explanation that 'they had left their packs in the valley below'. Airey and Lucan begged to be allowed to take up the pursuit on their own but their request was refused—probably rightly—for the force they could assemble was small and it could easily have been overwhelmed if the Russians had turned and made a serious stand. (They did in fact do so but it was not necessary.)

This is the bare outline of the battle. It reflects great credit on the soldiers and unit commanders involved but precious little on the higher command. Menschikov blundered in not realizing that his left was not in fact secure, but was extremely fortunate in that the French command was apathetic. Eight Russian battalions were sent from where they could have been very useful to a part where they were not used at all, and thus their possible contribution was entirely wasted. Gortschakoff, commander of the Russian right wing, had allowed himself to become too involved. He had behaved with astonishing courage, leading one of his columns personally; but a commander is scarcely in a position to make decisions about the best use of his troops when he is fighting desperately for his life or a piece of ground. Three of the four Russian generals in the centre were wounded. Total Russian losses were said to have amounted to six thousand; these were mainly due to withering fire from the Minié rifle. British losses were given as two thousand, many of which came from artillery fire. The French had taken little part and were relatively unscathed, but their turn would come later.

Few commanders-in-chief can have exercised less authority than Raglan did on this occasion. To crowd together the initial dispositions —as he did—is bad. To order your main force to advance over a river, up a slope, into a heavily defended position is not conducting a battle; it is gambling with your best troops at long odds. To isolate yourself from your force and put yourself in a highly vulnerable position is simply folly. It has been suggested that he had chosen a masterly vantage point; in fact he could have seen and done much better if he had stayed on the other side of the Alma. His crowning folly was not to organize his own and French troops into pursuit. Had he done so the bitter fighting for Sebastopol would probably have been avoided.

Of St Arnaud one can say little. He was a dying man; he probably knew better than anyone that he had little hold over his subordinate commanders. He may have thought that once a pursuit began he would lose all hold on events, his forces would stream away into unknown country, perhaps into traps, and be slaughtered; he saw no reason to believe that Raglan was not prepared to fight to the last Frenchman; after all Raglan was in the habit of calling the Russians 'the French' when he was outlining his plans. To both men the Napoleonic wars were more real than present events in the Crimea.

So the defeated Russians escaped. Seven miles from the Alma lay the Katcha River where they felt safe.

Individual accounts of the battle are naturally somewhat different from official versions made when the smoke has cleared. A feature of the description of the Alma battle is the good-humoured imperturbability that appears to have characterized the belligerents. Hume wrote:

Most of us for the first time found ourselves under a hot fire of round shot and shell—a curious and by no means pleasant experience. There was an involuntary movement amongst the men to cower and crowd together when the first round shot passed over us, and there were few who did not duck their heads. All, however, soon got accustomed to the sound and saw there was much more danger in crowding together than opening out, and the loose order we got into before crossing the river Alma would have delighted the drill reformer of the present day.

When clear of the village [Bourliouk], which was burning fiercely, the order to lie down was given, which we did without any cover, and under the fire of some of the enemy's heaviest batteries, which were throwing shot and shell very thickly. As we were lying down most of the shot passed over us; a few fell into our ranks; a round shot passed through a man who was lying in front of me and close to my brother. One of the guns in the large Russian battery was pointed exactly in my direction. Whenever I saw that gun fired I looked out a bit. I begged Major Whimper to get off his horse but he would not. A round shot, spent, rolled to his horse's feet. None of our field officers dismounted. Colonel Warren sat like a statue behind the centre of the line with a single glass to his eye; he never moved when the shot and shell passed close by him. Lieut-Colonel Daubeney on the right of the line was equally cool and collected. When lying down we could see the French advancing and swarming up the precipitous heights—very hard work but they were not exposed to the fire of the batteries as the British troops were. We could see the round shot, after they passed us, ricochetting over the plain, looking like cricket balls.

After lying down for about an hour we got the order to advance, which we did getting under the shelter of a low vineyard wall. We lay there a short time, our rifles touching up the Russian columns. We did not lose many men at the wall. Lieut Armstrong was dangerously wounded there. After leaving the wall we took ground to the right, moving across a road in front of a house which led to the bridge over the Alma. While crossing the road the fire was terrific; the ground was literally swept by grape and shot. It was near this that our captain, Brevet-Major Rose was mortally wounded by a grape-shot while gallantly leading his company.

We fortunately came on a ford; the water only reached our knees. We crossed under a shower of bullets. Major Whimper was dangerously wounded; his leg was broken and his horse killed by the same bullet.

A little later:

Lieut-Colonel Daubeney took the officers carrying the colours (Lieut Harkness and Richards), placed them a short distance behind the elevation, and called to the officers to form up the men on the colours. This was done at once showing the result of careful training and excellent discipline combined with perfect confidence in their officers, which can only be acquired by long and continual association in the same regiment, and the mutual attachment and *esprit de corps* thereby engendered in all ranks.

Finally:

All were glad to halt when the heights were crowned, tired after the hard day's work. My brother Gustavus met us—the three brothers untouched. Great congratulations on all sides from those who had escaped the dangers of the day, and sorrow for those who had fallen.

Hume had a marked sense of humour. After they left the battlefield they camped in the open.

Very heavy dews wet us considerably as we lay like warriors taking our rest with our regimental greatcoats around us. We had great difficulty in finding soft stone for pillows but we managed to sleep well when we got a little hay or straw to lie on.

Some kind individual put his foot through my shako, which I had carefully preserved up to the time, not liking to set a bad example by getting rid of it. My brother thought that we should look more uniform in forage-caps, so we hung our full-dress headgear on one of the shrubs. No doubt they now figure as trophies in some Russian or Tartar cottage.

Lieut-Colonel John Adye, writing in 1857, considered that Prince Menschikov had set out his army skilfully. 'Fearing for his right, as affording fewer natural obstacles, it was there he had concentrated his chief strength to command the road; and beyond this flank again numerous cavalry was held in readiness for such contingencies as the battle might create.' He was critical of the French plan: 'de Bazancourt states that the design originated by Marshal St Arnaud was' that:

The English should turn the enemy's right, at the same time that General Bosquet's division, reinforced by the Turks, should climb the steep heights at the river mouth, and turn their left. The 1st and 3rd French divisions (with the 4th in reserve) then to attack the centre. But the troops in this last attack were not to advance until an hour after the others.

Such a plan is at once open to great objection. The forces would have been divided into three distinct parts, besides which it is at all times dangerous to attempt to turn simultaneously both flanks of an enemy, unless the attacking force is very superior in numbers (which in this instance was not the case) but more particularly would it have been so with an enemy posted and entrenched on strong ground of their own choosing, and with a river in their front.

Adye supports Raglan unreservedly:

When it is considered that the base of our operation was the sea-shore, and that our safety depended on free communication with the fleets, it will probably be admitted that Lord Raglan showed good judgement in not attempting anything so dangerous as an inland flank movement; and therefore when de Bazancourt calls the direct advance of the English an 'heroic' error he produces an unjust libel on one of the most brilliant feats ever performed by an army.

Clearly no criticism of Raglan is justified in Adye's eyes, nor is he prepared to hear a good word for the French strategy. He may perhaps have been right. A balanced judgement may often be quite inaccurate about both sides. Adye, however, respects a brave man when he sees one. 'In personal appearance the French Marshal was pale, thin, bent and emaciated, but he seemed in good spirits, and pleased when the English cheered him heartily when he passed. There was certainly something touching and chivalrous in the feeling which induced him, even in his last hours, when suffering from a mortal disease, and daily growing more feeble, to remain still at the head of his army, and lead it in the field.' Futhermore he gives credit to the French for their enterprise and persistence on the heights:

St Arnaud, taking advantage of the success of this manoeuvre [an attack on their left], and in order to prevent General Bosquet from being overpowered, on the firing of the first gun at once ordered the columns of General Canrobert and Prince Napoleon to attack in their front. In advancing they were warmly received at the river by the Russian skirmishers, and by their infantry on the slopes. The French artillery was brought into action, the batteries of Prince Napoleon being placed on the right of the village of Bourliouk. The French column soon forced the passage of the river, and began to swarm up the heights, the enemy gradually retiring before them, but disputing every inch of ground. It was about two pm when the French gained the crest [this would be very soon after the English attack had begun], and Canrobert then found himself face to face with the left centre of the Russian Army, consisting of powerful columns, concentrated near an unfinished telegraph tower. His own artillery had been obliged to make a détour to gain the heights, and had not joined him; that of the enemy, hitherto engaged with Bosquet, now turned and concentrated their fire upon his columns. The Prince Napoleon, on his left, also met with equal opposition. St Arnaud then ordered forward General Forey's two brigades of the reserve. Arriving with their artillery, they gave timely support to General Canrobert and Prince Napoleon; at the same time Bosquet continued to advance along the heights and threatened the Russian left, which enabled Canrobert to order an attack to the front, and the enemy were driven back, retreating with heavy loss.

Thus far the battle in this direction was gained; the French having accomplished a most difficult and gallant advance, for which their activity and dashing qualities were well suited. But a sterner and far more terrible struggle had commenced upon the left.

W. H. Russell, *The Times* correspondent was, of course, highly critical not only of Lord Raglan's conduct of the battle but also of some of his subordinate commanders, Sir George Brown and Brigadier-General Buller in particular. Adye leaps hotly to their defence:

The Battle of the Alma affords a proof of the great advantage of attacking a position with troops deployed in successive thin lines. Fearful as was the loss of the Light Division, it would undoubtedly have been still greater had the advance been made in column; in fact it may be considered doubtful whether any troops in that formation could have stormed such a position. The great front of fire gained by deployment is another advantage; and although the line of the Light Division had become a good deal broken when they delivered them, still it was far superior to that of the enemy, whose crowded encumbered masses could not stand against it, but at once gave way. A comparatively very small amount of ammunition was fired away by the English in this battle.

Colonel Sir George Ashley Maude, KCB, was commanding 'I' troop of the Royal Horse Artillery, as Captain G. A. Maude. His second-in-command was Capt. J. D. Shakespear. There were three lieutenants, an assistant surgeon, fifteen N.C.O.s, eighty gunners, seventy-seven drivers, one trumpeter and nine artificers. There were twelve officers' horses and 180 for the remainder of the troop. They had four light six-pounders, two twelve-pounder howitzers, nine ammunition waggons, a rocket carriage and four other carriages. Maude wrote a series of letters to his wife, of which the following is one.

20 September. Today we have fought and won a severe general action, beating the Russians from a strong position they had taken up, to the number of about 40,000 on the banks of the little River Alma. Their artillery was much heavier than ours, and they were so much above us that, though we were under heavy artillery fire, we could not touch them with our guns. The infantry advanced in a most gallant way, and stormed the entrenchment, carrying everything before them, and taking several guns. We then advanced and pounded them well. You will see a much better account in dispatches than I can give you, only having seen part of it, and I am very tired. Again 18 hours on horse back, but thank God, to His other mercies He has added returning health, for though I have had no bed and no water to wash in for the last two days, I yet feel very strong and well. [There follows a few lines on casualties known to him.]

He wrote another, fuller letter the next day. It had the impressive address 'The Heights of Alma'.

We halt today so I can write you a clearer account of what we have been doing for the last two or three days. We left the beach, where we first landed, at 3 o'clock in the morning of the 19th, and the whole army was formed in line at right angles to the shore about 7 o'clock that morning. The French on the right or sea-coast line and the English on the left further inland, the whole facing south. We began to advance about 7 o'clock. Small bodies of Cossacks hovering about and falling back on supports till about three o'clock in the afternoon. We came to a body of about 2,000 of them, with 10 guns on some rising ground, just where we had intended camping for the night. The cavalry were ordered in to dislodge them, as their guns were not seen at first, but as soon as they advanced the guns opened on them and wounded five men, three of whom had their legs amputated, and killed several horses. Brandling's Troop (Thomas's) and mine were ordered on and we soon silenced them killing and wounding 35 men and 32 horses. They retired for the night, and we fell back to where the infantry had encamped. The next day, yesterday, we had a much more serious affair. After advancing about six miles we came to a very strong position, where the Russians had entrenched themselves, and had some very heavy guns. It was on the banks of the River Alma, on the north side of which was a fine plain, but the south rises steeply to about 300 feet. Up the side of the steep slope the enemy had entrenched batteries with some very heavy guns, and, as we now learn from a Russian general taken prisoner, 52,000 men and a strong body of cavalry. They began a tremendous cannonade on us when we came within 2,000 yards, which we could not return, they were so high up, but the plunging fire did not do much damage at that time. We silenced some of their lower batteries, and then the Light Division attacked them in the most gallant way with the bayonet, and in two hours from the time the first shot was fired, had carried the heights. We then gave them a great pounding when they were retreating, and if our cavalry had been stronger we should have got all their guns and completely routed them. As it was, they retired in the greatest disorder, and we advanced two miles beyond the heights we had carried. The French did the same on the left as we did on the right, and the result was all that could be desired. I am sorry to say that our loss was very severe. The 23rd, Fred's regiment, lost half their officers, the Colonel, and eight others. The Guards also suffered a great deal, but not in officers. Our total loss will be about 2,000 and the French 5,000. The Russian general said they had calculated on holding the place for eight weeks at least, and that then we should be too late in the year for the siege of Sebastopol. We advance again tomorrow. I can only tell you what I saw, of course, as our front extended three or four miles. Poor Captain Dew, of the Artillery, had his head shot off, and his lieutenant killed. Goodlake, of the Guards, is all right. I am so glad Freddy Vane was not there; his regiment was in a terrific fire and there is not more than half of it left. I lost three horses, one killed and two so badly wounded that I had to destroy them. We were in heavy fire for a long time, but God has mercifully protected me again. Compy Dickins has just come to my tent, and I have given him some paper to write home. He is all right and well. You will, I know, thank God with me for my preservation.

The letter gives no hint of the cool courage which had distinguished the writer in the battle. Clearly his information about French casualties was either wildly inaccurate, or—more likely—a mistake for five hundred. It was probably already clear to him—and if it was not it soon would be—that in a battle lasting two hours at a cost of two thousand casualties, the Crimean War had been won. Unfortunately for those concerned the victory was frittered away by not being followed up with a cavalry pursuit. In consequence the war was to drag on for two years, and there were to be nearly three hundred thousand casualties in conditions of the utmost misery and privation.

The Crimean War, like all campaigns up to the present century, had far less deaths in battle than from disease. The deaths in the British army storming the Alma heights amounted to three hundred and forty-two. But the wounded who would recover and be fit for battle again were very few; any serious wounds were probably fatal. One effect of being a casualty and taken out of the line was to increase a man's chances of cholera, for he would be sent back to the point at which infection was probable. The problem with cholera was that infection was so swift and lethal. It was thought to be caused by a cholera 'cloud', and the best prevention was believed to be a 'cholera' belt that would keep the stomach warm. Diarrhoea, dysentery and enteric were all confused with cholera, but only the first of these would benefit from a 'cholera' belt. Cholera rapidly dehydrates the body with vomiting and diarrhoea. If the victim recovers he may be several stone lighter in weight, although this will be regained rapidly. If he does not recover, his body and everything he possesses should be burnt, not thrown into the harbour as happened in the Crimea. During the Second World War Captain W. M. Shakespear, a descendant of the Captain J. D. Shakespear mentioned above, contracted cholera and cerebral malaria simultaneously while in the Thailand jungle. Although abandoned as dead, he recovered, and dragged himself along jungle paths until he reached the next camp.

The question of whether Raglan should have allowed the cavalry to pursue the Russians has been hotly debated in many discussions since. The criticism levelled at him for his conduct at Alma, and subsequently, was that he was too cautious. As mentioned above, if he had ordered a cavalry pursuit he could probably have destroyed the last traces of Russian resistance there and then, and have entered Sebastopol virtually unopposed. However, Raglan knew well enough from his own experience in the Napoleonic wars that battles can rapidly be lost again even when the first, and apparently final, round has been won. Furthermore there were plenty of well-known incidents in military history to confirm this view: the Battle of Hastings could well have been lost again by the Normans within a short time of their capture of Senlac Hill. Edgehill provided another example of what happens when a pursuit gets out of hand. As far as Raglan knew, large numbers of Russian men and guns had been withdrawn intact; the formidable Russian cavalry had been uncommitted and would be in an excellent position to cut off pursuing cavalry; there was no knowing what the ground was like and whether it had been prepared against the invaders in any way; and there was the certain conviction that once he launched his cavalry into the unknown he would have very little idea of what they were doing, whether they were routing the last remnant of the enemy, or whether they themselves had been cut to pieces. Communication was abysmally bad in the Crimean War, and many of the messages which were passed were misunderstood; the Charge of the Light Brigade is always taken as the outstanding example but there were numerous occasions which could match it.

There have been many campaigns in history when an army has fought to victory when ravaged with disease but few armies can have suffered as much as those in the Crimea. The effects of malaria in India, and of dysentery even as long ago as Crécy, have been recorded, but there seems to be no other occasion when an army pressed forward while cholera was thinning its ranks dramatically without any assistance from the enemy. Raglan was in the unfortunate position of not knowing whether he would have an army at all the following day. Capt. Hedley Vicars, of the Coldstream Guards, who was killed on 23 March in front of Sebastopol, had written a year before: 'I should think no disease except the plague, can be so horrible as Asiatic cholera. I saw its ravages in Jamaica, but that which has raged here seems to have been of a more virulent nature, and death has come on more rapidly; it so alters the countenance that I have been quite unable to recognize dying men whom I found, on asking their names, that I knew very well.'

However there were plenty of men on the spot who felt that Raglan should have pressed on. Among them was Colonel Charles Windham, who later became Lieut-General Sir Charles Windham. He had strong views on the conduct of the battle as well:

The more I think of the battle the more convinced I am that it might have ended the campaign. I thought so at the time and I think so more strongly now.

The battery should never have been attacked. Our left should have been thrown forward and to the left, and have turned the right of the Russian position.* Had the Russians then waited for our attack they would have been driven on to the French or into the sea. Had they not waited they must have abandoned their batteries and their position.

If it be said 'Aye, but they would perhaps have driven back our attack over the river and ruined it' I answer, 'If they could do this without their batteries, why could they not drive back our centre with them?' In fact, we flung away the great advantages of the attack, namely choice of time and place; and moreover, when the battle was over, did not follow up our success.

In a letter written to his wife from the Heights of Alma he mentions the Guards officer casualties, which read rather like a roll-call from Debrett. He adds: 'The Russian General we took prisoner, and who is now on board the *Agamemnon,* says of all the soldiers he ever saw he has never seen anything like the British infantry; they fought more like devils than men.'

But if Raglan was inept, Menschikov was more so. Having decided not to oppose the landing and not to harass the invaders on their approach march, he had staked everything on his ability to hold them on the Alma. He was fortunate in not having the French to contend with, for—as would be seen later—they were a formidable fighting force. He wasted the possibilities of his cavalry entirely, being completely put off balance by the disciplined fighting power of the British infantry.

* This was St Arnaud's plan. Raglan agreed but did not implement it.

The reasons why the opposing armies performed as they did makes an interesting study. The Turks who fought in the Crimea lacked organization and morale. The Russians who fought moderately well at the Alma, and magnificently later, were on their home ground but at a point so far removed from their own homes that they might well have been in a foreign country; the explanation for the difference in performance may well be that in the early part of the war the Russians were organized by discipline and in the later stages by leadership. The French were well-organized throughout, although there is some justice in the criticism that they allowed the British to bear the brunt of the fighting; nevertheless they clinched the final result.

The British, who were badly equipped in everything except rifles, and had minimal training, showed superb fighting spirit. Why was this so? The explanation seems to lie in the paternal/feudal attitude of their officers. For, if fear is infectious, so is courage. It may be unnatural, and even exasperating, to see a man expose himself to withering enemy fire but if he does not get killed—or even if he does, and someone takes his place—it is difficult for the onlooker not to find himself stirred to adopting a similarly nonchalant attitude to danger. There was, of course, also a conviction that if the officers thought it right then it must be so. Lastly, although enjoying their occasional luxuries the officers were as indifferent to hardship as they were to danger.

The scenes on the battlefield after the fighting was over were of the expected grimness, but lightened by humanitarian instincts. Windham wrote in his diary:

> Assisted some of our own, and many Russian wounded. Much pleased at the conduct of our men towards the latter, but greatly hurt at the want of exertion and system of getting the wounded away. The whole of the 4th Division ought to have been employed, as well as others, in collecting them; whereas hundreds of men are walking about giving them bread and water, but no fatigue parties were employed to carry them in, and bury the dead until nearly forty-eight hours after the battle. Cholera on the increase, I am sorry to say.

Although the conduct of the defeated Russian officers was above reproach the behaviour of the men was not conducive to a merciful attitude. Cases were recorded of Russian wounded being given water and then shooting their benefactors. W. H. Russell, *The Times* correspondent whose *British Expedition to the Crimea* has formed the basis of much that has subsequently been written said:

> There was more than an acre of Russian wounded when they were brought and disposed on the ground. Some of the prisoners told us they belonged to the army of Moldavia and had only arrived in the Crimea twelve or fourteen days before the battle. If that were so, the expedition might have achieved enormous results at little cost, had it arrived three weeks earlier. All the Russian firelocks, knapsacks, bayonets, cartridge-boxes etc., were collected together, near Lord Raglan's tent, and formed heaps about twenty yards long by ten yards broad. Our men were sent to the sea, three miles distant, on jolting arabas* or tedious litters. The French had well-appointed covered hospital vans, to hold ten or twelve men, drawn by mules, and their wounded were sent in much greater comfort than our poor fellows.

Russell went on to explain that 'The French return of 1,400 killed and wounded was understood to include those who died of cholera, during the passage from Varna and the march to the Alma', and he also had something to say of the Russian weapons:

> Our men broke all the enemies' firelocks and rifles which lay on the ground. As many of them were loaded the concussion set them off, and the balls were singing through the air in all directions on the night of the 20th, the 21st, and 22nd, so that dropping shot never ceased for about forty hours. The men were also busy clearing out firelocks which got choked or would not go off during the fight, and kept up a constant discharge all over the country.

(Other accounts mention that the British soldiers constructed fireplaces of the Russian arms; when these became hot any which contained a charge were promptly set off or exploded.)

Russell said:

> The Russian musket was a good one to look at; but must be rather a bad one to use. The barrel, which was longer than ours, and was kept polished, was made of iron, and was secured to the stock by brass straps, like the French. The lock was, however, tolerably good. The stock was of the old narrow oriental pattern, and the wood of which it was made, white-grained and something like sycamore, broke easily. From the form of the heel of the stock the kick of the musket must have been sharp with

* Rough local carts.

a good charge. Many forelocks were of an old pattern, and had been originally flint-locked, but were changed to detonators by screwing in nipples and plugging up the touch-holes with steel screws. The cartridges were beautifully made and finished, the balls being strongly gummed in at the end but the powder was coarse and unglazed, and looked like millet seed; it was however, clean in the hand, and burnt very smartly. The rifles we found were a better description of arms; they were two-grooved, and projected a large conical ball with two raised grooves in it. The ball was flat at the base and had neither hollow cup nor pin; its weight must exceed our Minié ball. These rifles were all made by J. P. Malherbe, of Liège. The bayonets were soft, and bent easily. Some good swords belonging to officers were picked up, and very effective weapons, probably belonging to drummers or bandsmen, exactly like the old Roman sword, very sharp and heavy, were also left on the field. Some six or seven drums were left behind, but nearly all of them were broken—several by the shot which killed their owners. No ensign, eagle, standard, of any kind was displayed by the enemy or found on the field. Our regiments marched with their colours, as a matter of course, and the enemy made the latter a special mark for the rifles. Thus it was so many ensigns, lieutenants, and sergeants fell.

# 4
# The March to Balaclava

On 23 September 1854 the armies were on the march again. They were wary, and expected to be intercepted on the Katscha River (seven miles beyond the Alma) or the heights nearby, but the expected resistance did not occur; it looked more than ever as if Raglan should have ordered that cavalry pursuit and cut the retreating Russian Army to pieces. The armies camped after this modest march, and went on a further six miles the next day. It took them to the Belbeck. There was no food or water for the horses in this barren area, and the men themselves were on 'hard tack', as the dry and tasteless biscuits of the army are known. At this stage the army was a mile and a half from the north of Sebastopol.

Whether an attack on the north side of Sebastopol was ever a practical possibility is a question to which much thought has been given. Defenders of Lord Raglan affirm that it was not; his opponents insist that it was.

Sebastopol Harbour was over a thousand yards wide and was defended by forts at the entrance and on the cliffs. Inland, to the north, was the 'Star Fort', with a ring of earthworks and batteries around it. These might have offered less resistance than was supposed at the time, for the Allied armies did not realize how far-reaching the effects of their victory at the Alma had been. An assault would probably have needed to be combined with a naval operation as the Russians had a number of warships at Sebastopol that could have shelled inland troops—or at least any attacking the forts. Raglan, writing a dispatch from Balaclava on 28 September summarized his views as follows:

> I have the greatest satisfaction in acquainting your Grace that the Army under my command obtained possession of this important place [Balaclava] on the 26th instant, and thus established a new and secure base for our future operations.

The Allied armies quitted their position above the Alma on the morning of the 23rd, and moved across the Katscha, where they halted for the night, and on the following day passed the Belbeck.

It then appeared that the enemy had established a work which commanded the entrance of the river, and debarred its use for the disembarkation of troops, provisions, and material; and it became expedient to consider whether the line of attack should not be abandoned, and another course of operation adopted.

It having, after due deliberation, been determined by Marshal St Arnaud and myself, that we should relinquish our communication with the Katscha, and the hope of establishing it by the Belbeck, and endeavour by a flank march to the left to go round Sebastopol and seize Balaclava, the movement was commenced on the 25th, and completed the following day by the capture of this place by Her Majesty's troops, which led the advance. The march was attended with great difficulties. On leaving the high road from Belbeck to Sebastopol, the Army had to traverse a dense wood, in which there was but one road that led in the direction it was necessary to take. That road was left in the first instance to the cavalry and the artillery; and the divisions were ordered to march by compass and make a way for themselves as well as they could; and indeed the artillery of the Light Division pursued the same course as long as it was found to be possible, but, as the wood became more impracticable the batteries could not proceed otherwise than getting into the road above mentioned.

The Head-Quarters of the Army followed by several batteries of artillery, were the first to clear the forest, near what is called, in Major Jarvis's map, Mackenzie's Farm*, and at once found themselves on the flank and rear of a Russian division on the march to Baské-Serai.

This was attacked as soon as the cavalry, which had diverged a little into a bye and intricate path, could be brought up. A vast quantity of ammunition and much valuable baggage fell into our hands, and the pursuit was discontinued after about a mile and a half, it being a great object to reach the Tchernaya that evening. . . .

The march was then resumed by the descent of a steep and difficult defile into the plain, through which runs the Tchernaya River, and this the cavalry succeeded in reaching shortly before dark, followed in the course of the night by the Light, First, Second and Third Divisions; the Fourth Division having been left on the heights above the Belbeck till the following day to maintain our communication with the Katscha.

This march, which took the enemy by surprise, was a very long and toilsome one and, except at Mackenzie's Farm, where two wells yielding

* Mackenzie was a Scottish farmer, who, with others, had been invited to Russia in 1820 to advise on agriculture.

a scanty supply were found, the troops were without water, but they supported their fatigues and privations with the utmost cheerfulness, and resumed their march to this place on the morning of the 26th.

As they approached Balaclava nothing indicated that it was held in force; but as resistance was offered to the advance of the Rifle Brigade, and guns were opened from an old castle, as the head of the column showed itself on the road leading into the town, I deemed it prudent to occupy the two flanking heights by the Light Division and a portion of Captain Brandling's troop of horse artillery on the left; movements terminated by the surrender of the place, which had been occupied by very considerable numbers of the enemy. . . .

The march of the French Army on the 25th was still more fatiguing and prolonged than ours. Being behind our columns they could not reach Tchernaya till the next day, and I fear must have suffered sadly from want of water. . . .

I regret to have to acquaint your Grace that Marshal St Arnaud has been compelled, by severe illness, to relinquish command of the Army. . . . Fortunately he is succeeded by an officer of high reputation, General Canrobert, with whom I am satisfied I shall have great pleasure in acting, and who is equally desirous of maintaining the most friendly relations with me.

Three weeks elapsed before his next dispatch, of which more later. St Arnaud was a dying man but had performed to the limit of his abilities. In spite of having a dubious reputation, and having acquired his job through politics, the French marshal had acquitted himself well. The vital decision—whether to attack from the north or the south—is, naturally enough, not mentioned by Raglan in this dispatch. Others have been less reticent. Hamley quotes Sir Edmund Lyons, second-in-command of the fleet, as urging Raglan strongly 'to try to take the northern forts by a *coup de main*'. Hamley did not consider this feasible for he notes that Menschikov had ordered warships to be sunk at the entrance to the harbour the day after the battle at the Alma. These would make it difficult, if not impossible, for the Allied fleet to enter the harbour. Of even greater importance was the appointment of Colonel de Todleben to supervise the defence. The dispositions, as described by Todleben, were as follows:

Prince Menschikov, when he concentrated his army in the Alma, left, as we have seen, but a very weak garrison at Sebastopol, composed exclusively of some troops belonging to the fleet of 4 battalions of Reserve of the Light Infantry Regiments of Vilna and Lithuania; of 4 battalions of troops of descent, and of two light batteries of the marines of 16 guns. It is evident these troops were insufficient, not only for the defence of the city, but for the numerous works which it was indispensable to execute on the line of defence; thus immediately after the landing of the enemy, in order to reinforce the garrison, the crews were formed into 4 battalions for service on shore. After the formation of these troops, the garrison of Sebastopol was, on 14 September, distributed in such a manner that the north side was occupied by 4 battalions with 8 guns, and the south side by 6 battalions with 8 guns; independently of the sailors placed at the three sections of the line of defence, and of the Admiralty and Hospital detachments.

The Russians fully expected the assault to come from the north side and made frenzied efforts to strengthen that area. It has been suggested that Todleben exaggerated the Russian weakness around Sebastopol in order to make his own contribution to its defence the more notable; this would scarcely seem necessary or likely.

On the north side was the permanent fortification known as the Star Fort. It was surrounded by a ditch twelve feet deep and eighteen feet wide and contained forty-seven guns. In order to reach the perimeter a would-be attacker would have to advance over ground that could be bombarded by ships in the harbour. However, if the Russians tried to make a stand in front of the fort in order to inflict a crushing blow on the Allied armies, they could have found themselves in very serious trouble indeed if they had to give ground. They therefore relied on the strength of their artillery, from the forts and from the Navy, to beat back an Allied attack. Fortunately for the Russians, the Allies felt that the north side of Sebastopol was too strong to be attacked. Not least of the considerations influencing Raglan at this time was the problem of supply. The only possibilities were from the mouths of the Katscha or the Belbeck, and neither could possibly be regarded as satisfactory. However, in the event they might have proved more viable than the disease-ridden harbour at Balaclava, particularly as they would have been needed for a so much shorter period.

Hamley mentions that Todleben considered the Allies could have staged a masterstroke by cutting the Russian line of communication —between Russia and the Crimea—but to do that they would have needed to establish themselves on the Upper Belbeck. This force would be vulnerable for its own line of communication—seventeen miles to the mouth of the Katscha—would be exposed to guerrilla attack.

Nevertheless, with the Allied Army of sixty thousand a mere three-and-a-half miles from the citadel it was hardly surprising that the Russians applied themselves to defensive works with considerable zeal. They worked night and day in the face of extreme difficulties. Only twelve of the forty-seven guns faced inland, and in some places the masonry of the fort was so old and weak that it crumbled away when sacks of earth were placed on the parapets to raise them to a height at which they would protect the heads of the artillerymen. As the defenders of these somewhat precarious works were mainly sailors, in a total force of 11,500, the outlook for the Russians seemed poor.

Todleben analysed what would happen if the attack took place. He considered that at the most the Allies would have had to contend with the fire of twenty guns, but would more likely have been facing seven only.

> Whilst every one at Sebastopol was persuaded that the enemy would immediately attack the north side, the Allied Army . . . suddenly quitted its position upon the heights of the left bank of the Belbeck, and bore towards the east in the direction of Mackenzie's Farm. The garrison, being deficient in cavalry, could not observe the ulterior march of the enemy. They supposed that the Allies had come to the resolution of moving upon the Chersonese Peninsula; and that they intended, after having changed the base of their operations, to attack the south side of Sebastopol. The fortifications of this part of the city, scattered over an extent of nearly seven versts, were still almost as weak as they were on the day of disembarkation; because after the invasion of the Allies our efforts were exclusively concentrated upon the north side, which it was wished to shelter as much as possible from the enemy's attacks. The garrison of the south side was only composed of 6 Battalions of the Reserve of the 13th Division of Infantry, and the 44th Battalion of the fleet. These forces when united did not exceed 5,000 men. Nachimoff, having recognized the impossibility of preventing the Allies from invading the southern side, made all necessary arrangements to sink the ships of his squadron, so that they might not be taken by the enemy in the event of the fall of Sebastopol.

According to this account by Todleben the Allies need not have landed north of the capital at all but could have gone straight to Balaclava, fought a similar battle to the Alma on more advantageous terms and captured the city without further delay. However, without absolutely reliable intelligence of the situation, the Allies would have been exceptionally rash to have taken that course. Todleben was at a loss to understand why, if the Allies did not intend to attack Sebastopol from the north, they should ever have landed on that side at all. He was not alone in his opinion. Prince Gortschakoff, who had commanded the right wing of the Russian Army at the Alma, and fought with distinctive courage, said subsequently, 'There was nothing to stop the Allies marching into the town.'

The Russian view that the Allies missed a golden opportunity in September 1854 is hotly refuted by many, including Sir John Burgoyne. He affirms that:

A look at the plan of the place will show how strong that front was: in extent about 2,400 yards, across a ridge of bold rocky heights, intersected by steep ravines, with a fort conspicuously situated on a commanding feature of the ground, the approach to the whole front subject to enfilade by heavy guns and the right of the position open in flank, and even in the rear, not only to the fire of several men-of-war including steamers in the harbour, but to the heights on the side of the town, as far as the valley of the Tchernaya; and defended by an army which, although recently defeated, was still very powerful, as it showed itself to be very shortly after.

It could hardly be said that such a position was assailable by an army but little superior to the defenders with nothing but its field pieces in aid, and which had no retreat.

To be sure, it is said that 'these forts are not even tenable, although they have been working at them for a year, and they can never be made so as they are commanded', all of which is specious, but quite inapplicable to the problem of immediate assault.

In the first place, the expression of not being tenable is indefinite; a work which, left to itself, may be deemed untenable, may be of great importance and strength, when forming part of a defensive position, as in this case. The particular fort alluded to, although of a very inferior character as a permanent work, was revetted and flanked, and, at all times, superior to the Malakoff, Redan, or Mamelon, at their best, and they were found tenable enough, till after the most enormous siege operations.

Burgoyne, who was writing in a period when life and argument, proceeded at a somewhat slower pace than at the present time nevertheless has a point. He comments that if the defences were as poor as Todleben describes them to be this is 'not very complimentary to the Russian engineers, nor to their commanding generals; but in this, in fact, introduced for the sake of criticizing the Allies, he does not do justice to his own side.'

Burgoyne went on to castigate Todleben's reference to the lack of defence on the south side of Sebastopol. He quotes Todleben's words 'when there was nothing to stop them' and goes on:

Now we will see what this nothing consists of:

1. A series of very strong positions, whose flanks were perfectly secure round a common centre [the town], from which each was easily accessible, and the mutual communication not difficult; whereas the attacks were to be made from a much more extended and diverging circumference, which was broken by deep, and, in part, almost impracticable ravines, some of the most important of which were raked by men of war in the harbour.
2. The positions were greatly strengthened in parts by the old time walls, towers, and strong buildings, affording, even in their dilapidated state, formidable obstacles against a *coup de main*, and to them the enemy were adding earthen redoubts on the most influential points, and on which, even then, some heavy guns were mounted.
3. A garrison, or rather a *corps d'armée,* as above described, to defend these positions.
4. The attack to be made by an army of no very great superiority of strength to the aggregate amount of that of the Russians, to be supported only by field artillery of a peculiarly light nature, and without any retreat in the case of a reverse.
5. That such a garrison was in the place (the other advantages for defence being indisputable) cannot be doubted from the circumstances above mentioned, and from the firmness and activity shown by the garrison on our appearance.

Sir John Burgoyne, as one of the advisers whose ideas Lord Raglan had accepted, was doubtless bound to try to justify his recommendations subsequently when they appeared to have been mistaken. Nevertheless, these arguments seem remarkably flimsy; to assume that a garrison was in place because it was needed is a degree of optimism unlikely to be shared by any student of military history. A more reasonable assumption about any campaign would be that the strength, disposition and terrain of the enemy would be known and the logistic arrangements for the attacking force would be adequate. This however did not apply in the Crimea.

Burgoyne goes into considerable, and laboured, further detail to convince his friends and enemies that the attack should not have been made from the north.

The situation immediately after the Alma suggests that both commanders-in-chief had completely lost their heads. Russell expressed it thus: 'The Allies, as we say, hastened away from a place they had fought a battle to get at, and were marching round it, while Prince Menschikov, in order to save it, was marching away from it.'

But having made the wrong decision on the north side, and not attacked there, the Allies made a second mistake when they arrived on the southern front. Russell checked every gun site and reached the conclusion that:

The total number of guns available for the defence on the south side was 145 pieces, which were spread over a space of nearly five miles. To these were added 27 guns in different places after the news of the loss of the Alma. The only part of the whole line capable of resisting an assault was at the 6th and 7th Bastions. Field works of the feeblest profile, the open spaces and unfinished works armed with light guns, were all that could be said to defend a city, garrisoned by only 16,000 men and 32 field guns. Neither the exultation of the troops nor their resolution to fight to the last extremity could have saved Sebastopol, if the enemy had attacked it immediately after the passage of the Tchernaya. To this Sir John Burgoyne says there was a series of very strong positions, much strengthened by walls, towers, and strong buildings, with a corps d'armée to defend it, almost equal to the assailants who had only field artillery.

Let us now see what the Russians did on the south side whilst we were waiting. Previous to 14 December the armament of the works on the line of Careening Bay to the sea, consisted, as we have seen, of 145 guns, many of which were carronades and pieces of twenty-four, eighteen, and twelve pounds. On 27 September, when the Allies made their appearance, there were 16,000 men and 32 guns on the south side, there were 3,500 men on the north side, and 3,000 sailors on board the ships. Todleben, availing himself of the delay which took place on the part of the Allies, proceeded to fortify the place. The principle on which he proceeded was to occupy the least extended position, and the nearest to the city, which would satisfy the necessary conditions to arm the principal points of the line so selected with the most formidable artillery which could be procured from the fleet, to connect those points with trenches for musketry, and to enable the separate batteries to concentrate a powerful fire on the front and flanks, to sweep the sinuosities of the ground as much as possible. One obstacle to the choice of the best line was presented by works already constructed, to the line of which he was obliged to conform, as there was no time to rectify the errors in trace which they presented. The besieged had only time to throw up the soft earth, as they could not excavate the rock, and the guns were put in position before the batteries were ready to receive them. Men, women, and children, laboured at the defences. Even the convicts and felons took their share. It was rarely they could dig as deep as two and a half feet without coming on the strong subsoil.

The orders to the commanders of the different sections show that the defence would be conducted in deadly earnest. Their instructions were as follows:

1. Concentrate his troops and move the reserves towards the points threatened with an attack, striving at the same time so to dispose the troops that they might be sheltered as much as possible from the fire of the enemy's artillery.

2. Order the artillery to open fire with round shot and shells at a distance at which it can effectively tell upon the enemy, and on his coming within grapeshot range, to fire as rapidly as possible. That the fire of the artillery might be sure to pace the ground beforehand, and mark out the distances of the surrounding objects on the ground in front of the batteries, as well as the range of the grape.

3. The infantry, thickly dispersed along the trenches, in two or more files, must keep up a rapid fire from a distance of 200 yards. The first to fire through the loopholes, the others to charge and hand the muskets.

4. If the enemy should succeed in breaking through our trenches at any point the battalions in columns of attack are to meet him with the bayonet. At the same time the scattered companies are to form rapidly in columns of companies and also to fall on him with the bayonet. The artillerymen are to collect in groups on their batteries, and to defend their guns at the point of the bayonet. [The greater part of the artillerymen consisted of sailors armed with muskets.]

5. On the repulse of the assault on no account to follow the enemy beyond the line of our intrenchment, so as not to hinder the fire of our artillery and infantry.

The companies formed for the bayonet attack will again disperse and direct a powerful musketry fire on the enemy. The artillery will follow him with grapeshot, and then with round shot and shells.

Provided the Russian officers did their job of surveying the area thoroughly the subsequent bombardment of the assault party should have been very effective. There was every reason to suppose that they did.

The garrison was reinforced until by 5 October 1854 there were thirty-two thousand soldiers in position. The later reinforcements included field guns and Cossacks. Nevertheless Todleben still considered the defence and the garrison too weak to withstand a thorough assault if the Allies should launch one. He found that at no point would the Russians be able to concentrate more than two-and-a-half thousand men against whatever force the Allies launched, and that if the Allies once broke the lines of the defence that would be the end, for there was no possibility of a successful counter-attack. The defence was thought to be particularly vulnerable to surprise attack with a feint, or to a daybreak assault when the artillery would be able to distinguish its best targets. In order to boost the defenders' morale Korniloff rode around day and night, watching, encouraging and even supervising. The words of his address to one unit are characteristic of many encouraging speeches in many different countries. 'Men of the Moscow Regiment, you are on the frontiers of Russia; you are defending a precious corner of the Russian Empire. The Tsar and all Russia have their eyes upon you. If you do not fulfil your duty to the utmost, Moscow will not receive you as her sons.'

The Russian urgency was not as important as it appeared to them at the time for the Allies showed no determination or energy in their approach to their task.

The reason for the Allied inertia was in fact, very simple. Just as the Allies had approached the Alma without a trace of subtlety, now they were going to approach Sebastopol with an equally outmoded stereotyped approach. Raglan's thought processes were clearly so slow and conventional that nobody could really believe he could be so unenterprising; in this perhaps there was an element of surprise. It all became obvious. Faced with a citadel he approached it and gave battle to the troops guarding the approach. He made no attempt to lure them out of the position they had chosen, and in fact made no attempt to control the battle he presented to his army on the worst possible terms, but merely contemplated it as an observer. He may or may not have been wrong about this for it could be argued that the original plan, with the French ready to made an encircling attack would have won the battle anyway if the Russians had driven the British Army backwards. He may well have been right about the cavalry pursuit because the cavalry were clearly going to be difficult to control, might misinterpret orders—as they did later in the famous Charge of the Light Brigade—and might well get themselves lost as they did on the flank march around to the south of the city. Possibly his words, 'I will keep my cavalry in a bandbox' may be interpreted to mean that he planned to keep them intact and in reserve—of more value as a potential threat than as a committed force. Possibly, in view of his lack of intelligence about the northern defences, and his own insecure base, he was entirely correct in refusing to hazard an army in such a situation. Had he been repulsed and had the Russians followed up, the rout of his disease-stricken army could have been one of the great catastrophes of history.

Equally predictable was his approach to the siege of Sebastopol. Sebastopol was a city. It was protected on the north by a five-mile-deep inlet, Russian warships, various defences and rugged ground; presumably there would be something similar on the southern side. At least he thought so, and Canrobert, who had succeeded St Arnaud, apparently thought so too. A besieged town could only be approached in a certain way. There was an established technique of siege that had developed steadily from the Middle Ages onwards. Various ingenious engineers had contributed to it; the most notable was Vauban. It was complicated and frequently successful; the only drawback to it was that it was slow. It involved digging trenches towards the besieged town, and at intervals branching off side trenches, known as parallels. From the distance heavy siege guns would bombard the walls; further in lighter artillery would add their contribution. Finally the trenches would creep up to and under the walls which would then be breached by mining. It was slow, laborious and, because of the endless bombardment and counter-bombardment, inclined to produce a steady flow of casualties. It was of course meant for strong, well-garrisoned towns, and was quite out of place here. Sebastopol was the ideal place for a quick assault, as the Russians well knew. Unfortunately the Allied higher command was slow-thinking and completely lacking in enterprise. They could easily have won—and in fact would have found it difficult to lose—but preferred to play safe. The result was two years of misery. Nevertheless, it should not be forgotten that the Allies never had a major reverse—

and a major reverse in their exposed position could have been absolutely disastrous.

It is of course easy to scoff at military pedantry, particularly if one does not happen to be on the scene at the time. But it should not be overlooked that the arts and sciences of attack and defence have been evolved over thousands of years, and although an unorthodox method sometimes achieves surprising and spectacular results it has much more frequently ended in a bloody defeat. Nevertheless, the ponderous progress of the orthodox military mind when in a position of higher command has produced untold frustration and ineptitude. When it is linked with stupidity, obstinacy and prejudice, the results may well prove disastrous. However it can be successfully argued that bold and dashing manoeuvres may produce short-term impressive gains but rarely win wars. Boer tactics in 1899 caused punishing setbacks to British forces but did not achieve total victory.

Once the military mind gets set in its groove it takes a lot to dislodge it. Nowadays it is inconceivable that England, France and Germany should have accepted the losses they did in the First World War 1914–18 but the interesting feature of it all was that the military concepts of both sides were equally unenterprising. Britain accepted huge losses at Loos, the Somme and Passchendaele; France and Germany settled to a war of mass extermination at Verdun. But in view of the conditions, resources, weapons and attitudes of the time it was all predictable. On this basis the Crimea campaign and in particular, the approach to Sebastopol, is much more easily understandable. However, it needs to be taken in conjunction with the development of fortification.

The earliest form of fortification was a mound and a ditch. The mound would probably have a palisade of thorns on top. This type of fortification developed into town walls. For many years these remained simple in form, and the advances in defensive technique were accomplished with the stone castle. Castle defence became a highly sophisticated matter but its main contribution to town defence was in the nature of the outer curtain walls. These were made high and thick. At the base they had a battered plinth, that is an outward projection, and along the line of the wall would project semi-circular towers. These walls would be difficult to approach because of the fire from the parapet and towers, difficult to damage because of their thickness, and impossible to undermine because of the surrounding ditch. The flanking towers, or bastions, which would be built at the corners as well as along the line would make attempts to scale the wall very hazardous.

Nevertheless defence was never passive; the besieged did not treat their secure walls as a refuge but as a suitable base for launching harassing attacks. There was never a stage in which the defender waited for the attacker; as likely as not the attacker would be harassed more often by the defence than he could mount his own assaults. In consequence his own offensive had to be reasonably defensive. With the invention of gunpowder this interesting balance of the attacking defender and the defending attacker became more noticeable than ever. The miner would obviously approach from underground, or at least from a trench, and so, after a while, did the infantryman and the artilleryman. But the attack would become most vulnerable just as it approached the walls, for the bastion towers, or even the walls themselves, would jut out in what was called the 'indented trace'. This soon progressed to what was known as the 'bastioned trace' by which the city was defended by a series of complicated outworks with towers, projections, covered passages, and every device that could be thought of to make flanking fire easier.

Towards the end of the seventeenth century Vauban turned the art and science of defence into something almost resembling a religion. In spite of saying that 'one does not fortify by systems but by good sense and experience' he designed a large number of fortifications which were so elaborate that no one could have commanded them successfully with the existing system of communications. After Vauban the defence aided by well-screened artillery obtained a temporary ascendancy over the attack. Vauban's principles of attack—which made successful assault certain even if very slow—were therefore followed meticulously.

Knowing that the methodical application of Vauban principles would cause any citadel to fall, experts in defence gave further and deeper thought to their problems. Montalembert looked critically at Vauban's defensive outlays and modified them into what eventually became known as the 'polygonal' trace. Carnot took this a stage further by giving the defenders every facility to make sallies and harass and destroy the besiegers. The method became almost sacrosanct after Torres Vedras in 1810, Linz Towers, Austria, in 1830 and the Paris defences of 1844.

At Sebastopol the Russians had the great advantage of a thirty-six-year-old Engineer, Lt-Col Todleben. Although young in years he was not so in experience; he had been commissioned at the age of eighteen and had recently shown that he was that rare commodity—a military genius. When given the task of defending the town he said—and probably believed—that his task was impossible for he had insufficient time. The basis of his belief was that even if the Allies failed to attack the vulnerable north front they could not possibly fail on the south where there was five miles of virtually undefended line. To his astonishment and gratification the Allies delayed so long before making their assault that he was able to make a formidable defence against them. As he put it:

We immediately proceeded to strengthen our artillery on that part of the line which faced the French trenches, as it was evident that the enemy intended to erect batteries there. Judging from the extent of the work, about forty guns could be placed on it. On our part measures were immediately taken to oppose a superior artillery to the enemy's batteries and for that part it was resolved to pierce embrasures in the 4th, 5th, and 6th Bastions towards the enemy's trench, while favourable places were chosen for new batteries.

Todleben proved to be right. In the opening exchange of fire the Russians completely silenced the French artillery at that point. They were less successful against the more distant English battery and suffered so much damage that even at this stage a swift Allied attack would probably have penetrated the city. But this sort of immediate action, taking advantage of unexpected opportunities, was not within the concept of war as seen by Raglan and Canrobert.

Raglan's dispatch on 18 October 1854 read as follows:

My Lord Duke

It was arranged between General Canrobert and myself that the batteries of the two armies should open immediately after daylight on the morning of the 17th and we invited Admiral Dundas and Admiral Hamelin to attack the enemy's works at the mouth of the harbour, with the combined fleets, as nearly simultaneously as circumstances might permit.

Accordingly upon a signal being given from the centre of the French lines, the batteries of the two armies commenced their fire about a quarter before seven yesterday morning.

On this occasion we employed about 60 guns of different calibres, the lightest being 24 pounders.

It may be here proper to observe that the character of the position which the enemy occupy on the south side of Sebastopol is not that of a fortress, but rather of an army in an entrenched camp on very strong ground, where an unlimited number of heavy guns, amply provided with gunners and ammunition are mounted.

The guns having opened as above stated, a continuous and well-divided fire was carried on from the works of the two armies until about ten o'clock am when, unfortunately, a magazine in the midst of one of the French batteries exploded and occasioned considerable damage to the works, and I fear many casualties, and almost paralyzed the efforts of the French artillery for the day. . . .

British Batteries, however, manned by sailors from the fleet, under the command of Captain Lushington and Captain Peel, and by the Royal Artillery, under the superintendence of Lieutenant-Colonel Gambier kept up their fire with unremitting energy throughout the day to my own and the general satisfaction, as well as to the admiration of the French Army, who were witnesses of their gallant and persevering exertions, materially injuring the enemy works, and silencing the heavy guns on the top of the loop-holed tower to which I adverted in my dispatch of the 13th instant, and many of its guns at its base, and causing an extensive explosion in the rear of a strong redoubt in our immediate front; the enemy, notwithstanding, answered to the last from a number of guns along their more extended line.

In the remainder of the dispatch he mentioned that, 'The English, French, and Turkish fleets moved towards the mouth of the harbour about noon, and kept up a heavy fire upon the enemy's forts for several hours.'

After some details of the success of this naval bombardment he went on to say, 'Since I wrote to your Grace on the 18th, six battalions of Turkish infantry, and 300 Turkish artillery have been added to the force in front of Balaclava (and placed under my command).'

The arrival of these reinforcements, the knowledge that the Russians had not yet had time to dig in but were frantically doing so, the certain knowledge that the Allied superiority was dwindling every day in the face of the Russian effort; none of these had the slightest effect on Raglan's plan. His inertia may probably have been entirely due to the facts mentioned above, that is, that a siege could only be tackled in the traditional way, but a kindlier view would be that knowing how completely unaccustomed to warfare most of his troops were, he thought it folly to commit them wholesale to action. However, although his own troops were unaccustomed to battle so were the Russians, and with disease at work on all sides it could have been wise to use them before they were hopelessly weakened.

But it is clear from his next dispatch, dated 23 October that there was never any possibility of his making the right decision for he did not see the campaign in these terms at all. He wrote:

> Our fire has been constant and effective; but the enemy having at their disposal large bodies of men; and the resources of the fleet and arsenal at their command, having been enabled by unceasing exertion to repair their redoubts to a certain extent, and to replace many of the guns that have been destroyed in a very short space of time; and to resume their fire from works which we had succeeded in silencing.
>
> This facility of repairing and rearming the defences naturally renders the progress of the assailants slower then could be wished; and I have it not in my power to inform your Grace, with anything like certainty, when it may be expected that ulterior measures may be undertaken.

This last paragraph, with its wonderfully inept conclusion, spelt the doom of many a man who was still walking around in England, for it showed that Raglan was happy to settle down to a war of attrition at a pace to be directed by the Russians. The Russians, however, were not content to conduct the war at the leisurely pace which Lord Raglan seemed to prefer, and attacked his forces two days later.

5

# The Balaclava Battles

One feels on reading his dispatches covering the events that followed the initial Russian attack that Raglan felt the Russians were somewhat unsporting in the vigour with which they kept up their onslaughts. A sally or two would be reasonable by his standards but the constant pressure kept up by Russians who should have been more concerned with defending than attacking was clearly not suitable to a besieged enemy. Both his dispatch of 28 October, which describes the famous charges of the Heavy Brigade and the Light Brigade, and the dispatch of 8 November which describes the Battle of Inkerman, are masterpieces of understatement.

Before describing the incidents it is necessary to give some account of the general situation.

The besieging force was on the south side of Sebastopol, with the French on the left (western flank) based on Kamiesch and the English on the right with a right flank extending as far as the Heights of Inkerman. The English forces were some six miles from their supply base at Balaclava to which they were linked by an indifferent road. Balaclava, and the road, were almost entirely open to Russian attacks for scarcely any attempt had been made to fortify this vital position. The layout of the ground and the disposition of the troops will be seen on the Appendix map. It will be seen that there were two lines of defences around Balaclava; the inner was on steep ground and contained naval guns and marines, the outer was weak. It lay along the line of the Causeway Heights with the exception of one which was opposite Kamara on a site known as 'Canrobert's Hill'. All the redoubts in these positions were clumsily constructed and weak. They were garrisoned by Turks, who, being badly commanded and knowing that they were in a vulnerable, exposed position, did not live up to their former reputation as fighting soldiers. Beyond the heights lay the north valley which was flanked on the left by the Fedioukine Heights. In the south valley, that is, the valley within the weak defensive system, were the 93rd Highlanders, and the cavalry commanded by Lord Lucan; the cavalry consisted of the Heavy Brigade under General Scarlett, and the Light Brigade under General the Earl of Cardigan.

On 25 October the Russians, commanded by General Liprandi, moved on to Balaclava with a force of twenty-five thousand infantry, thirty-four squadrons of horse and a total of seventy-eight guns.

The attack should not have been unexpected, for its imminence had been reported by a Turkish spy. Then, as later, spies brought in so many conflicting reports that the more valuable tended to be thrown out with the worthless. At dawn on the 25th however, the Russian advance was clearly seen and steps were taken to meet it. In the circumstances it will come as no surprise that the steps taken were too few and too late and the task of holding the Russian attack fell on one unit only.

The Russian advance was in three groups. The left flank came to Canrobert's Hill, the centre came to the Causeway Heights and the third took up a position on the Fedioukine Heights. The Turkish outposts were soon overwhelmed by a combination of artillery fire and massed infantry attacks. Those on Canrobert's Hill who resisted had 170 killed out of 500, the remainder did not stay to be massacred but fled to what they hoped would be the safety of Balaclava. It is said that the only person who tried to stop them was the wife of a Scottish soldier who struck everyone she could reach with her broomstick in an attempt to sweep them together and turn them back to face the enemy. Eventually they were rounded up by a naval captain and formed into line behind the 93rd.

The 93rd (who with the 91st became the Argyll and Sutherland Highlanders) numbered a mere 550 and were drawn up two deep. They were commanded by Sir Colin Campbell, who said to them 'Remember, there is no retreat. You must die where you stand.' His words were greeted with a cheer. As the Russians approached, some of the 93rd pressed forward as if to charge, but were steadied by Campbell.

This absolute steadfastness and resolution communicated itself to the Russian cavalry as it advanced. The first volley from the 93rd was at long range. Surprised, the Russians checked, but rode on. Then came the second volley. Somewhat disconcerted, but with the intention of outflanking the 93rd, the Russian cavalry commander wheeled away to the left. As he exposed his flank the 93rd picked their targets again; the Russians rode away. It was not a great or bloody battle, but a supreme test of nerve. As the only unit which stood between the Russians and Balaclava the 93rd had saved the day, and earned their distinguished title 'the thin red line'*. Had it been required they would undoubtedly have been wiped out to a man, and the knowledge of that—and the cost of it—was not lost on the Russians. It seems that no Russians were killed but a number were hurt.

Elsewhere there were other tense conflicts of strength and will. The main body of the Russian cavalry was beginning to come over Causeway Heights, and there was little to check them. But that little was Scarlett's Heavy Cavalry. As Scarlett moved up to the Causeway Heights he had no idea of the forces opposing him. Even when they appeared over the crest of the hill he did not know their full numbers, which were, in fact, three thousand. He himself had six squadrons (a total of eight hundred) and they were advancing in two parallel columns. On the left was one squadron of the Inniskillings and two of the Scots Greys, and on the right was another squadron of the Inniskillings and two of the 5th Dragoon Guards. To the rear were the Royal Dragoons and 4th Dragoon Guards.

Scarlett's success was due to his swiftness of decision. Seeing that the Russians were virtually at a halt he decided that a quick assault would be productive of considerable results. To accomplish this he wheeled into line the left column, which consisted of only three hundred sabres (swordsmen on horseback) and led the charge himself. He headed straight for the centre of the Russians and, when he arrived, set to with the best of them, although sixty-one years old. He himself received five wounds, and his ADC fourteen. Fortunately, three British guns found the range of the rear of the Russian force at this time and contributed considerably to its discomfiture. But the main effect was caused by the vigour, speed and determination of the charging squadrons, not only as they arrived but in the way they fought when once among the Russians. The latter, perhaps thinking that another similar charge must be on the way at any moment, gave ground, broke up, and finally rode fast away from the scene. It was an incredible situation, eight hundred men putting

* To receive cavalry, infantry usually formed up four deep, or in squares. The 93rd had no time to do this—even if they had wished to—and the thinness of their line gave them their distinguished epithet.

three thousand to rout. But this was a war of surprises, and they were not limited to one side. In all fairness it must be acknowledged that the way the Russians built the defences and subsequently fought for Sebastopol, the way the French stormed the Malakoff, and many individual or sub-unit performances, showed great heroism. Unfortunately the magnificent achievement of the Heavy Brigade, which was a genuine and much needed victory, has been overshadowed by other less valuable but more publicized events in the war.

The most famous incident of the war but, in truth, one of the least important, was the Charge of the Light Brigade which was soon to follow. Had there been any control or cohesion in the British force Scarlett's magnificent repulse of the Russians would have been made into a complete rout by the Light Brigade. But, unbelievably, Cardigan sat watching the Russian retreat through a gap in the heights and never moved. His brigade numbered 675, and according to Lucan, Cardigan had been told to attack everyone and everything. Cardigan, when subsequently criticized for his inactivity, denied this strenuously and affirmed he had been instructed to remain on the defensive. Cardigan's virtues and defects have been minutely analysed elsewhere, and there is no point in going into them here. The only relevant point is that as war is such an unreasonable matter there have been many occasions when utterly unreasonable—even scarcely sane—commanders have brought their troops to such a pitch of bewilderment and frustration that even the wildest demands have been met without appearing to be particularly excessive.

Raglan, who, as might be expected, was observing the whole scene from the highest point, was far from pleased at this display of apparently sullen ineptitude and sent a message to Lucan telling him to occupy the ground which the Russians were vacating. Lucan did not accept the message as an order for he knew very well that the correct way to occupy that ground was by a combined infantry action. As he had no infantry to combine with he sat and waited for it. No infantry was forthcoming, so another golden opportunity was allowed to slip away.

The next order was clearer, and of great importance. The Russians, pleased at not being harassed, decided to send out horses and drag away the guns in the redoubts they had overrun earlier. Raglan observed this and realized that if they did they would have the fruits of apparent victory. Feeling that his recent verbal instructions had been misinterpreted, he put his next in writing and sent his ADC

Captain Nolan with a message to Lord Lucan. It directed the latter to 'advance rapidly to the front and prevent the enemy from carrying off the guns.'

From his position Lucan could not see the guns to which Raglan referred, and assumed that the latter meant the Russian guns further down the valley. He considered, not surprisingly, that such an attempt would not merely be suicidal, but also futile, and said as much. Nolan, of whom much has also been written replied–insolently as Lucan thought, 'Lord Raglan orders that the cavalry should attack immediately.' Lucan turned to him in disdainful irritation and said, 'Attack, Sir. Attack what?' In reply Nolan waved airily down the valley and said, 'There my Lord is the enemy, there are the guns.'

Lucan by this stage was in a towering rage at this unreasonable order, delivered by an insolent and conceited captain, but nevertheless decided to obey it. He rode up to Cardigan and told him to advance. Even the imperturbable Cardigan found this order a little strange. Having received the order, and nodded assent, he added 'Permit me to observe that we are advancing against a battery with guns and riflemen on our flanks.' 'Yes, I know,' was Lucan's answer, 'but it is the Commander-in-Chief's order.'

That, of course, was that. Cardigan, who had the skin of a rhinoceros but the heart of a lion, gave the order to move: 'The brigade will advance.'

Cardigan led the charge, closely followed by his ADCs Captains Maxse and Wombwell. The brigade consisted of the 13th Light Dragoons and 17th Lancers, followed by the 4th Hussars and the 11th Hussars, with the 8th Hussars in the third line. The pace was a steady trot in perfect formation. As it began Nolan galloped obliquely across the front waving his sword and pointing. He was killed by a shell splinter almost immediately–although he remained rigid in his saddle for a few seconds longer–but it was subsequently decided that he had suddenly come to his senses, and realizing the fearful catastrophe his ill-tempered bad manners was about to cause, made a heroic effort to prevent it. Nolan was a complex character, of distinguished record, and was but one of several people who contributed to the disaster of the charge.

The event was of course absolutely heroic, and in its immediate results utterly futile. The general impression is that six hundred men advanced and two or three emerged. It was not quite like that. Of the 673 men who took part in the charge 247 were casualties: 113 of them being killed. Nearly all the horses were killed or had to be destroyed subsequently. From start to finish it took twenty minutes. The brigade was not merely shot to pieces by gunfire, it was also intercepted by Russian cavalry and had to fight its way out. It reached the end of the valley, it reached the unattainable guns, killed the gunners, and even rode past the guns to face a huge Russian cavalry force behind. There was nothing to be done but to turn round and ride out again—what was left of them. Cardigan was apparently unmoved by this monumental feat of British courage, of which he was a vital part, and rode back to his yacht grumbling at Nolan, had a bath, drank a bottle of champagne and went to bed. It was all in the day's work as far as he was concerned.

Was it merely a futile, flamboyant, expensive gesture? The answer is no. Elite armies have to be capable of such feats if they are to be of the finest quality. The Charge of the Light Brigade was an example of what courage, determination and discipline will do, however misdirected. The spirit that enabled the charge to be made also made the victories of Marlborough and Wellington possible. It was the spirit of Isandhlwana and Rorke's Drift, of the Marne, Landrecies and many another occasion of British arms. It was a pity that it achieved no victory and took place on a day when the Russians took all the valuable prizes. They carried off the Turkish guns, they held the Causeway Heights and they gained command of the vital Woronzoff road which would have enabled the British to move supplies easily from Balaclava to the front line.

The Charge of the Light Brigade has been so publicized that certain features of it are overlooked or distorted. The first is that brave though it was, it was by no means unique. There have been numerous other occasions when battalions have unflinchingly advanced to their almost certain death. Secondly, it might not have been such a classic blunder as it is popularly supposed to be. Already, on that day, spectacular courage had been found to give results vastly beyond expectations. There was a chance—though admittedly a slight one—that the Russians might have abandoned their guns and fled. Cardigan—who of course had no option about accepting the order—might well have expected this; after all, Russian resistance had collapsed very suddenly on the Alma. Thirdly, it was not a charge in the accepted sense of the word; the distance was a mile and a half, and although the pace increased as the Brigade neared the far end, the order to charge was never given.

Nolan, who being dead could give no subsequent explanation of events, has been thoroughly blamed. Had he survived, his memory for fragments of conversation might have equalled that of the other participants. The clarity with which vital conversations were recalled is as remarkable as it is incredible. It is, of course, true that in conditions of great stress tiny details are forever imprinted on people's minds, and it may perhaps be that the traumatic nature of the occasion caused all these casual words to be recollected perfectly. The fact that they have been repeated faithfully by writer after writer since the first person recorded—or perhaps invented—them, gives a wonderful touch of authenticity. Unfortunately, history is full of inspiring words which turn out, on examination, not to have been used by the people to whom they are ascribed. Usually the clearest statements are made by those who died in the process. 'Kiss me, Hardy' (or was it 'Kismet, Hardy') 'How is the Empire' and so on; however it is of some importance to a person's family to know whether or not a certain form of words was used. Cardigan, who was not renowned for either intelligence or memory, was able, in future years, to recall perfectly what had been said.

The only person who could have elucidated the matter was Nolan. He had delivered a vague message of considerable urgency; he was a superb horseman and the ride down the slope which he had just accomplished was one which few men would have been able to do at the speed. He was an Irish Italian, passionately fond of his profession and desperate to see his beloved Light Cavalry at last play their rightful part in the war. He hated Cardigan as much as Cardigan despised him. It is possible that the exertion of what had been a highly dangerous ride, and the feeling that even now Cardigan was going to do something—or not do something—which would prevent these élite horsemen going into action, made him gesticulate wildly. Possibly he may not have understood Raglan's order himself, or, more probably, he was so nettled by Cardigan's evident disdain for him that he indicated the Russian guns as a taunt. Subsequently, seeing what was about to happen he undoubtedly tried to redirect the charge. The most likely explanation is that he arrived with the idea that Raglan wished for a quick charge to the Russian guns, but after he had delivered the message realized that it was the former Turkish, not the Russian, guns which were intended. The mistake would be natural enough. Most people can recall thinking one thing in the heat of an excited moment, but something quite different after a moment's calmer reappraisal. There is also no real reason to suppose he did give Cardigan the correct order but that the latter misinterpreted it. The difference in the two directions has been variously calculated as being between twenty and thirty degrees.

The most restrained account of the above events occurs in Raglan's dispatch of 28 October. It ran:

My Lord Duke,

I have the honour to inform your Grace that the enemy attacked the position in front of Balaclava at an early hour on the morning of the 25th instant.

The low range of heights that runs across the plain at the bottom of which the town is placed was protected by four small redoubts hastily constructed. Three of these had guns in them, and on a higher hill, in front of the village of Camara, in advance of our right flank, was established a work of somewhat more importance.

These several redoubts were garrisoned by Turkish troops, no other force being at my disposal for their occupation.

The 93rd Highlanders was the only British regiment on the plain, with the exception of a part of a battalion of detachments composed of weakly men, and a battery of artillery belonging to the Third Division; and on the heights behind our right were placed the Marines, obligingly landed from the fleet by Vice-Admiral Dundas. All these, including the Turkish troops, were under the immediate orders of Major-General Sir Colin Campbell, whom I had taken from the first Division with the 93rd.

As soon as I was apprised of this movement of the enemy I felt compelled to withdraw from before Sebastopol the First and Fourth Divisions, commanded by Lieutenant-Generals His Royal Highness the Duke of Cambridge and the Honourable Sir George Cathcart, and bring them down into the plain, and General Canrobert subsequently reinforced these troops with the First Division of French Infantry and the Chasseurs d'Afrique.

The enemy commenced their operation by attacking the work on our side of the village of Camara, and, after very little resistance, carried it.

They likewise got possession of the three others in contiguity to it, being opposed only in one, and that but for a very short space of time.

The farthest of the three they did not retain, but the immediate abandonment of the others enabled them to take possession of the guns in them, amounting in the whole to seven. Those in the three lesser forts were spiked by the one English artilleryman who was in each.

The Russian cavalry at once advanced, supported by artillery, in very great strength. One portion of them assailed the front and right flank of the 93rd, and were instantly driven back by the vigorous and steady fire of that distinguished regiment under Lieutenant-Colonel Ainslie.

The other and larger force turned towards Her Majesty's heavy cavalry, and afforded Brigadier-General Scarlett, under the guidance of Lieutenant-General the Earl of Lucan, the opportunity of inflicting upon them a most signal defeat. The ground was very unfavourable for the attack of our Dragoons, but no obstacle was sufficient to check their advance, and they charged into a Russian column which soon sought safety in flight, although far superior in numbers.

The charge of this brigade was one of the most successful I ever witnessed, was never for a moment doubtful, and is in the highest degree creditable to Brigadier-General Scarlett and the officers and men engaged in it.

As the enemy withdrew from the ground which they had momentarily occupied I directed the cavalry, supported by the Fourth Division, under Lieutenant-General Sir George Cathcart, to move forward, and take advantage of any opportunity to regain the heights; and not having been able to accomplish this immediately, and it appearing that an attempt was making to remove the captured guns, the Earl of Lucan was desired to advance rapidly, follow the enemy in their retreat, and try to prevent them from effecting their objects.

In the meanwhile the Russians had time to re-form on their own ground, with artillery in front and upon their flanks.

From some misconception of the instruction to advance the Lieutenant-General considered that he was bound to attack at all hazards, and he accordingly ordered Major-General the Earl of Cardigan to move forward with the Light Brigade.

This order was obeyed in a most spirited and gallant manner. Lord Cardigan charged with the utmost vigour, attacked a battery which was firing on the advancing squadrons, and, having passed beyond it, engaged the Russian cavalry in its rear; but then his troops were assailed by artillery and infantry, as well as cavalry and necessarily retired, after having committed much havoc upon the enemy. They effected this movement without haste or confusion but the loss they have sustained has, I deeply lament, been very severe in officers, men and horses, only counterbalanced by the brilliancy of the attack, and the gallantry, order and discipline which distinguished it, forming a striking contrast to the enemy's cavalry, which had previously been engaged with the heavy brigade.

The Chasseurs d'Afrique advanced on our left and gallantly charged a Russian battery, which checked its fire for a time, and thus rendered the British cavalry an essential service.

The dispatch continued with the mention of Lieutenant-Colonel Ainslie of the 93rd and Captain Barker of the Royal Artillery, the

Earl of Cardigan and Brigadier-General Scarlett. As the Russians made no further attacks the British forces reoccupied their original positions but, he went on to say:

> The Fourth Division had advanced close to the heights, and Sir George Cathcart caused one of the redoubts to be reoccupied by the Turks, affording them his support and he availed himself of the opportunity to assist with his riflemen in silencing two of the enemy's guns.
>
> The means of defending the extensive position which had been occupied by the Turkish troops in the morning having proved wholly inadequate I deemed it necessary, in concurrence with General Canrobert, to withdraw from the lower range of heights, and to concentrate our force, which will be increased by a considerable body of seamen, to be landed from the ships under the authority of Admiral Dundas, immediately in front of the narrow valley leading into Balaclava, and upon the precipitous heights on our right, thus affording a narrower line of defence.

The reactions of the home government on reading the last paragraph are not recorded but it is not difficult to surmise what they might have thought on reading that the force which had been dispatched to conquer Sebastopol, and had had a considerable victory at the Alma, should now be withdrawing into a narrower perimeter around their base, which was a good six miles from their objective.

Raglan enclosed reports from Sir Colin Campbell and the Earl of Lucan with his own. Lucan spoke very highly of the attacks by the Heavy and Light Brigades but made no distinction between their relative importance in the conduct of the campaign. Of the Heavy Brigade he said 'Upon every disadvantage of ground these eight small squadrons succeeded in defeating and dispersing a body of cavalry estimated at three times their number and more', but he seemed more impressed by the Light Brigade: 'The attack of the Light Cavalry was very brilliant and daring; exposed to a fire from heavy batteries on their front and two flanks they advanced unchecked until they reached the batteries of the enemy, and cleared them of their gunners, and only retired when they found themselves engaged with a very superior force of cavalry in the rear.'

His concluding paragraph mentioned Maude and Shakespear, whom we referred to at the Alma: 'The conduct of the Royal Horse Artillery Troop, first under the command of Captain Maude and, after that officer was severely wounded, of Captain Shakespear, was most meritorious and praiseworthy. I received from these officers every possible assistance during the time they respectively commanded.'

Campbell's report was more numerically factual:

> When the enemy had taken possession of their redoubts their artillery advanced with a large mass of cavalry, and their guns ranged on the 93rd Highlanders, which with 100 invalids with Lieutenant-Colonel Daveney in support, occupied very insufficiently from the smallness of their numbers the slightly rising ground in front of No 4 Battery. As I found that the shot and shell began to cause some casualties among the 93rd Highlanders and the Turkish battalions on their right and left flank I made them retire a few paces behind the crest of the hill. During this period our batteries on the hills, manned by the Royal Marine Artillery and the Royal Marines, made most excellent practice of the enemy's cavalry, which came over the hill ground in front. One body of them, amounting to about 400 men turned to their left, separating themselves from those who attacked Lord Lucan's Division, and charged the 93rd Highlanders, who immediately advanced to the crest of the hill and opened their fire, which forced the Russian cavalry to give way and turn to their left, after which they made an attempt to turn the right flank of the Turks, who were placed there, upon which the Grenadiers of the 93rd, under Captain Ross, were wheeled to their right and fired on the enemy, which manoeuvre completely discomfited them.
>
> During the rest of the day the troops under my command received no further molestation from the Russians.

Nevertheless the Russians, although content with their work for one day, did not relax their efforts. They realized much too well for English comfort that attack is the best form of defence, at least as far as siege warfare is concerned, and were not content to sit still and be reduced slowly. Two days later they were out again with large, though unspecified, numbers. De Lacy Evans described the Russian force as 'several columns of Infantry supported by artillery. Their masses, covered by large bodies of skirmishers, advanced with much apparent confusion.' They were stopped by accurate artillery fire and pushed back by vigorous infantry attacks in which eighty were taken prisoner. The English losses, coincidentally, also totalled eighty. Raglan's subsequent dispatch estimated the Russian force as numbering six to seven thousand men. He was not present at the time, through no fault of his own, being occupied at Balaclava when it took place. He enclosed the Adjutant-General's (J. B. Estcourt) casualty return which records that Lucan and Brigadier-General Scarlett were both wounded slightly.

The Russians had by no means exhausted their efforts and were now preparing for the Battle of Inkerman.

# 6
# Inkerman

Inkerman is well known as 'the soldiers' battle' and owes its name to the fact that the British Army was taken by surprise and won the fight without higher direction. It was the biggest and longest battle so far. Although a reverse at the Alma could have been a disaster, it was unlikely that the Russians would have moved forward and taken advantage of it. At Balaclava the Russians were taken as much by surprise at their success as the Allies were; but at Inkerman the Russians were out to win, and if they had done so would have made the victory devastating.

For all practical purposes the Allies might not have had any previous victories at all. They were in a weaker position, relative to the Russians, than they had been a month before, and the Russian generals knew it. The Russian command was also aware that the Allied forces were affected by a sort of paralysis that prevented them from taking the initiative, although they probably did not appreciate its cause.

The Russian forces, under Generals Soimonoff, Pauloff and Gortschakoff, totalled 55,000 with 220 guns. There were 63,000 Allied troops on the peninsula but in the event only some 16,000 were available for the battle, and only 12,000 were actually engaged. Troops were committed piecemeal to the battle, and the earlier fighting fell almost entirely to the 2nd Division, which totalled only 3,000 men.

It was fortunate for the Russians that their approach march took them to one of the most weakly defended parts of the Allied position—the English right flank. The position of the 2nd Division had for some time given concern to many, notably to its commander Sir de Lacy Evans. Raglan was well aware of the isolated and exposed position of the Division and would have liked to send it more men and also to furnish it with a line of suitable defence; unfortunately every available man had to be used in the tortuous conventional approach to the siege of Sebastopol. This was reasonable enough if one saw the primary task as reducing the town by a formal siege but somewhat incautious in view of the constant reports—some of them from friends in Russia—of large Russian forces bearing down on the Allies for imminent attack. The only possible support for the 2nd Division was a brigade of the Light Division on the adjoining (Victoria) ridge but a very rough ravine separated the two forces. Nearly a mile to the rear was the Brigade of Guards and nearly three miles away were the 3rd and 4th Divisions whose assignment was besieging Sebastopol. There was a French army corps under Bosquet but this could not be used quickly. There was no possibility of reinforcements for there were no other troops who could be brought up in time.

The Russian attack was launched in two columns, with a combined strength of thirty-five thousand, using just over half their available guns. They planned to join up on the northern slopes of Mt Inkerman after having destroyed all local resistance. These columns would be led by Soimonoff and Pauloff. They would subsequently be joined by the remainder of the Russian forces, under Gortschakoff who up to this point would have been fending off any attempt by the French to interfere by coming to the aid of the English. Fortunately for the Allies the proposed battlefield was too small to employ all this number of men, and was also very rugged, making any sort of large-scale movement in formation almost impossible.

The battlefield itself will be seen to be a ridge, running north-west. Parallel, but separated by a ravine—the Carenague—was the Victoria Ridge. The Inkerman Ridge was crossed by a smaller ridge—the Home Ridge. Four hundred yards on the inner side of the Home Ridge was a low stone fortification known as 'the barrier'. To the north-east of this—but a little lower down the slope on a spur about four hundred yards off—was a gun emplacement holding two eighteen-pounder guns. It was known as the Sandbag Battery. It was a very difficult battlefield for not only was it rough but it was also covered with scrubby vegetation, rocks and large stones.

In spite of warnings the Russian attack had the advantage of complete surprise when it came. It was initiated by Soimonoff at 5 am with all the advantages of morning fog and darkness. As the outposts clashed, the Russian guns started shelling the rear area. The English —or rather the Irish Commander of the 2nd Division, Pennefather— behaved somewhat unpredictably. Instead of falling back—which would have permitted the Russian guns to take a heavy toll—he pushed forward. The Russians were somewhat disconcerted to find that they themselves were being attacked by numbers which they could not estimate, but which presumably must be large for such an action to take place at all, and the English set to merrily without the vestige of an idea that they were completely isolated and unsupported. The original attacking force numbered only three thousand, but they were well positioned, and fired with such accuracy and speed that the Russian column—which had expected no such thing—was broken up and retired behind its own guns.

Soimonoff had not however gone to all this trouble to be repulsed as easily and quickly as that. Next he made a drive straight for the centre of the British line, using nine thousand men. Fortunately for Pennefather, elements of the Light Division were now coming up, and among them the redoubtable Connaught Rangers (the 88th Regiment). There were only four hundred of them, but for a while they stood the whole weight of the Russian attack. When the Russians moved on, as inevitably they must, they were by no means the better for the experience of meeting the 88th, and when caught in the flank by the 77th (the Middlesex), began to fall back. By this time it was the bayonet rather than the bullet. In the thoroughgoing melée that followed, General Soimonoff, his second-in-command and a number of his staff, were all killed. The Russians fought with great courage and determination, but were put out by the vigour, wildness and unexpected nature of the charges they had to sustain. The last chance of rallying was dispersed when the 49th (the Berkshire Regiment) put in a vigorous attack.

But the destruction of Soimonoff's column was by no means the end of the battle. Pauloff was doing considerably better and had captured the Sandbag Battery. Pennefather had few enough forces to dispose of but he committed the 41st (the Welsh Regiment) to this attack. They advanced in an impressive but vulnerable manner, widely extended. The Russians assumed there must be more of them, and, after the first devastating volleys, decided to fall back. When inexperienced troops fall back, that is the end of the matter unless the officers are of exceptional quality, and the Russians at this moment were not. The Sandbag Battery was recaptured.

Meanwhile, what was left of Pauloff's men were now approaching the Barrier with every intention of reversing the trend of the fighting elsewhere. Here they met one wing of the 30th (the East Lancashire Regiment), a mere two hundred men. Unfortunately for the East Lancashires their guns were wet and the caps would not explode. There was nothing for it but close quarters and the bayonet. Again it was completely unexpected—the Russians had come forward for an entirely different form of fighting. While they were confused they fell back, and once they began to fall back it was soon over. It was still only 7.30 am.

But good though these results were they were by no means enough. The Russians were not deterred by large losses, and there were, in any case, ten thousand men who had not yet seen any fighting. These numbers could not possibly be matched by any English reinforcements, in number at any event. But some reinforcements were on the way. They included the Brigade of Guards, about 1,200, the Fourth Division, about 2,000, and another 1,500 from the Batteries. There were also two French battalions but, owing to a misunderstanding, these were not committed till later.

The Russians were now reorganized under General Dannenberg. He made his first objective the Sandbag Battery, and though the 41st defended it stubbornly, after a time they had to fall back and leave it to the enemy. As it happened it was not a particularly valuable asset either strategically or tactically, but once it began to change hands it was given a totally unmerited importance. A first-class general quickly distinguishes which ground is vital, and should be held at all costs, and which is merely useful; unfortunately there was no one to make these vital decisions at this point and, as a result, the Guards recaptured the Sandbag Battery, only to vacate it for a better position immediately behind. However, once they vacated it the Russians re-occupied it, and were very pleased to do so. The Guards, thinking they had missed a trick, attacked and recaptured the position only to decide to vacate it again. But as soon as the Russians reappeared the Guards decided it had been a mistake to leave, and, by tremendous efforts, fought their way back in again.

However, the situation, which had gone remarkably well for the English, could not be relied upon to continue in that way. Curiously enough, disaster occurred when they were on the offensive. As the 4th Division (Sir George Cathcart) came up, its troops were committed where they seemed to be most needed. There were only two thousand of them and apart from one-fifth, who were kept in reserve, they were sent in detachments at what seemed to be key points. Cathcart took the majority and, thinking there was an opportunity for a decisive flank attack on the Russian left, set off down the slope to exploit it. He was joined by elements of the Guards, of the 20th (Lancashire Fusiliers) and 95th (Sherwood Foresters). Unfortunately he would have been better advised to have plugged the gap which had always existed between the Guards and Pennefather's extreme right—and indeed this course of action had been suggested by Raglan who had now come up. Unfortunately Raglan had not made his suggestion an order. The gap was soon filled by Russians who were thus able to come in the rear of Cathcart's small force. Cathcart was shot dead in the early stages of the fight so did not have to justify his action. His troops fought like tigers, and managed to extricate themselves and join their fellows, but it was a bad move and weakened an already overstretched effort.

Just as the East Lancashires were meeting forces of vastly superior numbers they were reinforced by the Rifle Brigade. The fighting was now on the edge of a quarry. At this point in came the 21st (Royal Scots Fusiliers), 63rd (Manchester Regiment), 20th (Lancashire Fusiliers) and 57th (the Middlesex)—'the Die Hards'. The French were now in action and although Allied forces were pitifully weak, there was no slackening of effort or morale.

Nor was there on the Russian side. Dannenberg pushed forward on to the English centre with the spearhead of a force of six thousand. Against this Pennefather had a mixed force that consisted partly of remnants. It included the 55th (the Border Regiment), the 95th, the 77th and the 7th Leger (French) and a sprinkling of Zouaves. It was not enough, and they were gradually driven back. At the critical moment, when the retreat could so easily have begun to speed up, a force of thirty Borderers, led by Colonel Daubeney, charged into the centre of the nearest Russian battalion. It was more of a symbol than an achievement, but it was enough. By bayonet, butt, and even fist, the forlorn hope drove its way through the middle of the Russian column and out at the other side. It was a completely senseless manoeuvre, but so unexpected that it threw the

Russian column into complete confusion. As the Russian column recovered and began to re-form, a charge by the 21st and 63rd completed the work. The Russians, having lost impetus and direction, began to fall back. It was now 9 am; the battle had been going on for four hours.

The fighting, though less bitter, continued. Around the Barrier the bodies began to pile up. Goldie, who succeeded to Cathcart's command, survived his predecessor by a bare hour. So far the Russians had had the benefit of artillery superiority. However, Raglan, who displayed more initiative on this than on any other occasion—probably because he allowed himself to be influenced by his own good military sense and not by any preconceived ideas—had ordered up guns. When they arrived they were eighteen-pounders, unfortunately only two—but devastating in their effect, for they were far superior to anything the Russians possessed. The Russians were not beaten, they were still attacking, but the tide of battle was now on the turn. At this point either side could have thrown a small force into the battle and tipped the scales if it had been done promptly. The Russians still had reserves, Gortschakoff had twenty thousand still uncommitted and the French were also fresh. If both had come in there is no knowing what might have happened, but in the event neither did.

At about midday there was a lull in the fighting. The eighteen-pounders were still thumping away at the Russian rear and the Barrier was still being fought over. Seeing what looked like an opportunity to improve the situation the remains of the Scots Fusiliers, Middlesex, and Rifle Brigade, decided to push forward. The Russians withdrew and the movement communicated itself to their whole army. They had not exactly been their own worst enemies but by concentrating on too narrow a battlefield they had formed a perfect target first for the Minié rifles, and then for the eighteen-pounders.

Raglan sent a telegraphic report of the battle on the 6 November in which he spoke of an attack by the enemy by 'immense forces' but in which he gave most of the credit to the division of General Bosquet, and other corps of the French Army, 'which by their gallant conduct contributed essentially to the decided success of the day'. His subsequent dispatch—on 8 November—stated that he knew large numbers of Russian troops had been sent to the Crimea but did not know till afterwards that in the final stages every possible man had been sent up by using the lightest and swiftest of conveyances.

The dispatch is not very informative, although it contains many glowing tributes to all the troops on the battlefield. Of the Russians he said:

I am led to suppose they could not have been less than 60,000 men. Their loss was excessive and it is calculated they left on the field near 5,000 dead, and that their casualties amount in the whole, in killed, wounded, and prisoners, to not less than 15,000.

Your Grace will be surprised to learn that the number of British troops actually engaged little exceeded 8,000 men whilst those of General Bosquet's division only amounted to 6,000, the remaining French troops on the spot having been kept in reserve.

I ought to mention that, while the enemy was attacking our right, they assailed the left of the French trenches, and actually got into two of their batteries; but they were quickly driven out in the most gallant manner with considerable loss and hotly pursued to the very walls of Sebastopol.

By the time Raglan wrote on the 11th the situation was much clearer, and there were many recommendations for bravery. The casualty lists were, however, not only long, but included the names of many experienced men who would not easily be replaced. There were of course other regiments, apart from the ones mentioned above, who took part and distinguished themselves.

Captain Temple Godman was not in the Battle of Inkerman, and, although he stayed for the entire war, saw little of the type of action he was longing for. His account of Inkerman where his regiment was in reserve—although it could never have been used owing to the nature of the ground—slightly exaggerates the casualties but is realistic enough in other ways. He visited the battlefield the following day.

I hear the enemy loss is computed at 10,000 *hors de combat,* ours very large, they say 38 officers killed and 96 wounded. The attack was made on our extreme right, near the valley and castle of Inkerman. The enemy came on under cover of thick fog, it was some time before supports could come up and our men were near being beaten. The enemy were in tremendous force, part of the army of the Danube having arrived, also the one from Odessa; the Grand Duke Constantine and Prince Menschikov are said to be here also.

Although the battle was won it was a near thing and he expresses the doubts that many were then beginning to feel about the direction of the war. (Inkerman, although won, may well have prolonged the war because it delayed the next Allied offensive.)

Everyone seems to say we are doing nothing with the siege and there are grave doubts if we shall take the place. With such a tremendous force against us we ought to have large reinforcements, especially if the Russians pay us such visits often as 5 November. They are said to muster 150,000 men; this however must be over the mark. We were not engaged though we could see and hear the battle raging, and an intensely anxious time it was.

We were in the rear of the fighting but not under fire. The field of battle is a terrible sight, near a battery round which there was a great struggle the bodies lie so thickly one can hardly walk. Some poor Russians yesterday were still on the field wounded and made signs for water. They were so thankful when we gave it to them. They are mostly fine, stout men but their faces are broad and flat and betoken great ignorance. They say their generals tell them never to spare the wounded; the consequence was they bayonetted all they came across. I wish they could see our men giving them water, and their own rations of rum and biscuits. Our officers are much too conspicuous. The Russian officers can hardly be distinguished from their men.

He returned to the same themes in his letter of a week later, both with regard to the conspicuousness of officers and the brutality of the Russians:

They say the Russians tell off ten men a company to shoot the officers. We sent them a flag of truce to tell them they had better not kill our wounded next time or we should have to do the same. Just fancy, one of their *Majors* we caught killing all the wounded. They are perfect savages. One of their men being wounded, long after the battle shot at one of ours (also wounded) hit the breast plate and the ball glanced off and went through his shoulder. So he crept up to him and with the only arm he had left he pinned him to the ground with his bayonet: served him right.

The Russian attitude was somewhat different from, and less chivalrous than, that of the British and French, but their attitude would undoubtedly be explained on two counts: one was that a wounded man may recover and it is therefore just as important to kill him as it is an unwounded soldier, the other was that he might not recover but would only linger on in appalling suffering; it was better therefore to finish him off right away and save him from further misery. There is a third explanation which many hesitate to give and that is that in many armies there are sadists who take a pleasure in finishing off the helpless. The Hitler Youth, the Gestapo, and certain Japanese units, were guilty of this during the Second World War. The Japanese massacred the inhabitants of two hospitals, one on Singapore island, the other in Burma.

# 7
# Everyday Life Before Sebastopol

After Inkerman it is interesting to look at the battles from a slightly lower level than that of generals or members of the Staff.

Captain G. A. Maude wrote to his wife on 26 September mentioning that he was going on to Sebastopol but did not anticipate too much trouble as he felt that 'the Russian army were so thoroughly licked at Alma, and in such a complete state of disorganization that no general on earth will make them face us in the open again'. However, on the march forward they saw a lot of Cossacks, three thousand at one point. On the mountain road his store cart turned over and rolled down fifty feet but neither horses nor driver were hurt. He gave a brisk account of the flank march of which he said 'the cavalry with their wise heads lost the way and I got rather praised for not having followed their example'. He was highly critical of the cavalry: 'We were quite unsupported, owing to the cavalry having lost their way', and 'we could not get the cavalry to the front to take prisoners'. . . . (This was when they overlapped the rear-guard of the Russian army and had a small skirmish.)

General Strangways and General Airey were much pleased with the conduct of my troop, and reported it to Lord Raglan, which I hope will do us good. They said on the ground, 'Now, Maude shall have his choice of one of these waggons' and I picked out one, but the cavalry got hold of it after I retired, and ransacked everything. There were a great many valuables taken: plate, watches, linen, champagne, beer, fur coats, etc. but I got very little, as I had pressed on in front, and those who were behind got everything. They call it the 'Skirmish of Mackenzie's Farm' a Scotchman of that name having tried his luck out here. After this affair we marched in a southerly direction and halted last night at a place called Duvankoi, on the River Tchernaya, which supplies Sebastopol with water. Today we have again established our communication with the fleets, and we are now going to commence the siege. The train is to be landed tomorrow. This is a curious place, a narrow, deep bay enclosed by high grey rocks, with water enough to float a line-of-battle ship, though not 200 yards across. . . .

Two days later he wrote again:

We arrived on the heights above the town on the south side at 3 o'clock, and Lord Raglan and all his staff took a long look at the place. It does not appear to be very strong on this side, but the fortifications on the other seem to have been strengthened lately and look very formidable. It was the intention, I believe, to have summoned the place to surrender yesterday, and to have told them our force and means for the siege, and also if they liked to fire a few guns, for the honour of the thing not in our direction, we should take no notice of it. The French objected to this, and want *'La Gloire'* of a siege so I suppose we shall have the trouble of bringing up the siege train.

This last incredible statement must have been true, and not rumour, for Maude was close to Raglan and was not a man to pass on mere hearsay.

He went on: 'I have not changed my clothes since we landed. Once I got a good wash at Alma, but I have not been able to do so since . . . we have the hardest work of any of the artillery, being at the outposts, and very often not being able to unsaddle even at night.'

On 1 October he wrote:

I have had a nice quiet Sunday, and able to read prayers to the men and to think of dear little *home*. The Russians keep firing away big guns at long ranges, which have not as yet hurt anybody, as the hill we are on is considerably above the town, indeed, we can look down into some of their streets. Still, it is not pleasant to have great 32lb shots pitching about in your neighbourhood. Last evening they found a very good plan of Sebastopol in one of the houses close here, which was just what they wanted as they were in total ignorance of the fortification. . . . The Russians are appearing in force again on our right flank, and we are to go with the cavalry to watch them, most likely tomorrow. We have got a most nice fellow landed now, General Scarlett.

On 4 October he reported without complaint, 'I turned out of my snug farm house yesterday as Lord Raglan goes in today, and am now on a rather dirty piece of ground, occupied before by the Turks.

We have constant alarms and turns-out now, so that we have to keep our horses saddled and our clothes on.' He went on to describe the problems of handling the heavy guns, but was still full of confidence.

The navy are landing 50 of their heavy guns. We have 80, and the French a like number, so that will be upwards of 200 powerful guns playing on the place at once. It cannot last a week. . . . Compy Pickins and I are now separated, but I met him today on the road. He seems to stand his work manfully, though such a thin, weak-looking fellow, and if his tidy father could see him, with his coat stained more than any hunting coat that ever was seen, and his epaulettes half torn off, and all to pieces he would hardly know him. . . . Everyone remarked on the field of battle how clean and smart the dead and wounded Russians were. Even their linen, which in our own men was filthy, was beautifully white and clean. It appears from a journal of an officer, that was found and brought to Lord Raglan, that the day of the battle [the Alma] was a fête day. The journal says they had all been given double rations that day, and that they were going to take a French colonel, who had been taken prisoner, and who seems 'a good sort of fellow' to some place of amusement. It winds up rather abruptly by saying 'Here are these —— English, coming to attack us; this will spoil our fun.' Whether the poor fellow was killed or not is not known. The French colonel was a man attached to Lord Raglan's staff and, during our skirmish on the Bulganac, had been sent on a message to Lord Raglan, but being rather short-sighted had ridden right into the Russians and been taken prisoner. There is a great deal of talk of course in the camp about the Battle of Alma, and everyone seems to agree there was not much generalship on our side, though the usual determined English courage which caused so much sacrifice of life. It seems now more than ever to be regretted that the two fresh divisions of infantry, which had not been engaged, and the cavalry and horse artillery were not allowed to push on that night a few miles or, at all events, next morning. It appears that all the Russian guns and material of every description were left on the Katscha that night, which was only four or five miles from the heights we took, and would most certainly have fallen into our hands. . . .

Maude's optimism was undiminished in his letter of 5 October. Referring to the Russians he said 'They are working away at their fortifications, and we have not yet tried to molest them in any way, but as the works they are throwing up are chiefly earth, and from being so dry is in a crumbling state, they can only stand a few hours against our heavy guns.'

On 7 October he wrote a letter which throws some light on the attitude of Lord Lucan. It ran:

This morning I was awoke at 5 o'clock by hearing the cry of 'Turn out, turn out!' and hearing popping shots. It appeared our outposts were engaged. I keep my horses saddled at night, so I was soon out, and, with the cavalry, we proceeded up the hill which separates us from the valley of the Tchernaya, or Black River. As we went up the shots increased, and the cavalry picquets were falling back in every direction. I rode on to see where the enemy was, and found a large body of their cavalry in the valley below, at about 1,000 yards distant, forming the attack. Lord Lucan was all hesitation, and for doing nothing but watch them, but I got leave to go and have a shot at them, and after a few rounds they all began to run away in confusion. When they got all together there were about 5,000 or 6,000, and two or three regiments of infantry in support. They all retreated towards the Tchernaya River, and failed in their object, which we supposed to have been a reconnaissance. We then all came back to breakfast. . . .

On 11 October he wrote:

I have nothing much to tell you. . . . The Russians fire all day and all night at some batteries we are making, but have done hardly any damage, and our men work away as coolly as if they were not firing at all, though the large 68 lb shot pitch very near to them sometimes. We have been delayed by the French, who, however, are now working hard, and everything promises to be ready for a general cannonade by Friday next, when the English and French batteries will open at once, and it is supposed the place cannot last many days, if even hours. As yet we have not fired a single shot at them and treated them with the greatest indifference.

It was getting colder, and much of his letters is taken up with minor successes in acquiring warm clothing and thoughts of home. 'I got a pair of warm gloves. I am glad you are getting a piano for our darling little girl, and I am sure she will work hard to get over the difficult part of it, and be able to play me a tune when I come home again.'

On the 13th he wrote, 'Tomorrow it is expected that a general cannonade will be opened on the place', and on the 16th continued:

We have had a tedious time of it since I last wrote to you, nothing but alarms night and day, the Cossacks appearing every now and then in small bodies, and making off as soon as they see we are prepared. This breaks our rest and gives men and horses hard work without any satisfaction. . . . The Russians still fire away all day and night at our trenches, but the cover is so good now that there have only been two or three men killed. This morning, at 10 o'clock, they opened a tremendous fire with their heavy guns, which was one continuous roar for half an hour, and then ceased. They did no harm.

All sorts of reports are going about as to where we are to winter. The army is fearfully reduced in numbers, hardly 15,000 effective infantry now out of nearly 30,000. The Guards have suffered more than any. The men, and even officers, are suffering from dirt, being ordered to bring on shore only what they could carry; and thinking they could get their things from the ships, several of them only brought what they had on their backs and carried their cloaks and blankets, which was a good weight for them.

His next letter described the opening bombardment, of which he said 'Some of the principal works have been silenced, and one of the towers, which was considered a great obstacle, has already fallen. It is not supposed that the town can last many days under the terrific fire which is now open on it.' The tower concerned was the Malakoff, which, of course, was soon repaired, and proved one of the principal objectives of the war.

On 17 October he gave Shakespear's report, which included the successful shelling of the French:

It was ascertained that their principal magazine had blown up, destroying a great many men and a great part of their works. They hardly fired a shot after this, and seemed completely discouraged. The Russians kept up a tremendous fire on them, and they were not able to make any repairs. . . . About 4 o'clock one of our shells from the land batteries exploded a large magazine in the redoubt in the centre of the Russian position, blowing out all the face of the work, and no doubt causing great loss of life. Our casualties have been very few. Everyone is very sanguine as to the result now, and I think a few hours will make an assault practicable.

This optimism was slightly diminished in his next letter. 'I have very little to tell you in the way of progress. The heavy firing goes on night and day, but as fast as we demolish any of the Russian guns they bring another out of the arsenal, and it is all right in half an hour. They open fresh batteries every day, and strengthen themselves continually, so we shall find it a harder job than we expected.'

Maude now felt that before the attack went in a combined land and naval bombardment would be necessary. He now said 'I fear there will be a great loss of life when the place is taken by assault, but there is no help for it unless we make up our minds to winter on the heights.'

On 21 October hopes of it all being over, and being home for Christmas, are receding fast:

> We had another weary night of watching. I was just going to ride up to the batteries to see how the fire was going on when I saw one of the cavalry vedettes circling on the ridge in front of us, and as this is the sign of an enemy approaching, I rode up to see what was the matter. . . . The troops we have down here, besides the cavalry, are chiefly Turks, marines, sailors, and a few Highlanders, and are not very steady at night. First of all the Turks began to fire away in a great hurry at an imaginary enemy about 12 o'clock. As the night was very dark it was some time before they found out their mistake. Then again about 2 o'clock, the marines fired muskets and guns, thinking the Russians were advancing, so we had a wretched night of it. . . .

This letter was sent off unfinished and before he could write another he was wounded. The next therefore came from the transport 'Exchange', and was written in pencil.

> 26 October, My dearest wife, We had a very hard fight yesterday and the Turks ran away from their forts and left us, so that we were overpowered and our cavalry got dreadfully cut up. It has pleased God that I should be wounded this time. A large shell burst alongside my poor old mare and killed her, and I am wounded in the left arm, hand and eye, the latter nothing. I am shipped off to Constantinople. I am doing very well but suffer a good deal of pain, as the wounds are so lacerated. . . .

That was the last of his letters. His wife went out to Constantinople and returned home with him. The medical report on him said 'A splinter struck him on the left leg, making a deep incised wound to the bone, about two inches above the patella, completely dividing the vasti muscles; in the left arm it tore away the muscles and lacerated the radial artery, from which he had severe haemorrhage; his left hand was also lacerated, and he also received some contusions on his brows, by which he has since lost the vision of one of his eyes.'

Maude's work as a gunner officer had earned widespread praise. The Maude family had a distinguished military record in many spheres. Another member, who later became General Sir F. F. Maude, won a VC for being first into the Redan and holding on, though dangerously wounded. Another VC was won by Captain F. C. Maude in the Indian Mutiny in 1857. Rather earlier, a member of the family had distinguished himself by capturing the King of Scotland in 1147. The Scottish king's name was William the Lion so the Maude family thenceforward had a lion behind bars on their coat-of-arms.

Maude did not describe what it felt like to be wounded in the Crimea—he may not have been conscious at the time—but there is an informative account in the Burgoyne Diary (edited by Brigadier Peter Young, DSO, MC). Burgoyne had been wounded a little earlier, at the Alma, where he was with the Grenadiers:

> We received orders to advance and before we had gone six paces I felt a blow on my right shin, and, on putting my foot to the ground, fell. Young Hamilton took the colours from me, and the battalion went on, leaving me lying on the ground, with the shot tearing it up all round me. After I had laid there some minutes Sergeant Davies took me up in his arms and carried me out of fire, and placed me under a bank in safety. . . . After lying for half an hour under the bank some of our pioneers came with a stretcher and carried me off to the surgeons. When we found our surgeons after a long walk I was laid down and had to wait nearly an hour for my wound to be dressed. When the doctors came near me and I saw their bloody hands and knives I felt sure they would have my leg off but they contented themselves with bandaging it up after torturing me with that detestable instrument, the probe, and booking me in return as severely wounded. After lying some time in the open plain and night approaching, I sent George off to pick up the greatcoat and blanket of the first poor fellow he found dead. He had not far to go for a man of the 33rd was lying within fifty yards with his head blown off. I was moved before dark to the Fusilier hospital in the village, and had a bed made of hay under a wall in the main street. Around me on all sides were wounded men, and close to me was a guard and a batch of Russian prisoners. Rolled upon blankets and greatcoats, with my wounded leg propped up with hay, I passed the night (a sad long one) as best I could. The excitement, pain, and moans of the wounded prevented all possibility of sleep.

Temple Godman was a captain in the 5th Dragoon Guards. He arrived at Balaclava on 30 September. The journey from Varna had taken four days:

We towed a ship with the Royal Dragoons on board, we had not been long out when it blew a gale and we parted from the ship we towed, the two enormous cables snapped like string. We fully experienced the truth of Byron's lines:

There is no sea the traveller ere probes in
Whose waves are more deceptive than the Euxine.

I am not sure my quotation is quite correct.

We have had a tremendous tossing but are fortunately all right, with the exception of the loss of horses.

I am in great hopes we are in plenty of time yet. It was a severe trial to our temper to hear of all that was going on, and be obliged to wait for the Brigade being embarked.

Optimism about the result of this campaign, confidence in British superiority and anxiety lest all should be over before he should see action are the characteristics of these letters, as of many other writers who would see all the action they wanted before it was over. In this—as in other wars—notably the First and Second World Wars—there was a strong conviction that all would be finished before the very first Christmas. Hearing of the result of the Alma, Godman wrote:

I really believe nothing can stand the British.

The cholera prevails here, but chiefly among the newly arrived and unacclimatized regiments. The Greys have lost an officer, and the 21st Regiment, which landed from England a few days since has buried 200 men, but then I suppose their strength is about 1,000; they have not been in action. The disease has greatly abated in the last few days. The Russians, I hear, have it badly in the town. Everyone is in the best spirits and no one doubts but that the place will be taken. They say if they had cavalry at that engagement the other day, an immense number would have been made prisoner, or at all events prevented from entering Sebastopol. They certainly should have waited for the cavalry, for a few days could have made no difference as far as the weather goes.

(Godman was then unaware that cavalry had been present at the Alma but had not been used.)

He went on:

The cavalry are encamped about 4 or 5 miles from the town, and we are harassed night and day with picquets and patrols. We cannot have much to do with the siege, unless in case of a sortie, or in clearing the streets when they get in. An army of some 30 or 40,000 men is expected up to the relief of the town, in which case there must be a good stand-up fight. Our inlaying picquet has just turned out in a great hurry after two squadrons of Cossacks but the latter know better than to stand a charge of even a dozen of our men. They came near and shot at us. There are about 1000 sailors dragging up guns out of the fleet which are to be put in position for the siege. The grand attack will not commence till Friday. Our infantry are close to the walls, just out of shot. Shot and shell constantly come bowling in, just up to their outposts. They say it won't be an easy job, this side of the town is not so strong but the west side is very strong. We came across plenty of forage and miles of splendid vineyards, the grapes are famous, and the French carry them away in faggots. We are just ordered to be ready to turn out, some Cossacks or someone are coming so I must finish as the post may be gone on my return. In great haste. Your affectionate son, Temple Godman.

Subsequent letters give an excellent insight into the life and duties of a young cavalry officer at this place and time. On 6 October he wrote:

My last letter ended rather abruptly as we got the order to turn out the Brigade, but though we remained saddled all day we were not called to go out. It was merely that our Patrol had been driven in by a large body of Cossacks. These gentlemen keep us well employed, though often two or three-hundred together they never dare attack even a picquet of 30 men of ours. I am longing to have a go at them and I hope to get a chance before many more days. There is such a scarcity of officers in the Brigade that we are on duty nearly every day. Tomorrow I am on inlaying picquet but I must tell you what this means or you won't understand. An outlaying picquet is a body of men, perhaps 30 or 40 (or stronger or weaker as the case may be) who go about five miles out in front or rear of the army, to give an alarm of any approach of the enemy, and if driven in keep them (the enemy) in check as long as possible to give the main body time to get under arms. From this body detached men are again placed forward to give notice of anyone coming from the enemy, these are Videttes*.

The picquet is commanded by a captain or lieutenant. You may imagine it is a responsible and often harassing post, you are personally out for 24 hours, and of course must not ever be off the alert especially near so untiring an enemy as the Cossacks. An inlaying picquet is a body which remains in the lines, ready, under arms, to turn out at a moment's notice in support of the outlaying picquet. A 'patrol' is a body which is sent to

* Godman's spelling was sometimes highly original.

reconnoitre the country. We have daily skirmishes with the Cossacks, they nearly surrounded our patrol yesterday, and drove them in before they saw them but tho' supported by a considerable body of cavalry they did not even fire at us, though we were only about a dozen strong. Today our patrol was fired on, some shot and shell. . . .

I rode about three miles up to look at Sebastopol the other day, from the hill above you can see, at about a mile off, right into the town and harbour. There lay the fine ships of war and there are the inhabitants walking up and down and the enemy working hard in their trenches outside, for they are very busy fortifying themselves, and doing much this way day and night. You can see the great black guns on the forts and looking through the embrasures, and if you show yourself too much a puff of smoke curls from the walls and a shell hisses over your head, they have all the ranges very well and drop them very close. . . .

Godman continues by recalling the Alma.

I regret extremely we were not at the Alma, if we had been we must have taken all their guns and lots of prisoners and cut them to pieces. Though the Light Cavalry were there they will get a medal for doing nothing. The Cavalry may say what they like about that affair but they were hardly under fire. I would have given anything to have been there. I saw a horse in camp today which had a bullet through his ear which first passed through the body of the adjutant of the 23rd.

Godman frequently recounts interesting though macabre details. His letters were not very well punctuated, and rambled wildly, but that is part of their interest; the reader sees the scene as he saw it and almost thinks the same thoughts.

I can't bear to hear of our servants being so fastidious, it really is too bad, and here are plenty of the sons of the highest men in England living on biscuit and salt pork, and so far from complaining are glad to get it. When we landed we had a lump of pork to carry, about three times the size of one's fist, not the better for being carried about, and some ship biscuits. This was all we had for three days. Yesterday we got some very skinny mutton, and tomorrow pork again, no bread here. Our mess when cooked, for we put 3 or 4 fellows' rations together, put me in mind of what Keeper collects in buckets for the dogs, however, it agrees very well with me.

You will see that we are what they call dis-regimentized, and attached to the 4th Dragoon Guards, all this is most absurd but Colonel Hodge behaved very well and I don't think he came once into our lines or interfered with us in any way. We have no more to do with them or they with us than you have.

The people about here are very civil, always take their hats off to us, their countenance is not at all like the Turk, but more flat, and the women have rather the look of the Chinese, tho' some are very good looking.

Our dinners are cooked by wood, brought from the houses. Doors, tables, floors, and even a piano has been seen on the fire, it is a pity but the French are great destroyers. You may often see a good fire of a mahogany bed or chest of drawers, they think nothing of pulling down a house for fuel.

On 12 October he wrote to his mother.

Here we are still *before*, not *in*, Sebastopol. Every day we hear the siege will commence 'tomorrow' or rather that the batteries will open. There will be an awful row when they do commence.

Two days ago the enemy kept up an incessant fire on our works from about 7 pm till 8 the next morning, we could see the flash of every gun in the night sky and could hear every shot and shell hissing in the flight. The result of all this fire was *one* rifleman killed and 2 or 3 wounded.

This was, of course, an ideal letter to send to a mother who would be worrying about her son's safety—lots of shot and shell, but the only person killed was someone in a different regiment; very reassuring.

My servant has got a famous house, a large cupboard he has got out of a house; this he gets into and shuts the door and goes to sleep. [However, there are hints of ominous matters] It is said that 40,000 men are on the march south to raise the siege; these, if joined to the 30,000 now in our rear will be a formidable force. . . . People must not be impatient about the siege, no one knows but those engaged what infinite work and trouble must be undergone before the fall of such a place can be effected. We have had daily skirmishes lately, yesterday our patrol had to retire before a force of 300 cavalry or more. We were but 40 strong. They did not hit one of our men but we knocked over 2 of their horses and one was an officer. About 40 or 50 shots were fired.

Today our picquets were attacked by Cossacks but soon driven back by our skirmishers, several shots were exchanged but no one hit. I went out to see them. These Cossacks will never show a front and are not in themselves formidable but they give us much trouble by their constant attacks. I am still Adjutant. I would rather not be just now as I should be more engaged in outpost duty, but if all reports are true we shall have enough work soon. I could not bear to go home without a good decided action. I am sure if we get them in the open they will remember it.

By the 12th he is beginning to get the action he has been eagerly awaiting, although at this stage it is mainly an artillery duel: nevertheless things are moving:

I believe we have sunk the Twelve Apostles, their largest ship. One of the Lancaster guns has burst, I believe without harm, they are doing great execution.

You must know that our army only encloses the town from the south east, to where the main creek runs up past the town, so the rest and other side, which is by far the strongest is open to the enemy. They say every inch is mined.

It is a puzzling and frustrating situation for Godman. All they do is skirmish and patrol, the artillery exchanges shots, and the assault which they have been expecting daily seems indefinitely delayed. Meanwhile vast Russian forces are moving up and it looks as if so far from besieging Sebastopol they are themselves likely to be besieged in Balaclava. However he does not criticize or complain, but merely explains:

We have been saddled all day in expectation of a turn out, and Lord Raglan expects an attack daily so that the sooner they come the better and let's have it over. We were confined to camp all day and threatened with arrest for leaving it but I could not stand hearing and not seeing the work so rode up this afternoon. It was a splendid sight.

We have not got it all our own way as some expected and I think today the besiegers and the besieged are about equal.

I hope the next mail will send you news of the fall of the place but unless we get on much faster and are let alone in the war I don't expect it.

In his letter of 19 October he refers to the extraordinary report, which had appeared in the London press, that Sebastopol had fallen: 'Your letter reached me this morning. I read the letter while a tremendous cannonade was going on and it seemed such a mockery to think that on the 2nd inst the news of the fall of Sebastopol was posted over London, and announced in *The Times*; how such a report could appear authentic seems strange.'

He is now ruefully recalling the exaggerated optimism which had characterized the invasion force earlier:

When we landed we made too little of the great work before us, and everyone said we should be inside the place in about 24 hours. Confidence is all very well but I think no one ought to boast before operations are commenced.

Sir Colin Campbell, the Highlanders' brigadier, commands the infantry about Balaclava; he is said to be a good officer. I hear Lord Raglan has given positive orders that no engagement should be risked at Balaclava while the siege is going on, and I think he is quite right.

Nevertheless this and other letters are full of accounts of false alarms and skirmishes that broke up before anything serious happened. But it was exciting enough:

At about 9 pm one of the Turkish forts commenced to fire musketry and the shape of the earth fort in which they were could be distinctly seen by the bright flashes sparkling out all round it. I immediately jumped on my horse, making sure the enemy were advancing up the hill. If they had we should have been in a bad way, having no infantry except 2 or 3 regiments of Turks (who are of course not to be trusted much in the open) and half the 93rd regiment. Cavalry are of course no match against unbroken infantry, and of course nothing would be easier than to put cavalry in confusion. These are attacks on a dark night. About an hour or two later I was just going to lie down, being very sleepy, when a bright flash lighted up the houses. I at first thought it was lightning but on turning round saw that the sailors' battery in our rear on the hills above Balaclava had opened fire. Of course I immediately mounted again, thinking the enemy were close on us; in the meantime the shell came tearing up the ground and rolling along and bursting very prettily in the dark night. The round shot too were making a tremendous noise as they went through the air. The Turks on the hill, seeing the Artillery open, immediately commenced to fire at what they knew not. Then, a fort with Turks, on this track where the enemy were supposed to be coming, opened their musketry fire also. You may imagine that this soon ceased and we waited till morning not knowing what had happened. We afterwards discovered that the Turks, who keep a very sharp look-out, discovered some drunken footguards who had lost their way. They puffed off some powder—their way of giving an alarm—which the sailors saw, and, taking it for the Russians advancing, they opened on them as I told you, supposing their front clear; it is well we were not further out in the plain. This shows what a little thing puts an army on the alarm.

Conditions for the troops around Sebastopol were clearly hard, for if they were not lucky enough to share a tent they slept in the open. Sometimes it rained, sometimes it was foggy and there was always a heavy dew. They were in the saddle much of the day and also often turned out at night.

> It is dreadfully harassing work and is telling on the men, most of whom sleep without any shelter at night.
>
> I shall not say much about the siege, which is still going now though the place was taken by *The Times* 10 days ago.
>
> Everyone you ask tells you a different story. One says: 'Oh we have it all our own way', the next tells you, 'The Russians are firing two guns to our one', and so everyone tells you what he thinks and so you hear 50 different accounts, nor can you tell much better by looking on.

Already the news is getting back to Balaclava that all is not as it should be at Scutari:

> I believe you think in England that every preparation has been taken to make the sick and wounded as comfortable as possible. Such is not the case. Indeed anything so disgraceful as the whole department it is impossible to imagine. The other day I was told on good authority that 500 men went to Scutari after Alma, sick and wounded in one ship, and attended by *two* surgeons and five men, one of whom died on the way, and the poor fellows had no one to assist them or look after them. On their arrival no preparations for their reception had been made. There are 1,200 wounded at Scutari, and 4,000 in hospital altogether there. I heard from one hospital sergeant who went on board one of the ships at Balaclava the other day that the state of things there is just as bad or worse, the ship crowded with men shouting for water, and no one to attend them . . .

There is more of this but of course much worse was to come. It was partly the inexperience which comes from not having fought a war for forty years, and partly sheer incompetence. Even so there are many living today who can tell stories of breakdowns in medical services, often from sheer pressure of work, in the Second World War, when conditions became by no means pretty.

The standard and boring ration was pork: 'We get lots of salt pork and beef here, the latter hardly eatable, especially when one is not very well. I shall be glad when the place is taken.'

Then came full-scale action at last. He wrote to his father on 26 October:

My dear Father—Yesterday the attack which I thought must take place came off and here I am Thank God, safe and sound, though the loss the cavalry have sustained is very severe. We were on parade as usual yesterday 25th an hour before daybreak, and soon after it was well light a gun from the Turkish forts (their outposts) told us something was going on. The cavalry immediately advanced across the plain, and halted behind the forts on our side of the ridge; by this time the fire along the whole line of batteries was continued with great quickness; this time we knew we were in for it. The H. Artillery and Battery soon opened but the former soon shut up for want of ammunition and the Captain [Maude] being wounded severely by a shell which burst inside his horse. Soon the unmistakable sound of shot over our heads told us they were advancing in force, indeed so fast did they come on that our outlaying picquet was near being cut off and the officers on picquet lost their cloaks, a serious loss here. They now began to ply the forts with shell, many of which, missing the hill-top, fell among us, one could see them drop, and in another moment the fragments flying far and wide causing one by an involuntary impulse to bob one's head, though well knowing it was of no use, as the pieces whistled and hummed over our heads. Odd to say, though several shell fell within a few yards, neither man nor horse was hurt. Soon the Turks outside the fort, on their extreme right commenced to fire musketry, and as we were only about 300 yards off, with my glasses I saw everything. Up the hill came the Russian infantry, meeting a warm fire from the Johnny [Turk] who at that moment turned and rushed up again under their fort. On came the Russians, shouting and running up in column in fine order, and giving a heavy fire. The Turks again showed a front, rushed at them, then wavered, and in went the enemy over their works, the Turks retreating down the hill into the plain in the greatest confusion. I saw a few braver than the rest close with the enemy but only to meet their death. And so, in less than half an hour, the strongest fort was in their hands. The Turks all along the range seeing this threw down their arms (at least many did) left their guns and ran like the rest to Balaclava so that the enemy quickly got the whole range of forts, and turning the guns on us peppered us well as we retreated, which we did at a walk, frequently halting and fronting, but what could we do without infantry against numbers and the round shot too much too thick to be pleasant. The poor horses running about loose, dreadfully wounded were sad to see, one with *three* legs, belonging to the Royals, would throw itself into our ranks, till at last I put an end to him with my revolver. We retired to our camp, which had been struck, and everything was nearly packed. We had no sooner formed in rear than the enemy who had formed all along the heights sent down their cavalry in two masses into the plain. One went at full split at some Turkish infantry, but the 93rd, who were lying down, jumped up and gave them such a volley that they wheeled to the left and rode off as hard as they could go in good order the artillery pounding them all the way. They never expected to meet English there I am sure.

This version of the 'thin red line' is particularly interesting because it is an unprejudiced eyewitness account by a fighting soldier. It is clear that surprise paid a considerable part in the Highlanders' success (Godman calls them 'English'). Russell, *The Times* correspondent, who made the occasion world-renowned, used the words 'that thin red streak, tipped with a line of steel', and followed it by: 'As the Russians came within six hundred yards, down went that line of steel in front and out rang a volley of Minié musketry.' This volley, according to Russell, was too far off to check the Russians—though they should have been well within range, but 'ere they came within two hundred and fifty yards another deadly volley flashed from the levelled rifles, and carried terror among the Russians.' Russell went on to say that 'the 93rd never altered their formation to receive that tide of horsemen, "No," said Sir Colin Campbell, "I did not think it worth while to form them even four deep." The ordinary British line, two deep was quite sufficient to repel the attack of these Muscovite cavaliers.'

It would appear from this last sentence that Russell was so carried away by enthusiasm that he reported what he wanted to see and not what actually happened. The first volley, when everyone was taken by surprise, including the Russians, was not as accurate as it might have been. The second, when Campbell had steadied the ranks, was more than the Russians expected, and convinced them that this was no minor obstacle to be brushed away in one charge. And of course only fools, or men in the last stages of desperation, charge the cavalry at accurate rifle fire from long distances.

Godman continues with an account of the Heavy Brigade charge, in which he personally took part:

At this time a large mass of cavalry came over the hill in front of our camp and would in a few minutes have been in our lines, and have cut down the few men left, when we got the order to advance. The Greys and Enniskillens went in first, then we came in support of the Greys. Their [the enemy's] front must have been composed of three regiments, and a very strong column in their rear, in all, I suppose, about 1,500 or 2,000 while we were not more than 800, however the charge sounded and at them went the first line; Scarlett and his ADC well in front. The enemy seemed quite astonished and drew into a walk, and then a halt. As soon as they met all I saw was swords in the air in every direction, the pistols going off, and everyone hacking away right and left. In a moment the Greys were surrounded and hemmed completely in. There they were, fighting back to back, in the middle, the great bearskin caps high above the enemy. This was the work of a moment. As soon as we saw it the 5th advanced and in they charged yelling and shouting as hard as they could split; the row was tremendous and for about five minutes neither would give way, and their column was so deep we could not cut through it. At length they turned, and well they might, and the whole race as hard as they could pelt back up the hill, our men after them all broken up, and cutting them down right and left. We pursued about 300 yards, and then called off with much difficulty, the gunners then opened on them and gave them a fierce peppering. It took some little time to get the men to fall in again; they were all mixed up together of course, all the regiments in one mass. The enemy being gone, and we all right, we had time to look round. The ground was covered with dead and dying men and horses. I am happy to say our brigade lost but 7 men dead, but had a considerable number wounded, some mortally. The ground was strewn with swords, broken and whole, trumpets, helmets, carbines, etc, while a quantity of men were scattered all along as far as we pursued. There must have been some 40 or 50 of the enemy dead, besides wounded, for I went over the ground today to look at it. All the wounded were of course, immediately taken off. Lord Raglan, who was looking down from a hill close by sent an ADC to say 'Well done, the Heavy Brigade'. This is some satisfaction after all we have gone through this summer. The Russians seemed very steady and well-disciplined but our men made fearful havoc among them with their long, straight swords. The Russian swords were much more curved than ours and very sharp. Scarlett was wounded in the bridle hand, but not much. He and Elliot were in the thickest and his helmet was battered in and the shirt of his frock coat sliced down. Poor Elliot did not escape so well, he got a bad cut in the face and a very severe one in the back of the head having lost his hat. I hope, however, he is not dangerously hurt; he is better today. He is a very brave fellow and fought very hard—so did Scarlett who is as blind as a bat. Swinfree was run through the hand and poor Neville, being a bad rider and too weak to use his sword well, was soon dismounted and had it not been for one of our men (Private Abbot) who stood over him he must have been killed. He was wounded in the head and three places in his back and they fear that his liver is injured in which case he cannot recover.

A corporal of ours was killed (Corporal Taylor) and one man (Private Bernard), and another must die. We have nine wounded besides and have lost about 14 horses.

It had been well if this success had been all the cavalry did but some infantry having arrived we advanced, and, owing to a mistake in an order which Captain Nolan brought from Lord Raglan, the Light Cavalry then charged down a valley under a fire of Minié rifles and guns on each side the valley and a battery of—I believe—20 guns in front. They drove all before them, took the guns, cut down the gunners and killed an immense number. They then retired but were perfectly annihilated by the cross fire. The Brigade Major told me that directly after the brigade numbered under 200, having turned out that morning 6 or 700 strong: It was a terrible sight to see them walking back one by one and the valley strewn with them. Our brigade came in also just then for a heavy fire and the Greys alone lost 40 killed and wounded, all for nothing. The Russians still have possession of two forts and spiked the guns of the other.

This calm, unemotional, account of three important actions, contrasts strongly with Russell's style which at times nears hysteria. Referring to the Russians concentrating their guns on the retreating Light Brigade he says 'With courage too great almost for credence they were breaking their way through the columns which enveloped them when there took place an act of atrocity without parallel in the modern warfare of civilized nations. The Russian gunners, when the storm of cavalry passed, returned to their guns and poured murderous volleys of grape and canister on the mass of struggling men and horses.' (Had he been reporting for the Russians he would probably have written 'With great presence of mind our gunners returned to their task, and in spite of being badly shaken, added fresh laurels to their glory as excellent marksmen.')

The above letter was to Godman's father. A week later he wrote one to his brother which gives a few of the details omitted from the earlier one; although both would doubtless be passed around the family circle. Of the Heavy Brigade's charge he said the Russians

. . . were so close to our camp and would soon have cut down our servants. The Greys and Enniskillens charged first but they were so close to our old camp we could not get up any pace to the charge and they met nearly at a walk. The Greys and Enniskillens were immediately surrounded, which, we seeing, the 5th and the rest of the Enniskillens went in with a shout and a yell. For about five minutes we were all hacking away at each other, pistols discharging and the devil's own row, then they turned and ran up the hill again as hard as they could.

Then the details

. . . we had time to look about, there were over 40 lying dead and dying in pools of blood with most fearful cuts. We lost a corporal, quite hacked to pieces and one man was shot, another must die, his lungs came through his back.

I had one or two shaves for it during the day, my coat sleeve was cut through and my wrist bruised but not cut as I had on some very thick jersies.

He relates that his coat was torn by a lance thrust and he was narrowly missed by cannon fire on a number of occasions. It was clear to him that although the cavalry and infantry occasionally took part in a spectacular feat of arms the main work of the war was being done by artillery fire which took a steady toll. He gave the Light Brigade one brief reference: 'Later in the day the Light Brigade charged down the valley. They had no business to have gone there. They lost about 300 but can't get the numbers exactly. They took 25 guns and killed an immense number but were totally annihilated by batteries on each side of the valley.' He went on,

The weather is fearfully cold and if it were not for a Russian officer's coat I found after the charge lined with fur I don't know what I should do. We lost a man today. The doctor said he died of cold; another is dying. . . . I hope we may get a real good charge at their cavalry again but I think they will funk to cross swords with us after their licking. They have never licked the English yet, though they did the Turks . . . I think the brutes must have killed our wounded, they will get no quarter next time. I feel sure we must have another row and I may not get out so well next time but unless a bullet takes me off I think I shall be able to do something with them first.

The use of words like 'funk', 'licking' and 'row' (fight) give Godman's words an archaic, schoolboyish ring. 'Row' was still being used in some schools in the 1960s but the others seem to have been replaced.

In most of his letters he mentions that his 'box' has not arrived. Winter is coming on—'It is nearly impossible to keep warm at night. . . . We are so far from water we seldom get a wash, and everyone is covered with lice which I pick out every morning regularly. I never take anything off for weeks together but trousers and coat; it is too cold to take off more.'

These conditions, cold, discomfort, shortage of water and the presence of lice, bugs and fleas, have of course been familiar enough to many men in most of the campaigns through history. Many of them were familiar enough—with the exception of the water shortage—to people living in Victorian England, though not first-hand to people in Godman's social class. However, the upper-middle classes and aristocracy tended to make light of these discomforts, whether their own, or other people's.

In spite of delays on vital supplies, mail was unaffected. In a letter to his mother on 3 November Godman mentions that they 'have moved our camp within the French lines, nearer Sebastopol, and have given up retaking our late line of forts', and goes on a little later to say 'You say that you heard of the disorderly state of the 5th and that my letters confirm it. This, if I have, I never intended to do, nor do I think I ever said anything about the regiment being in disorder.' But he brings up an interesting point: 'The fact is we were cut up by disease and half-starved, men and horses, and then we met with very hard treatment from Lord Lucan, who was certainly jealous of the high character the regiment and our Brigadier have always borne—and like many others was glad to have a rap at us.' He urges his mother to contradict all rumours to the contrary, and says that Scarlett is going to write to the papers to contradict the reports.

He wrote of a splendid meal he had on board a ship, 'boiled mutton and bread, which I have not tasted but once since I came here. It is of no use to send me anything. We shall be at Scutari or winter over before it could arrive. The horses will never be good for much after this.'

As Godman suspected, the army was going to have another 'row', and the biggest one yet. In his last letter he had mentioned that forty thousand Russian troops were in the neighbourhood, 'but I suppose Lord Raglan knows what he is about'. Whatever happened he had no doubts about his men. 'The cholera was a far greater trial than any fight can be, and anyone who saw the orderly and quiet manner in which they behaved during the cholera, when about half of them were ill, would never doubt for them afterwards.' Only a person who has seen a cholera epidemic at work will appreciate those last words.

There were, however, lighter touches. Chodasiewicz, a Pole serving with the Russian Army wrote that:

> One of the men of our regiment, Ivan Grigorieff, lying behind a stone, took a shot at a French soldier who was lying before him only partly concealed, and missed him; he acknowledged the compliment by waving his cap, and immediately fired at Grigorieff, who acknowledged it by standing on his head and waving his legs, in token that he was unhurt. It was a very pretty sight from the bastions to see the two lines of *franc-tireurs*, marked by little puffs of white smoke, as they lay and comfortably took shots at each other; something amusing happened almost every day. Our men had orders to fire at anything visible, no matter what the distance.

Of Chodasiewicz and his views we shall have more later. They make an interesting contrast with those expressed by Godman who writes:

> The enemy are far superior to us in number and weight of their artillery; ours are mere useless popguns compared with theirs . . . all idea of storming the place is abandoned and I don't suppose it will fall for 2 or 3 months. Lord Lucan, who received the nickname of 'Lord Look on' from his having so often led us near the enemy without letting us have a go at them, quite retrieved his character at the action of Balaclava, when he showed he had plenty of pluck but not, I fear, much besides necessary to qualify as a general. The greatest dissatisfaction is expressed at the inactivity of the fleet, who don't help us at all. The Admiral has received the appellation of 'Admiral D—d Ass'*. We hope he will be recalled and Lyons put in his place.

Godman's box has still not arrived. He hears it is on a boat called the *William Pitt* which he hopes has not been sunk. However he has received a parcel of pens, which he had requested for sketching, but he says 'I don't want any more at present as I have no time to draw. I have enough wafers but you may send more from time to time.' The same letter gave news of the hurricane which had struck Balaclava and ruined all hopes of warm clothing and better conditions for the winter.

> This mail will give you a bad account from the seat of the war. On the 14th, soon after our morning parade was dismissed, a violent hurri-

* This was Admiral Dundas.

cane accompanied by tremendous rain broke over our camp. In a few minutes every hut was levelled and all our things drenched, while we turned out of house and home and had to weather the storm as best we could. Away went cooking kettles and all kinds of things. One officer's air bed I saw flying high away over the Turkish camp, hardly a tent was left standing. After a little while the wind moderated but the rain continued and then snow, till the ground was covered an inch thick. Of course no fires could be lighted, therefore we had nothing but biscuit and rum and water all day.

The next day was fine and so it has been ever since, though very cold. I could see about 6 ships on shore near the Katscha River and I fear some were men of war. I hear that a million and a half of damage has been done to the fleet. At Balaclava, even in their land-locked harbour, surrounded by high steep hills, the vessels were jammed together and most of their masts gone, while those outside which could not get to sea were driven on the rocks and went down with nearly all hands. There are said to be about 500 men lost at Balaclava alone. *The Prince,* a fine steamer from England, sunk with all the warm clothing for the army, the *Polytechnic* men and diving apparatus, and two large mortars, etc., etc. The harbour is full of hay, rum barrels etc. *The Prince* had been in ten days so there is no excuse for not having her unloaded. All the rice and sugar are used, the former a most necessary article with so much salt meat. We are getting much infected with scurvy in consequence. Some of the troops I hear are worse off still, and there is no saying how soon the biscuit or anything else may be stopped.

In view of the cold, the frustration and the discomfort, the letters are remarkably restrained. Others may have railed at fate for the freak storm which removed the chance of any comfort in the winter but Godman was not unprepared for such catastrophes. What irks him is the lethargy—or incomprehensible strategy—of the Higher Command:

All sorts of rumours about here. The Commissary-General is positively stated to have told Lord Raglan that he would not undertake to forage the cavalry, but he said not a soldier should leave the Crimea till Sebastopol is taken. Some talk of storming again now that large reinforcements are arriving. All seem to expect an attack on Balaclava daily, in which case I suppose we should take the enemy in the flank—I expect soon to be engaged again. Many say we can never outlive the winter in tents, but I hear no huts can be built for us so we must do our best. One thing is certain, if we stay here we shall be quite unfit for service in the spring, while the French Heavy Cavalry will turn out from Bourgos. It is out of the question for an army to take the field without the branch, when the enemy are so strong in the same arm, besides guns are nearly useless without cavalry. It is all very well for Raglan living in a house with plenty of coals. We, and all the army, have an immense number of sick and I am sorry to say I am too frequently called on to read the burial service.

I am sorry to say the Duke of Cambridge is reported to have gone quite mad. He was on board a man of war which was near being lost in the storm.

He spoke of his horses: 'The Chestnut does not turn out a very good charger though a useful handy horse. I don't want a better mount than my brown in action. I can manage him so easily, his mouth is so good.' In his next letter he was not so happy. 'I fear most of the horses will be dead before they get them under cover. Glanders, farey and lung complaint, are killing a good many.' (Glanders is an unpleasant disease which can be transmitted from horses to man; it would have seemed they had a large enough selection of diseases: cholera, dysentery, diarrhoea, rheumatism, scurvy, without needing reinforcements from the animal kingdom.) But the much-scorned Turks are being made into a labour force:

The Turks are to be set to work to build us huts—this sort of work and scraping the mud off the roads is all they are good for. Everyone out here (in spite of what *The Times* may say to the contrary) hates the name of a Turk while a Russian is certainly a more noble and a braver man. I can't think how the Turks ever beat the Russians, for they seem to fight well and be well led; they are most determined-looking fellows, while all the former I have seen (which are not a few) are the most rascally-looking rabble in the shape of an army that any nation could produce. French and English look at them with contempt.

The French, on the other hand, seem popular with their allies. 'These French are very jolly fellows. I get French bread nearly every day, only they require us to give them such an immense lot of biscuit for a loaf, but we generally settle it somehow.'

In his next letter he says, 'The report of the Duke of Cambridge having gone mad is quite untrue; he is still on board ship', and continues:

Many officers have lately sent in their papers, which have mostly been returned. Fisher, 4th D.G. [Dragoon Guards] sent in his after the gale but I hear they were refused and he withdrew them. For my part I shall stand by now for better or worse till we get through. Many here say that Lord Raglan is far too old and slow, and in fact he does not appear to give satisfaction, still he has a game to play and ought to be allowed to play it out; there may be more in him than there seems, certainly our head people are very slow. The French have had warm sheep skins served out to them and now our heads of affairs begin to think that such things might be useful to us, so I suppose we may get them towards spring, the same may be said of the huts.

Much of this letter is taken up by discussion of 'prospects'. This, of course, was the period of the purchase of commissions. The purchase system had a long history but a far from satisfactory record. In the Middle Ages gentlemen would raise a force from their own estates, and take it to battle. If they were defeated, so much the worse for everyone, but if the campaign was victorious there would be handsome dividends in the shape of ransoms and plunder. Woe betide the blundering over-enthusiastic retainer who killed an important opponent instead of taking him prisoner. From start to finish fighting was a business transaction, and also a considerable gamble. Troops had to be taken off other work, clothed, armed, trained and paid. Even in medieval warfare the cost of this was considerable. Even so, a commission was worth money, and, when the army was on a victorious campaign, might bring a man something approaching a fortune. This may appear a thoroughly bad system but in practice was not entirely so, for it meant that men took their profession very seriously, would not take arms against the monarch whose commission they held (thus making for stability), and, provided they had money as well as talent, could rise to a high rank at an early age. However there were abuses, and some of them quite fantastic. Rich parents could purchase commissions in fashionable regiments for their children, even when infants, and even if the regiment never went to war the pay over the years gave a good return on the capital investment. The effect on unmoneyed, passed-over officers was obviously disastrous, and there were cases of men serving for twenty or thirty years in the same rank.

Godman's position was worth £2,035, and he considered himself well placed, though many would not have agreed with him. But the outlook on these matters can only be conveyed by the following comments, made to his father:

> Thompson has joined us; he is as great an ass as ever, and perhaps more consequential. As to consulting him on matters connected with the regiment I might as well talk to a post. He always says 'Yes' or if he does not, 'I don't mind': in fact I do pretty much as I like with the direction of affairs. He makes sure of getting Le Marchant's vacancy. I hope he may, as being the less of two evils, for if not we shall be thrown over again with respect to promotion—but I fear we shall be done. Campbell has been laid up for a month with a bad leg (an old affair) in a little tent, not a very lively state of existence as you may imagine, and no wonder he has made up his mind to go; he does not want the price we give for troops at home though what it is I don't know. He is engaged to be married which is another reason. Now Halford I think won't give much over regulation as I expect he is waiting for Scarlett's step to go without purchase, as the Brigadier must sooner or later be promoted. But I must talk to Halford seriously about it, for it won't do to lose a step if it can be avoided, and if he does not get his money perhaps Campbell might exchange to half pay, bringing in a man to serve, which would completely do us. A letter from Mackinnon says that when Thompson went to the Horse Guards about his promotion a friend of his told him to apply for the majority and lt-colonelcy, which he promised to do; just fancy such a fellow. Mackinnon also says Le Marchant's brother told him that Le Marchant had been to a levée at the Horse Guards to retire but they advised him to take a little time to consider about it. I can't believe this, I think he is staying on with the chance of getting Scarlett's lt-colonelcy and then he would sell out, making a lot of money by the transaction. It cannot last much longer and it is a shame he is not made to sell directly.

Not everyone was as indifferent to the hardships, and as concerned about promotion prospects, as Godman was. He wrote:

> Thompson had a letter from someone in England to say that Le Marchant is not going to leave the regiment, he has good interests and has, I suppose, managed to do us somehow. I can't think he can stay long. I don't believe he has the pluck to come here, and if he did hardly anyone in the regiment would speak to him. You may fancy the feeling against him when I tell you the men have been heard saying that 'he would not come here because he would not like the noise of the cannon'. McNeile wrote for three months' leave and then to sell out but was told to join or sell directly, so he, I expect, will soon be out of my way for promotion. I shall be sorry when he goes but his health could not stand this work.

*Four contemporary cartoons from* Punch *illustrating the prevalent British attitude to the war. 'What it has come to', 'Bursting of the Russian Bubble', 'The Giant and the Dwarf' are dated 1854; 'All but Trapped' is dated 1855*

ALL BUT TRAPPED.

WHAT IT HAS COME TO.

*Aberdeen.* "I MUST LET HIM GO!"

BURSTING OF THE RUSSIAN BUBBLE.

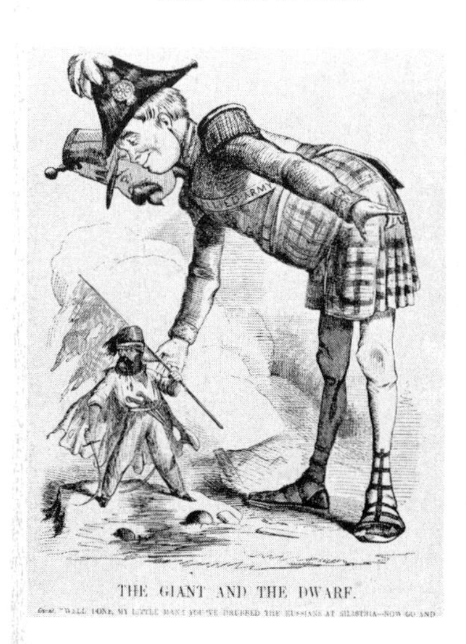

THE GIANT AND THE DWARF.

*Giant.* "WELL DONE, MY LITTLE MAN! YOU'VE DRUBBED THE RUSSIANS AT SILISTRIA—NOW GO AND

*The Battle of the Alma (Sir Colin Campbell leading the Highland Brigade) ended in victory for the Allies, but was ineptly handled by both sides*

*Guards regiment engaged in fierce fighting at the Battle of the Alma*

*Balaclava – Cavalry charging the Russian guns*

*Balaclava – Cardigan leading the Charge of the Light Brigade*

*Officers and soldiers of the 4th Dragoons outside an improvised hut. About six wives per company were allowed to travel with the troops and served as laundresses, cooks and nurses*

*Inkerman – G. Greatbach's engraving of 'General Cathcart's Death' (right)*

*A more realistic portrayal – 'Roll Call' after an oil-painting by Lady Butler (below right)*

*Stratford Redcliffe (Viscount Canning), Ambassador to Turkey*

*Vice-Admiral Sir J. W. D. Dundas*

*Lord Raglan*

*Lord Cardigan*

*Todleben, the brilliant Russian engineer who organized the defence of Sebastopol*

*Crimean hero:*
*Piper David Muir of the 42nd Highlanders (right)*

*The heroic view: a contemporary engraving of the guards fighting in the Crimea (far right)*

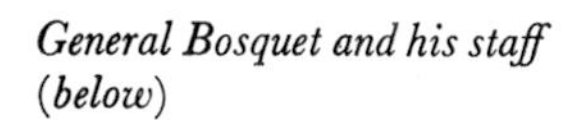

*General Bosquet and his staff (below)*

*General Brown and his staff (below right)*

*The ordinary soldier: Roger Fenton's photograph of a private of the 28th regiment in full marching order*

*Soldiers off duty – 'L'entente cordiale' – a photograph by Roger Fenton*

*'Near Sebastopol at the time of the big excursion, 24th October 1854'.*
*A contemporary Russian engraving*

*'The Bombardment of Sebastopol'. A contemporary Russian engraving*

*'The Guards working in the trenches before Sebastopol'.*
*An engraving by R. Hurd and G. Greatbach*

*'Sentinel of the Zouaves before Sebastopol'.*
*Lithograph by W. Simpson*

*The Bombardment of the Malakoff Tower. General Bizot fatally wounded while visiting the English trenches*

*The road from Balaclava to Sebastopol during wet weather. Lithograph by W. Simpson*

*Improved medical treatment.
A somewhat idealized
engraving*

*Interior of the Redan, Sebastopol,
which the Allies fought
so hard to take*

Burnand's leave expires this month. I don't know what he will do. I must say it is hard on me and others who have gone through the hardships of the campaign. If we went home tomorrow Burnand would get his troop before me and perhaps keep me back a long time; all who have the misfortune of ill-health ought to retire. Our surgeon from the 2nd Life Guards is much too great a swell for me, he does not like this rough work, and has been before a board to get a medical certificate, a regular case of shuffle. I don't like such chicken-hearted men, and the sooner these go home the better, especially the doctor, who ought to stick by one to the last, when affairs look bad and his services are likely to be wanted. The other day, in the gale, his tent like all the rest came down. He was in bed, though half-blown out of it, and rain coming down on him in bucketsfull. I though turned out of my house and home too, could not help standing by to admire the scene while he was shouting for help and for his servant, and when I asked him if this was as pleasant as Knightsbridge Barracks he seemed to think I was joking, and did not half like it. I could not help laughing in spite of our mutual misery.

However, as Godman would happily acknowledge, the doctor concerned was an exception, and there were many out in the Crimea who went well beyond the highest expectation of devotion to duty and their fellow men. Nor did he criticize many of his brother officers and regiments. In fact, it is astonishing that there were so few complaints in such conditions. He does, however, come down very sharply on some of the reporting of events in the Crimea, which, he says, credited regiments with achievements they could not have had, and denied them to others who had accomplished them. These letters, which have never been published, throw considerable light on life and attitudes, and also correct some of the false reports that have gone unchallenged for nearly a century and a quarter.

An interesting viewpoint on the Crimean campaign came from Captain John Codman, who commanded an American chartered transport. Codman considered that the Russians had been cleverly deceived by the Allies over the landing place and that the disembarkation took place before the Russians could assemble a force large enough to oppose it. He goes on to say:

They made, however, a gallant resistance after the invaders had debarked. The whole small garrison of Sebastopol came out to meet them upon the Heights of the Alma. There the first battle was fought. It was chronicled as the first great victory of the Allies. On the other hand the

Russians justly regarded it as the first check on them. It was reported in France, where we happened to be at the time, that Sebastopol itself had fallen, and for a week people believed it. . . .

The news of the Battle of the Alma and its want of entire success created an intense excitement in France and England. It had been imagined that this expedition into the Black Sea would have been sufficient to disperse the Russian forces from its shores, but all at once the Western powers awoke to the seriousness of their mistake. The capture of Sebastopol, though of course exceedingly desirable as the destruction of the Russian fleet would have ensued, was not of absolute importance. But it was now more than ever determined upon as a matter of pride. It could have been blockaded and all the operations of the war might have been carried on nearly as well by that means as by the final conquest of only a portion of the town. Thus many thousands of lives might have been spared but the pride of France and England was touched, and they were determined to enter Sebastopol, though obliged to wade through the blood of their own children.

Codman's belief that Russia could have been brought to her knees by the blockade of Sebastopol does not seem easy to substantiate. Furthermore he had already stated of Sebastopol that, 'The town was already impregnably fortified against all attempts from the sea, as the fleets shortly afterwards discovered on the occasion of their ineffectual bombardment.'

Nevertheless, although some of Codman's beliefs may seem debatable his observations on the contestants are extremely interesting and valuable. His ship, the *William Penn* was the first transport under a foreign flag chartered by the French Government. He left Marseilles on the first of November with a cargo of stores and ammunition and a detachment of troops for the Crimea. The voyage seems to have given him much artistic pleasure, and its only mishap was treated philosophically.

We were entering the Dardanelles, the ancient Hellespont. It should not have been attempted on a foggy night especially as the narrow and crooked strait was unlighted. But our orders were imperative to follow the French gunboat which bore us company. The result of this temerity was that we both found ourselves snugly ashore before morning. We grounded on Nagara Point, the very spot where Leander landed when he swam the Hellespont, and where Leander had more occasion to be pleased in getting ashore. We were unable at the time to back off, but fortunately the ground was soft, and no damage was eventually done to either of the ships. It was, after all, perhaps a fortunate accident. Had not this detention occurred we should in the ordinary course of the voyage have been off Balaclava in the destructive gale of the fourteenth of November.

Codman has the highest praise for the Pasha of the Dardanelles who came in person to give assistance in getting the boats off, and rather more important, produced a fleet of boats to take the cargo off and numbers of Turkish soldiers to do the work. The Pasha was deeply religious, and prayed regularly and long. Assuming that his religion extended to the prohibition of alcohol Codman served no wine at dinner. He was disconcerted when the Pasha gently suggested that a little champagne would be acceptable. Codman apologized for not having produced it before but explained as he did so that he had been under the impression that wine was forbidden to the true believer. 'Wine was forbidden by the prophet, not champagne' was the reply. 'Champagne did not exist in his day; how then could he have forbidden it? God is great. Pass the bottle.' The Pasha, incidentally, made no charge for his services in refloating the *William Penn.*

One of the most revealing statements—as far as the British were concerned—was in the following paragraphs:

Receiving renewed orders from the agents of the French Government, we proceeded up the Bosphorus and entered the Black Sea. After the Battle of the Alma, when the Allies had discovered that Sebastopol was not so easily to be captured as they had imagined, they made their preparations to invest it. For this purpose they took advantage of convenient harbours to land their munitions and troops. A nearly equilateral triangle may be supposed, having for its points Sebastopol, Balaclava and Kamiesh. The first was occupied by the Russians, the English took possession of the second, and the French of the third. The area of this triangle served during the war for the outposts of the Russians, and the encampments of the Allies, and the neighbourhood on the inland side was the great battlefield on which all the subsequent actions were fought.

Balaclava is completely land-locked, having an exceedingly narrow and crooked entrance, which makes it when enclosed one of the best harbours in the world. But it is very small. This did not seem an objection to it at that time, for no idea was then entertained of the extensive use to which it would afterwards be applied. The English accordingly, with the consent of the French, appropriated it for their vessels. The disadvantage arising from this error was proved first in the terrible hurricane of 14 November, in which so many English transports, unable to find shelter in the inner harbour, were wrecked upon the rock-bound coast. At the same time the French loss was slight, their harbour being sufficient to retain all their ships. Subsequently I have seen twelve hundred sail of vessels safely moored within it.

So, it seems, the great hardships stemming from the hurricane—of which more later—could have been avoided if the harbours had been shared.

Codman went on to say:

> At the time of our arrival there prevailed the famine and distress which the survivors of the English Army still hold in sad remembrance. There was absolute starvation in their camp, while at four or five miles' distance provisions were rotting on the beach. Much has been said of the mismanagement of the British Government and the superiority of the French commissariat. There is a certain degree of truth in this, but the neglect was not so extreme as has generally been supposed. The English made many mistakes. Their first and greatest arose from a misapprehension of the enemies they had to deal with—the Russians and the Russian climate. A summer's cruise was projected to capture the little town of Sebastopol and to return with the guns of its fortress at about the same time as those from Cronstadt were expected to arrive. . . .
>
> The English were unfortunate in the selection of Balaclava for other reasons besides the smallness of its harbour. It was at a greater distance from their camp than was Kamiesh from the headquarters of the French, and the road to it was chiefly of clay. While therefore the French managed with difficulty to keep up communication with their port, that of the English was nearly cut off. Four miles was sometimes a day's journey for a man on foot. The road was packed with animals that had died in their tracks. Under such circumstances it was absolutely impossible to transport sufficient provisions for an army. While the French barely succeeded in doing it on account of a better road and a shorter distance, the English could not do it at all.

These observations on the harbours and conditions in the Crimea throw a revealing light on a situation which is normally only seen from the somewhat obscure landward view. Codman's views were detached but discerning. . . . But whether he is correct in the following viewpoint it is up to the reader to judge:

> There was another reason for their greater suffering which observation warrants me in believing important. A Frenchman can live upon what is starvation to an Englishman; he can adapt himself to short allowance as

no other mortal can. But an Englishman remembers his roast beef and his beer, and if he cannot get them he will growl and lie down and die. Three or four Frenchmen can live upon the rations of one Englishman and be more jolly upon their empty stomachs than he would be with a tight waistband. When everything else fails they can live on ragouts made of remembrances of the past and seasoned with hopes of good times to come.

This might not seem to be entirely true, or even fair, but he went on to illustrate the point:

Once after a toilsome tramp to the English headquarters, my purser and I entered the tent of an officer with whom we were acquainted. Woebegone he looked, as he gave us a grouty welcome. 'Come in,' said he, 'sit down. I wish I had something to offer you but I have not. Expected a dozen of porter and pair of fowls up today. Couldn't have cooked the fowls if they had come. No coal. However, might have lived a day or two on the porter, but done out of that too. Infernally miserable, by Jove!' And so he was. He looked it all.

Feeling little inclined to accept the only hospitality he had to offer—that of a camp stool—we pursued our way tediously to the French camp, where our gay friend, Lieut Courtois was quartered. Before reaching his tent we heard a snatch from an opera. With what *empressement* he rushed to embrace us, invited us to dine. Insisted upon it, and sent for some of his comrades to meet his guests. His larder was scarcely better stocked than that of the Englishman, which had nothing in it. But roots were grubbed up, and a fire was made, some rough boards were laid out and a clean cloth spread upon them. On came the soup, hot, at any rate, if it was homeopathic. And in the other courses, which were numerous, beans, the material of the soup, were disguised in infinite variety with such skill that they served for fish, roast, entremets and dessert.

This view of the comparative merits of the British and French at improvising in the field may well not seem entirely fair. The two officers concerned were not necessarily typical, and, in any event, it is the private soldier who shows ingenuity in improvising (he would probably, rightly, call it scrounging). Any soldier who has had some experience of active service is likely to become expert at making himself comfortable in difficult conditions, even if it does cause him to be indifferent to the honesty of some of his activities. British, French, Turkish and Russian would all be adept at acquiring any scraps of food or fuel that were available, but the French would probably serve theirs up in a more palatable way.

However, the fact that Codman unburdens himself of some opinions which are not easily acceptable to British ears does not mean that his other views should be dismissed. He was, of course, in closer contact with the French than anyone else. They had saved his command from disaster. The *William Penn*, a 613-ton boat with accomodation for up to thirty passengers, had had a disastrous maiden voyage as not a single berth had been sold. The *William Penn* made for Marseilles in the hope that there it might pick up passengers for the return trip to New York. Its arrival at Marseilles coincided with a violent outbreak of cholera so that Marseilles and every other Mediterranean port was in strict quarantine. Cholera raged through the city in suffocatingly hot weather—there was a drought for six months. When therefore the French Government offered to charter the *William Penn* to take troops to the Crimea the offer was scarcely likely to be refused.

Codman's compassion was aroused for the Turks whom he visited in the trenches before Sebastopol.

> The condition of the Turks was in some respects more pitiable than that of their allies. No one seemed to care for them; for their ignoble retreat at Balaclava they were heartily despised by their friends as well as by their enemies, and till they redeemed their character at Eupatoria, were treated with scorn and neglect. I have actually seen a mule and a Turk harnessed together in a cart, and a Frenchman riding upon it and whipping up the team.

Contrary to the general view, he considers that the French administration was impeccably honest.

> I can truly say that in all my business intercourse with the Government I never saw the least sign of bribery or corruption. I believe that nearly all the money disbursed by France, nominally for the expenses of the war, was actually expended for that purpose. I wish that the same could be said of my experience in the transport service of our Civil War, to prosecute which an enormous national debt was incurred—no small part of it for individual benefit.

However, the French honesty was in no way connected with laxity, and the thirty-berth boat plied between Marseilles and the Crimea carrying shells in the hold, four hundred soldiers between decks and horses on the decks, from which the stalls were occasionally washed overboard in heavy seas. In one storm 'two of the horses were pitched through the skylight upon the heads of the cylinders, necessitating a stop of the engines until we could hoist them and throw them overboard.'

Having seen the destruction that was caused by the hurricane, Codman was always on the alert for a man-made catastrophe, which, fortunately for the Allies, never occurred. There were twelve hundred sailing vessels in Kamiesh harbour alone, and if the Russians had introduced saboteurs and set them alight the destruction would have been immense as there would have been little chance of escaping from the crowded harbour. He himself was so convinced that the Russians would try this manoeuvre sooner or later that he always berthed the *William Penn* as near to the mouth of the harbour as he could, and kept the engine room in a state of constant readiness.

It was the privilege of sailors to be able to see what was actually going on, then to read about it in the newspapers. Both French and English were equally misleading. Raglan for the Army and Admiral Boxer of the Royal Navy both reported that 'sanitary conditions were excellent' right up to the time they both died of cholera. The purpose of these mendacious dispatches was to convince the people at home that all was going well, that it was a hard struggle and that they should redouble their support. All this in spite of the fact that in Eupatoria numbers had been reduced from thirteen thousand to six thousand without a battle being fought.

The most significant statement of all was the one in which Codman explained why cholera never broke out on his ship:

> The secret of our immunity was that we never drank any water that had not been filtered elsewhere or distilled on board. In the naval fleet the water was never brought on board from the shore but was always distilled. On land this precaution was perforce not taken. Still, something might have been done to prevent the soldiers from drinking the water of stagnant pools and streams polluted with the carcases of dead animals that had been dumped into them to save the trouble of burial. It really seemed as if the Allies were not content with being killed in their engagements with the Russians, but were determined to add to battle, and murder, the sudden death they brought upon themselves.

The simple but vital precaution of boiling all drinking or washing water might have been difficult to apply through the entire army, but was by no mean impossible. It would certainly have been easier than coping with cholera and its effects. But even years later cholera continued to claim victims in other campaigns through lack of this simple precaution. It seemed to be one of the discoveries–like drinking lime juice–which prevents an appalling scourge and then is forgotten, only to be rediscovered and re-used years later when many have since died.

Nevertheless it still seems somewhat of a miracle that the *William Penn*, which must have been typical of the better transports, did not have an outbreak of disease. As the war progressed the ship would carry 'four hundred cattle, two thousand sheep, seven hundred soldiers, or two hundred and fifty sick and wounded'. The cattle were, however, light–being supplied by the contractors by number and not by weight–'so thin that they could be easily stowed away and so light that they were always hoisted in and out by their horns'.

It seems surprising that any of the sick survived at all. They were taken on to the beach on carts or mules–if the latter one man would be slung on each side of the animal, and there they would lie for hours before being taken off. Needless to say many of them died either on the beaches or while being transported on board. The only heartening feature of these unnecessary agonies was the conduct of the Sisters of Charity who came to the boatside under any conditions in summer and winter, and spared no effort to alleviate the last moments of the dying. None of their names are known, let alone remembered, and yet the work they did was certainly braver, and in all probability, of more value than that of the 'heroes' of the war.

# 8
# The Russian Defences

The reason why wars are won or lost is usually discovered by intelligent hindsight. This is clearly a simpler task than for a general to decide how they may be won by imaginative foresight. But even with hindsight it is sometimes difficult to know exactly why a campaign was successful. This is because battles are sometimes won by armies with inferior numbers, or when very little, if any, advantage seems to have been gained. Casualties may be approximately equal, and low, at the turning point. It is only when one side gives way that the heavy slaughter begins. Even then the ensuing casualties may not be limited to one side. Although the losers are almost certain to have large numbers of killed, casualties may also sharply increase among the winners, who become careless and underrate the desperate efforts of an enemy fighting for life itself. Therefore the explanation of the victory may not lie in comparative casualty rates. Probably it comes from a loss of confidence by the higher command, which rapidly transmits itself to the troops. Frequently the event which destroys this may seem trivial. The Battle of Hastings was touch-and-go until Harold was wounded, the Battle of Barnet was lost on the cry of 'treachery', the Battle of the Slim River in 1942 in Malaya was lost when the Japanese were retreating but no one on the British side realized what had happened, and so on. The Crimean War appears to have been lost because the tactical defensive had been broken.

The military theory of the Crimean War would be that the landing, the Battle of the Alma, flank march and battles around Balaclava were offensive strategy. Once Sebastopol had been invested, the policy of the Allies was presumably to shell the town and exhaust the Russians at a tactical level by letting them try to probe the encircling defences. The Russians of course could have interpreted their actions as being a series of delaying actions inflicting the greatest losses and wear on the enemy who would therefore become so exhausted militarily and economically that he would be glad to make peace on terms favourable to the defender. As it happened, the decisive act of the war was the successful French attack on the Malakoff. From this the Russians concluded that there was no point in trying to hold a town which—in spite of its advantages—had failed to keep the Allies out, and therefore moved back to a second strategic position—the Mackenzie Heights. From this point they could bombard the Allied positions in Sebastopol and, if necessary, draw the Allies further inland—1812 all over again. But, upsetting their calculations, the tactical success at the Malakoff proved sufficient to convince all concerned that there was no point in anyone pursuing further aims in this essentially 'limited' war.

The factor which put the result of the Crimean War constantly in the balance was the intense activity of the defenders. In the very early stages Todleben had inspired and, of course, driven the Russians into building earthworks and defences at a speed which the Allies could never have imagined. During the appalling conditions of the winter of 1854–5 the Russians could have driven the Allies out of their trenches but they did not realize the advantage they had at this point and concentrated instead on perfecting their own defensive works. They did, of course, mount counter-offensives at Balaclava and Inkerman but did not appreciate their tactical opportunities later in the year.

However, once the winter was over the defence displayed as much offensive spirit as the attack. The Russians had the unfortunate experience of being more exposed to artillery fire than the Allies were, for they had to have working parties continuously exposed while repairing the damage done by Allied gunfire. Forward trenches had to be fully manned against the possibility of a surprise assault. But this did not in any way lessen their morale, although it is doubtful whether it enhanced it. But they did not accept a merely passive rôle. Forward and diagonal trenches were dug so that the English and French positions could be raked by enfilade fire. This was in addition to the skirmishers and sharpshooters who were always strategically posted. As the Russians worked intensively at night the light of the following day often brought surprises.

In the morning the French saw with astonishment a work thirty feet long, with a parapet five feet thick, formed of barrels and sandbags, within 300 yards of their trenches, from which twenty riflemen immediately opened up on their working parties. A second lodgement was thrown up in the rear of the first on the night of the 3 December, and on the following nights five lodgements were established on the right of these, which were finally connected, and constituted, in fact, a parallel made by the besieged to attack the works of the besiegers. The approaches of the French on that point were at once arrested, and they proceeded to direct their attention towards the Quarantine Battery. But the Russians were equally active. Between 7 and 22 December they had checkmated the French by establishing no less than fourteen lodgements between the Cemetery and Quarantine Battery. They also strengthened their right wing with new guns and batteries. The French, checked on the left, then directed their energies to Bastion No. 4, and began to blast the rock to force their approaches. The Russians, between 6 and 7 December, made two lodgements on one flank of it, and on the night of 10 December threw up two other lodgements on the other flank, of which the most advanced was only 150 yards from the third parallel. Rifle pits were also established to harass the English in their works, which were further off than those of the French.

Todleben recorded that the French were much more vigilant against sorties than the British, in the early days at least.

In all sieges, from the very earliest times, the mine and countermine have been very important factors. Sebastopol was hardly likely to be an exception. The means of detecting the approach of mine or countermine are simple but ingenious. A bowl of water placed on the ground will often suffice to show if anyone is working underneath, and there are a variety of sophisticated listening devices. As Russell put it:

Both sides displayed intelligence and indefatigable zeal in the approaches and counter-approaches, but the Russians had the best of it as regards information. Now it was a deserter from the Légion Etrangère who gave them such intelligence as enabled them to calculate the day when the French would reach the spot beneath the counterscarp of the bastion. Another time Todleben received from Prince Menschikoff a plan of the mines, *lithographed in Paris,* very imperfect without doubt, but in which there was marked a gallery in the direction of the head of bastion No. 4, with a chamber under the *terre-plein* of the salient. Such indications gave the Russian engineer the means of disposing his galleries and countermines so as to guard against the impending danger; and the

French were astonished from time to time to find their plans defeated by news which, without their knowing it, was derived from themselves.

Mining was extremely difficult owing to the rock being so close to the surface; in some areas it was covered by a mere two feet of earth only. Nevertheless, trench, sap and mine continued to be hacked out. Eventually the pattern of trench, traverse, sap, parapet, parados, lodgement, gunpit, etc. was so complicated and interwoven that it was almost as much a handicap to the attack as to the defence. This was when there was a heavy attack using supporting troops and large numbers of men who were unfamiliar with the ground. A confusing factor was that the engineers of both sides were not particularly orthodox in outlook; there was therefore no right adherence to a set pattern, rather the trace followed the ground instead of trying to ignore it, as has happened elsewhere with disastrous results. Nevertheless, where large numbers were involved—and fifty-five thousand were concerned in the attack on the last vital day—the crowding and confusion, not to mention the superb artillery targets thus presented, were a considerable liability.

This was a liability that was shared by the Russians who also had an extremely complicated network of forward trenches and communications. Their working parties were vast by any standard, on some days as many as ten thousand would be employed, and thus exposed to Allied gunfire. The total Russian casualties were given by Todleben as 93,625, although only 17,000 of these were killed outright; casualties in Sebastopol were 89,142.

As a shrewd tactician Todleben had made an assessment of what he thought were the many problems of the other side:

> All the imperfections of the administration of the English Army were brought out to full view during the campaign and it could be seen also to what an extent their mode of recruiting by voluntary enlistment was defective. There was no harmony between the different branches of the administration. The commandants of the troops took no care of the food or well-being of their soldiers, leaving that duty to the 'intendance' which could not know the wants of the men and had besides no means of satisfying them.

This view does not appear to be borne out by some of the officers and men whose writings are quoted later. But, it was undoubtedly true that:

The recruit enlists under certain conditions, and does not think it necessary to execute labours not provided for in these conditions. Moreover, the ranks of the British Army are filled almost exclusively by men unacquainted with any sort of trade and who have no other means of subsistence than by entering the service. Such a soldier is quite unfit to get on in the more difficult moments of campaigning, and so it was that the greater part of the miseries the English soldiers had to endure arose from the fact that the army, as a whole, was incapable, without receiving help from abroad, of overcoming obstacles, arising from the circumstances in which it was placed. Rain destroyed the roads and no one thought of repairing them. Transport and saddle horses perished of cold in multitudes, and their dead bodies were left to rot till the foetid atmosphere forced the authorities to order their removal. In March, 1855, the railway was finished by the English, for which not only materials but even workmen and engineers were sent out from England, which proves how unfit the English army is of itself to overcome the difficulties which are so often encountered in a soldier's life. A deplorable confusion reigned in Balaclava. Ships discharged their cargoes whenever they found it convenient. No one knew what had arrived or what was coming. Sometimes the soldiers were in need of the very articles which had been landed in the harbour.

A commission of inquiry, held after the campaign was over, disclosed a series of totally unnecessary hardships that had been caused by sheer incompetence in distribution. However, at all periods in the histories of armies, up till today when the situation at last seems to have changed, quartermasters have been famed for not issuing vital supplies. Either one excuse or another has been found, but the prevailing idea seemed to be that a quartermaster's store should always be full and then there were no problems with accounting. It was undoubtedly true in the Crimean, as it was on more than one occasion in the Second World War. At the battle of Isandhlwna in Zululand in 1879 two quartermasters refused to issue ammunition to messengers from different companies although the entire force was in imminent danger of being overwhelmed by thousands of Zulus; when the inevitable happened the two quartermasters–loyal conscientious men, no doubt–died with the rest. Sometimes the confusion stems from peacetime accounting systems still being used in a war situation. When Singapore Island was within hours of falling to the Japanese in February 1942 certain stores were still held on a peacetime basis, and could not be issued without 'proper authority'.

The fact that similar stores had been captured or were being burnt a few miles away made no difference. In 1964, when troops were fighting in the Radfan Mountains, accounting in Aden was on a peacetime basis and all bills had to be approved by the Colonial Office. In the light of mistakes which were still being made a hundred years later some of the anomalies of Crimean administration seem a little less grotesque.

Whether the Russian administration was any more competent seems highly debatable. The garrison of Sebastopol had shelter against rain, snow and cold, except when they were used on working parties, or held in reserve to cope with expected attacks—which was often enough. The remainder, such as those on the Tchernaya Heights, had the roughest of improvised accommodation even in the worst of the winter. Many would have suffered appallingly on the long march to the front. The supply of food was infinitely more difficult for the Russians, who had to transport it hundreds of miles overland. There was a perpetual shortage of bread and biscuit. Waggons broke down, horses died, the transport teams suffered from cholera and all the other ills made familiar in this campaign. The conditions for the evacuation of the wounded were, of course, completely inadequate. To some extent the food problems of the Russians were alleviated by the Cossacks who raided far and wide. They were said by Todleben to have carried off forty thousand cattle from the Tartar people living around the Eupatoria region. What happened to the poor peasant proprietors who had their means of livelihood removed is not recorded, being of no interest to the robbers.

It seems that it never occurred to the Allies to send a force, either from the north or the south, to cut the Russian supply lines. It would have been easy to do enormous damage, had they thought of it. The Russians were well aware of the threat, and kept small forces on hand to guard against it, but it seems unlikely that they would have been able to do much if the Allies had made a determined attempt.

On 17 February 1855 a Russian force under General Kroulew attacked the town of Eupatoria, which had been in Allied hands since the landing. The force included 500 Cossacks and 108 guns, but failed against a spirited defence by Turks, French, Tartars and a detachment of marine artillery. One French and two English steamers lay off the coast and fired into the Russian force. The attack was a complete failure, mainly owing to the heroic resistance of the inhabitants but partly because it was ill-conceived. The Russian attack cannot have been very determined for it broke off after sustaining losses of 769; the defence lost just over half that number (401) of which the Turks bore the brunt, losing 364. In a theatre in which the Turks were generally despised and maligned these figures are of interest but, as was seen at Kars, when there was any semblance of leadership or efficient organization, the Turks could perform with the best soldiers.

The failure of the Russian attack is said to have caused the Tsar 'intense mortification and disappointment', but Todleben regarded it with gloomy satisfaction; he had disapproved of it from the very moment it was suggested. The Russians reported on the battle as follows:

> Thus the principal object of our attack had not been attained. Eupatoria remained in the possession of the enemy, but the affair in itself was productive of advantageous results to our cause. This attack obliged the Allies to be always on guard and in readiness to repel others. It was from apprehension on this point that they always maintained at Eupatoria a large garrison and that they established here a vast entrenched camp.

It is well known that the views of commanding officers and members of the Staff are not always shared enthusiastically by those in the field. Captain Chodasiewicz, whose name has been anglicized to Hodasevich, and who has been quoted earlier in this book, wrote a somewhat critical account of the Russian efforts. He had served in the Faroutine Regiment of Chasseurs. His statements are written with tolerant cynicism. Before the Battle of the Alma, when the Allies were sighted on their way to land at Eupatoria—so it was thought —he remarked:

> Many of the younger officers expressed extravagant joy at the idea that God had given our enemies into our hands; the soldiers were also rejoiced at the news; they were burning with impatience to meet the enemy face to face, as well as for a change in their monotonous lives. Some few of the officers became sick, and required to be sent to the hospital but the number of these was small. I must say that I looked forward to fleshing my maiden sword with pleasure.
>
> There is no doubt that the men had confidence in their officers, who, they expected, would set them an example of daring and heroic deeds; but, alas, their confidence proved to have been misplaced. Those who were quiet in their demeanour, and said little about what they thought

of doing in the hour of danger, proved the first on the field of battle; while the boasters were for the most part to be found in the rear.

He mentioned this matter of boasting on other occasions. 'I remarked that I had little confidence in our leaders, as they were too fond of boasting, especially when under the influence of the bottle.' Hodasevich, in fact, had so little confidence in the Russians that he deserted to the Allies at the first opportunity. As a Pole he hated the Russians, though he had risen high in their service. Had he received any encouragement to do so he could have induced large numbers of other Poles to desert the Russians. He may have had a slightly idealized view of British justice at this time. He wrote 'In the Russian service it is impossible for a General to be in fault when only a captain of a company is in question. Russia is not the free country that England is, where a free press exists, and where every man can appeal for justice to public opinion, no matter who may be his oppressors.'

Hodasevich's writing is full of interesting information, not only about the Crimean War but about life and conventions at the time. Modern readers who are under the impression that the booby-trap is an invention of the present century will be interested to note that the Russians, on leaving a town, gave orders that all the flour should be mixed with lime. He says:

> A Russian soldier forms part of a machine, which is composed of enormous masses of men who never have thought and never will think. They are oppressed with blows and ill-treatment; their understanding is kept down by servitude, and the severe laws to which they are subjected. Sometimes a man more sprightly than his comrades will try to solve some knotty point, but he soon loses himself in the mystery, and only escapes by concluding that, as he knows nothing about it, it is the business of God and the Emperor, but none of his.

Some of Hodasevich's stories appear almost incredible, but he quotes time and place. 'Captain Gorieff flogged one of his men to make him laugh. It is hardly to be credited, but after receiving one hundred lashes the man managed to get up a laugh.' Certain regiments however, Guards, Artillery, Sappers and Rifles, being all picked men, are better treated than the men of the line.

The Russian Army was not cluttered up with what some might think unnecessary administration. 'In the Russian army there are no nominal returns of the killed and wounded, so that unless one happens to be a general or a colonel at least, it is very difficult to ascertain the fate of an officer who has ceased writing to his friends; the fate of a soldier it is next to impossible to learn.'

Hodasevich at times appears so critical that it is difficult to believe that he is not taking a jaundiced view. On occasion, however, he does give praise, but not for administrative ability. 'Prince Menschikov showed a great deal of personal courage; four officers of his suite were killed near him by the fire from the fleet while he remained unmoved. But for a commander-in-chief courage is not the only quality required; in fact it is a part of his duty not to expose himself, unless absolutely necessary, to the enemy's fire.'

Whatever may be thought about Raglan's decision not to order a cavalry pursuit there was no doubt in Hodasevich's mind of what it could have done as the Russians retreated from the Alma. He said:

It was extremely fortunate for us that the Allies were not strong in cavalry or not more than 15,000 would have reached Sebastopol. Horse artillery would have been very effective while we were crossing the Katcha at the village of Aranchi, where the greatest confusion reigned. At this time all were crowding together over the river at a ford—there were commissariat waggons, artillery waggons, with wounded artillery, infantry etc. in one mass of confusion. All these had to retire through a narrow pass surrounded on all sides by high mountains, from which had a shot or shell been thrown from time to time, it would have completed the disorganization, for none would have thought of resisting, so great was the demoralization of the men.

After the Battle of the Alma Hodasevich gave some thought to the reasons why the Russians had lost. This is his analysis:

First the troops were badly disposed upon the position; secondly during the action nobody gave any directions what to do, and everyone acted as he thought fit; the battalions of reserve began to retreat without any orders; our battalion also began to retire following the example of the reserves. During the five hours that the battle went on we neither saw nor heard of our general of division, or brigadier, or colonel; we did not during the whole time receive any orders from them either to advance or retire; and when we retired nobody knew whether we ought to go to the right or the left. In the centre of the line it was the same; and if the men fought it was solely on the responsibility of the colonels of the regiments, but certainly not from orders of Prince Gortschakoff; for who would have thought of sending a regiment to the charge without its being supported by artillery, when there were plenty of guns in reserve. Where there was some degree of order was on the left flank where Prince Menschikov was in person; but it was difficult for him to stop the advance of the French troops as he could not get up his reserves before they had crowned the heights.

Hodasevich had studied the battle carefully and referred to the plan he had made of it. He went on to say:

> With such confusion among the heads of the Russian army it is not surprising that the battle was lost; but a more ample proof of this will be seen in the sixth chapter [of this book, *A Voice from Within the Walls of Sebastopol*], where a large army with a numerous artillery surprised a small body of Englishmen at Inkerman with every prospect of success, but were beaten off through the blunders of the commanders.

He spoke highly of Admiral Korniloff, who all this time was working to improve the defences on the southern side of the harbour, but he blamed the Russian Army commanders for the lack of provision for the sick. Had he known that the Allies were no better Hodasevich might have been a little less scathing:

> The chiefs of the army are to be blamed for not having made any arrangements for taking proper care of the wounded. This proves that either the Prince never expected a proper invasion of the Crimea, or that forseeing the event, he was guilty of neglect in not establishing proper hospitals for the wounded that might have been expected to result from the struggle. During the night of the 20th–21st these unfortunate men arrived in the town, for the most part with their wounds undressed. Few of them were able to ride but dragged their mutilated limbs in the greatest agony on foot. To the honour of the Russian soldiers be it said that many tore up their shirts for the purpose of bandaging the wounds of their comrades, neglected and left to their fate from the want of proper arrangements for their accommodation.

Weird rumours circulated when the defeated Russians poured back into Sebastopol, 'drunken sailors wandered riotously about the streets and in some instances shouted that Menschikov had sold the place to the English, and that he had purposely been beaten at the Alma, where he had caused confusion by giving no directions during the battle; many similar ideas were current among the drunken populace and sailors. The Prince did not show himself about the town.' In order to restrict the drunkenness Korniloff stopped the sale of all liquor; as this had no effect on sobering up the town he took the further step of ordering all stocks of liquor to be destroyed. Menschikov gave the order to sink the blockships immediately after the Army's arrival but upwards of forty vessels were still left afloat.

Hodasevich confirms Todleben's statement that Sebastopol was wide open to attack on both sides after the Alma. But this defenceless state did not last for long. Everyone who could work was pressed into service, even Cossacks and convicts. Of the Cossacks he said:

> They have few words of command but all their movements are directed by signals. These signals are imitations of the cries of different animals found in the Caucasus; they howl like jackals and wolves, bark like dogs, mew like cats, etc. These signals are of course understood by the men. Their appearance in Sebastopol was anything but prepossessing, as their clothes were in tatters, so that in places the bare skin could be seen through the holes of their garments.

But even the Cossacks were not the most bizarre element of the defence force. That distinction was earned by the convicts 'who in their ordinary dress, minus the chains, were formed into a kind of forlorn hope, they were armed with cold arms only, such as long-handled axes, boarding-pikes, etc.'

Life under bombardment might have appeared to be active enough without additional hazards but this was not the way the Russians saw it:

> On the third day of the cannonade the fire was particularly hot, as the Allies began to throw in shell, which we had not hitherto seen. I suppose that during the first two days the mortars were not ready. In a confined space a shell is perhaps the most destructive thing that can be employed, and frequently one would put from 10 to 25 men *hors de combat.* Some were daring enough to rush upon them as they fell, draw the fuse, and thus prevent their bursting, thereby saving the lives of their comrades; whoever did this immediately received the cross of St George, which is only given for rare examples of courage, and is of the utmost importance to men, as it exempts them from corporal punishment and gives them an increase of pay.

Discipline, however, was maintained:

> On this day Captain Zorine, of the Navy, ordered a man to be punished for theft, which was done by tying the man to a cooled gun, and while

the bombardment was going on, he received 150 lashes with ropes' ends in the presence of his comrades and Captain Zorine, his commander, who paid not the slightest attention to the shot and shell that were flying about very plentifully in all directions, for this interesting ceremony took place about 2 o'clock in the day. I witnessed it myself.'

Todleben inspected all the defences closely and gave orders for modifications to be carried out during the night. During the hours of darkness a complete black-out was observed, but it was a voluntary one. So great was the danger of attracting the attention of an Allied gun crew or sniper that soldiers did not even light their pipes between dusk and dawn if their situation was in any way visible outside the town.

The art of fortification has fashions just like every other art but certain fundamentals prove their worth over and over again. Once gunfire was introduced the best type of fortification was soon found to be low, squat, and made of earth. This was certainly so in Sebastopol. Hodasevich had very interesting views on fortifications, and he was certainly in a position to form judgements:

This war has proved that the best kind of defence against a regular attack consists of earthworks, that can so easily be changed, altered, and increased to meet the attacks. The batteries at Sebastopol were at first nothing but earth, loosely thrown up with the shovel, the embrasures were plastered with moistened clay, but when it was discovered that this was not enough, they were faced with stout wicker work. Then fascines were introduced, and finally gabions were employed. The batteries were frequently found not to bear upon the required point, or the embrasures were not made so as to enable the guns to be pointed in the right direction. Whenever a discovery of this sort was made the whole was changed during the night. If no changes were required, new and more formidable works were added. In this respect Sebastopol offered unexampled advantages in the arsenal, so that there were always guns to mount in these new works. If one of the bastions of Sebastopol were to be taken, and a section made, suppose for instance of the Malakoff, it could then be traced through its different periods of existence till it became the mass of sandbags and gabions it is at present, with the enormous embrasures firmly revetted with two or three rows of gabions. Then were added the casemates, holes dug in the ground, and covered with enormous ship-timber that was again covered with earth to the thickness of eight or ten feet, and perfectly proof to the heaviest bomb. In these the garrison, and a part of the gunners, could always find shelter; though these casemates eventually caused the loss of the Malakoff, and consequently the whole town. By this means of defence it was possible to concentrate a tremendous fire upon any given point of the trenches. The commander of every bastion and every battery had his orders in which direction he was to fire, and what guns. All these arrangements emanated from Todleben.

Small wonder that Sebastopol proved such a tough nut to crack. The great advantage of earthworks over stone fortresses was that they could be repaired, strengthened or altered with little trouble. Stone, by contrast, was a much less suitable material.

Although Hodasevich seemed hardened to the point of indifference there were others who were only too well aware of the perils that surrounded them. He quoted some fresh effects of shells. One occurred when 'in the front room, before the open window were two cadets of our regiment, looking over the engravings of the *Illustrated London News*. [How they had obtained it is not stated; possibly it circulated freely in Russia during the war!] A shell burst in the street outside and a splinter entered the room. It carried away the left cheek of one of the cadets, a lad of eighteen who died an hour or two later, and travelled across the room to kill an N.C.O. who was writing at a table. A Major thereupon crept under the table. Hodasevich was very scornful as the next day 'the Major reported himself sick and left the town for the north side'. He went on to say:

> During a war no officer can resign or get leave of absence on any consideration whatever in the Russian Army, so that many who merely entered the service for the sake of something to do, or for fine clothes to wear, were obliged, against their wills, to remain and defend their country. . . .
>
> It must not be supposed however that there are no good officers in the Russian Army, that idea would be altogether false. The Russians themselves, however, must acknowledge that a considerable proportion of their best officers are men of foreign extraction, such as Poles, Germans, etc.

He speaks bitterly of those officers who know nothing and take little interest—'they spend their time in drinking, gaming, and other vices and depend entirely on their non-commissioned officers. I have seen men of this class nominally in command of companies, while they could do nothing without the sergeant-major, who oppressed and robbed the men with impunity.' The weak officer who lets his

N.C.O.s run his unit is well enough known in all armies, although few of the latter, whether warrant officers or non-commissioned officers, go as far as actually robbing the men. But the Russian Army was like any other, right up to the present day.

It is a great thing for an officer to study the character of the men under him, and to let them feel that he takes an interest in them, at the same time that he knows his duty, and will allow no one to oppress them. When you have once gained the rude affection and confidence of Russian soldiers they will follow you anywhere; but to do this you must first know their character, and, knowing that, a few words, two or three will do, that will excite some of their few feelings, and they will be cut to pieces for you.

Whether the system of utterly incompetent officers being forced to stay in the line was a good idea seems debatable but presumably it was maintained because of the sheer impossibility of promoting from the ranks or finding replacements elsewhere. By contrast—as emerges from Godman's letters—English officers were allowed to sell their commissions and retire when they wished; presumably it was assumed that they were naturally brave and the replacement would be as good.

Although Hodasevich was merely voicing his own opinions they were based on observation and experience. Just before he left and sought asylum in the British Army—which was granted by Sir Colin Campbell—he made a series of bitter comments on the Russian quartermastering system. For the enterprise and skill of the engineering works he had had nothing but praise; for the transport and stores side he had little but scorn:

I wonder what became of the regimental transport all this time, as we were supposed to have 240 horses in this regiment, while I can affirm that we never saw more than thirty of them, and these were seldom employed for the transport of provisions, which were brought chiefly on the backs of men. There was an order from Prince Menschikov for each regiment to provide itself with packsaddles, though I never saw one used during the four months I was at Chorgoun. I was told, however, by the officer in command of the transport company that eighty of these packsaddles were made. 'Then why don't you use them?' asked I. 'We are keeping them new and clean in case of a review', was the answer. This is frequently the case in Russia; as for instance the entrenching tools of a regiment are kept for show, but not for use.

But, if Hodasevich had a dislike for all things Russian and an admiration for all things British there were others who did not share his views. After the fighting was over a host of sightseers visited the scene. There had been plenty when the fighting was going on but it was nothing to what followed. Among them was R. W. Cook, who wrote a book called *Inside Sebastopol.* It was published in 1856 and describes a journey accomplished in the autumn and winter of 1855. He visited Lord Raglan's house and talked to an N.C.O. What, he inquired, had the N.C.O. thought of Lord Raglan?

He was a good man, Sir, and when he met an officer, he would always speak to him, and sometimes ride alongside of him and ask him questions; and for that matter, he'd speak kind to the men. But then, Lord, the men, not one in a hundred ever saw him, or he them. A man, Sir, to command an army ought to be able to tire all his aides-de-camp down, as the old Duke used to do when he was in the field. Poor Lord Raglan, Sir, couldn't do it; he hadn't the strength for it; and I think, Sir, he hadn't head for it. We did hear in our camp that at Inkerman he didn't know how far our trenches went, and asked an officer with him whether the batteries in front didn't do a deal of damage in our trenches; whereas the batteries were our own batteries, and had been pushed further on than the paper in hand told him of. I don't know whether it's true but that's what we used to hear. We all knew he couldn't help it, and we didn't blame him.

This view, although a normal slander on the ability and intelligence of commanding officers, is stated a little too tolerantly for one to believe readily. Doubtless any modern soldier could improve on it.

Nor did Simpson inspire any greater confidence. But the French, well—that was a different story. The only unusual part of this critical survey was that it was offered to a stranger. Most soldiers, while happy to condemn all and sundry to their fellows, resent and discourage prying or criticism by a stranger.

Cook was able to wander around freely. He was entertained in an officers' mess and he wandered, though not caring much for the experience, in the streets of Sebastopol. He found much that was harrowing. Of the Redan he observed:

The Redan is a strong mound, the last undulation citywards of the table-land on which the besiegers sat down. It overlooks the descent down into the harbour of Sebastopol. Approaching it as we did from the south side it appeared a very gentle elevation; but there were abundant evidences that it was an elevation very difficult to reach. For many hundred yards before we arrived at the foot of it the earth was scarred with trenches fortified with gabions, with heavy guns crouched between them, allowing us just room to pass between their platforms and the rock.

His guide was highly critical of the troops who had been used in the first assault, which he called 'All sorts of trash.'

Cook inquired why the English sap was not pushed up closer to the Redan, as the French had to the Malakoff. He received a brisk uncompromising answer:

It cost the French fifty men for every yard of the latter part of their sap, and we could not afford a loss of five hundred men a day on this work. It was cheaper, in matter of human life, to assault as we did assault; but it should have been done with ten thousand men, and with the Highlanders and the Marines, both of whom volunteered and were refused, or else with General Eyre's third division, who would have carried the place in ten minutes and held it for a century.

His informant did not in any way blame Windham for leaving the Redan. According to his story the support did not move up, and when Windham tried to lead a charge he could rally no support except from officers and N.C.O.s.

The moment of victory passed away. The Russian supports came up in vast numbers; instead of finding five thousand Englishmen on top of the hill protected by the Russian guns now turned on their former owners, the Russians found only the five hundred men who had first got in and these engaged in desultory sharp-shooting with the scanty garrison which lurked among the traverses.

There was clearly going to be controversy for years about the failure of the attack on the Redan. The troops who had failed to win the Redan were cut to pieces by Russian fire.

Then the shot and shell came over into the crowded trenches, and the poor innocent babes who didn't know a bayonet from a musket and were no more fit to act as soldiers than they were to act as parsons, were cut up by balls and splinters, and were got out of the trenches as quickly as possible.

The mystery of it all was why, when there were so many experienced troops to hand for this vital assault that new, inexperienced ones were used, although their inexperience was somewhat overexaggerated.

Cook's story, although somewhat disjointed, brings out a number of points that are not mentioned elsewhere. One is that the failure at the Redan was much more important than it is usually made out to be, for success there might have brought about a full Russian surrender; as it was their Army reclaimed its morale and the war dragged on another six months. Windham was blamed in many quarters, but this appeared to have made little difference to his subsequent successful career. He was nicknamed 'Redan' Windham and specially promoted to Major-General on 14 October 1855.

According to Windham's own account the attack went badly from the start. He was the first person into the ditch and went straight into the middle of the work:

> I was followed by no one to the best of my belief. I crossed the work and went into the chambers upon the proper right face of it, and patted many of the men on the back and tried to get them out of the openings towards the second line—it was no use: I was never followed but by one man of the 88th*, and two men of the Rifles. The man of the 88th came out most gallantly and was abreast of me, the first rifleman also came out well and it was to these two men, who would unfortunately fire and not charge, that I said 'Well, if you will fire, shoot that (a strong expletive)' pointing to a Russian officer, who was kicking away the gabions in front to give his men a good shot at us. Finding, notwithstanding my cheering and doing the theatrical that these three men were all that came, we fell back; and, on my getting on the parapet the men were nearly taking a panic. I accordingly ran along the top of it (amongst their muskets) and assured them that there was no cause for fear and implored them not to fall back; the men on the salient gave me a hearty cheer and all seemed right.

However, all was not right and the support troops were reluctant to accept his assurances that it was. He mentions that 'A sergeant of the Rifles would have been of great service to me, as he was active, cool and brave; but he was killed whilst I had my hand upon his arm, being shot through his black belt, and the blood spurting quite out from his body.'

This was not, of course, the first or the last time that a commanding officer would foolishly try to encourage his men by telling them there was no danger. Threats would not have availed either; the only way he could get them to move forward would be to convince them

* The Connaught Rangers.

that they would all be killed if they did not. They were not, in fact, all killed, but a far larger number were than would have been if they had followed Windham forward. Once Windham himself turned back it was inevitable that the line would collapse.

Windham was clearly a man of great courage and character. However he was not a 'lucky' commander. In 1857 when the Indian Mutiny broke out he applied for a command on active service. After a first non-active command he was appointed by Sir Colin Campbell to Cawnpore, which at the time was thought to be in no danger. The situation suddenly changed and Windham eventually found himself pinned down in Cawnpore, where he might have been overwhelmed had Campbell not returned. He was subsequently heavily criticized for having tried to defend too wide a front, and for having over-emphasized aggressive defence. Clearly Campbell thought Windham had muddled the operation and he returned to England in 1861 a 'saddened and disappointed man'. However, two years later he was made a knight and two years after that was appointed commander of the forces in Canada as a lieutenant-general. He died at Jacksonville, Florida, in 1870. Sir William Codrington, who was thought by many to have made a complete mess of the attack, was made commander-in-chief when Simpson resigned on 10 November 1855.

One of the explanations of the English failure at the Redan was that they were outwitted by the French who made the British wait until the French flag was hoisted on the Malakoff. This was said to have been arranged so that the French would attack while the Russians were eating but the English when they had finished; this seems somewhat improbable. Another excuse was that Windham should have been allotted at least five times as many troops, although at no time was there a complaint about the quantity but only the quality; there is no doubt that Windham, if instructed, would have been brave enough to tackle the Redan with a mere half dozen. His declining years were far from happy as his only relative, the last surviving member of the family, contrived to ruin himself physically and financially (he was eventually reduced to driving the Cromer coach for £1 a week). General Windham did his best to save the situation, but the family property, Felbrigg Hall, Norfolk was sold—and was bought by one John Ketton, a Norwich merchant who had made his fortune out of cotton-seed during the Crimean War.

There are two other views of the Redan battle which deserve mention. One is the Canadian view of Frederick Vieth. Although his parents wished him to go into the Church he managed to get himself nominated for a commission in the Army. This meant that he would be commissioned if he passed the requisite examination. The examination, which lasted 'five or six hours' took place at the Royal Military College, Sandhurst (now, after its amalgamation with the RMA Woolwich, the RMA Sandhurst). After being looked over by the RMC surgeon, the examinees were ushered in to four examiners 'all of whom in turn questioned us. Questions both written and *viva voce* were asked by a Mr Chepnell in Roman, Grecian, and English history; and Geography, Arithmetic, Algebra, Latin and English composition were undertaken by Mr Narrien; French and German by Mr Cambrier, and fortification and drawing by Mr Cole. The results were given to the candidate as he left the room, and if successful he would be asked what regiment he would like to choose.' Vieth had been at a military academy before so, presumably, he had some idea of his future. He mentioned that only nine of the twenty-eight candidates passed. 'One week from the date of my passing I found myself appointed an ensign in the 63rd or West Suffolk Regiment [now the King's].' Once with the regiment (for he did not have to stay at Sandhurst) his training began in earnest, every day, including Saturday, being a working day for the first two months: 'Touching this daily instruction I may say that no distinction was made between officers and men newly joined as far as "setting-up" and "company drill" were concerned; we all fell in the ranks together.'

In some ways the situation between then and now seems remarkably unchanged: 'One of the drill sergeants, Mayburn by name, of the 21st regiment, under whose tuition I found myself placed, was noted as well for his eccentricities in expression as for his capabilities in imparting instruction. His correction of a recruit for some glaring mistake, frequently took the form of what was intended for withering sarcasm, which it was no easy task to prevent one's self laughing at outright, and nothing but the impropriety of setting so bad an example restrained.' Inevitably there was the odd man out: 'when such an order as "right face" or "right wheel" was given, it was quite usual for him to turn in the opposite direction, and bumping up against his next-door neighbour with a staggering collision, jumble up the whole squad, and bring upon his head the ire of the exasperated instructor.'

Vieth arrived in Balaclava on 26 August 1855 so he was just in time to take part in the Redan battle. They were in the second brigade of the Fourth Division. His regiment was not, however, in the assault; most of his account of it seems to be based on Russell's report, which gives a full and graphic account of the horrors of the scene, then and subsequently. Russell's account of the carnage in the Malakoff and other Russian defences makes the normal horrors of the war, the cholera, the trenches and the hospitals quite mild by comparison. But of the Redan assault he says:

> Colonel Windham, who bore a charmed life that day—for he escaped injury altogether—had been indefatigable in urging on the men inside the fortress. Seeing how matters were trending [sic], as our men were dropping fast, he determined himself to go to General Codrington, and ask for additional assistance. He had already dispatched three officers on this errand to the General, but each had been stopped on the way by a Russian bullet, so, telling an officer close by (Captain Crealock of the 90th) where he was going and for what purpose, he got over the parapet of the Redan, again crossed the intervening space to the fifth parallel through a storm of bullets and reached it unhurt.

This movement was of course misconstrued, as well it might be, for if an officer encourages his men to follow him into action he can hardly be surprised if they also follow him when he leaves it. Vieth's regiment was due to make the attack the following morning but, as we know, the Russians evacuated the Redan and blew it up during the same night. However they were not without casualties for they had been exposed to a lot of Russian fire while moving up and waiting their turn.

The other account of the Redan battle comes from Temple Godman in a letter written on 10 September. It was addressed to his brother. After describing the preliminaries he says:

> On the 8th we were out at 3 am and then went to the front, four squadrons. I went with one squadron; we were only there to keep back the spectators from getting too near. I went in front of the picquet house, and saw all. The fire was heavier than I ever saw before, and the Russians hardly fired at all. At noon the French had sapped up over the parapet into the Malakoff with (it is said) the loss of only one man (the

Russians were apparently unable to live under the fire directed on the place). As soon as they were in they became heavily engaged for about an hour in the rear of the place, and we saw the Russians run out across to the Redan. The whole place became a mass of smoke and we saw no more except sometimes the immense supports wandering up from the Mamelon. Nearly at the same time our men stormed the Redan, and the storming party took it and spiked a lot of guns but the Russians were in such force in rear, and our supports not coming up in time, our men were driven out again. At the same time the French who entered on the left, near the Flagstaff Battery were not more successful but the Malakoff was secured. The wounded men now came flocking to the rear, and a great number of officers, and from them we learned for certain of our repulse. Lots of men who came up, with their limbs smashed, stopped and talked to us and seemed not to care the least for their wounds. The number of officers was out of all proportion to the men; these latter I may tell you did not behave quite so well as usual. I only say this as you are sure to hear reports about it but when the country trusts its honour to *children* who have been about 4 months in the army and know next to nothing of drill and discipline it cannot expect such deeds as were performed by old and trained soldiers. I was told by many that at one time about 20 officers held the Redan for some minutes against masses of Russians, but the men did not support them and nearly every one was killed. The fighting was desperate and when too close for muskets they dashed each others' brains out with stones. After we were driven back we kept up a heavy fire on the place. I saw the 97th march home, about 60 men out of 800 and one subaltern; they said that was all that was left but more turned up after. The officer had lost his cap and was covered with powder and dirt, and his clothes spattered with blood, and torn in several places by shell. Then the 88th marched by, nearly cut to pieces, six officers coming back out of seventeen. We saw all these men going down in the morning cheerful as possible. We got home about 7 in the evening, having had a very long day. In the night the Russians left the town and retreated across the bridge. I suppose they saw it was useless to remain when the Malakoff was taken. The town was now on fire in many places, and when I went up early yesterday it was on fire all over the large buildings by the water, the ships, and the docks. I rode to the head of Careening Bay, and walked into the town by the Garden Battery. The strength of the place is enormous and I can't think how we could take it. The Russians were springing mines with electric batteries. The Frenchmen were plundering the town, the houses were riddled with shot, and the burst shell and shot were enough to pave the streets with. I never saw such scenes of havoc; there were hundreds of new guns not in use and immense anchors, of course very valuable. Just after I came out a large magazine blew up in the dock and explosions constantly take place even now. . . . I then went to the Redan and it seems to me we should never have attacked it, for it is quite commanded by the Malakoff and could not be held when we were in but the French said we must go at it to draw off the men from other parts. The Russians were there in heaps and the ditch was nearly full of dead English piled one on the other—I suppose five feet thick or more. The Redan was terribly strong and bomb proof inside. There was not a place an inch large that was not ploughed up by our shot and shell. Guns, gabions and even pieces of human flesh of every shape and size were scattered about. It was absolutely torn to pieces and one mass of rubbish and confusion impossible to describe. Inside were some field pieces filled to the muzzle with grape, which they had fired at our men; when they got in some had not been discharged. The Malakoff too was an extraordinary sight; the French lay in piles where they had been mown down with grape from a steamer and then the Russians too were in lines where the French had brought up field pieces and sent grape among masses at a few yards. I could form no idea of the number of the dead which must be enormous; it beats anything I have ever seen before, I think even Inkerman, but it is all over now with Sebastopol, and the three or four steamers remaining must soon be burnt too.

Of the Malakoff he said: 'It is a wonderfully strong place and has bomb proof houses enough to hold some thousands of men. The ditch must be nearly 30 feet deep. The French must have taken it quite by surprise for they say there was only a working party in it at the time. If it had not been surprised I believe it would have stood an attack from any amount of men.

It was, as he said, all over with Sebastopol, which he and others still found a beautiful city, even though every building had been damaged in one way or another. But the campaign was not over. Godman saw no further action, though he was held in readiness and did not arrive home until 25 June 1856. He must have had one of the longest records of service of anyone in the Crimea theatre.

On Sunday 7 October there began another operation by the Allies. On 8 October the Allied fleet was anchored off Odessa. The expedition had not, however, been planned against Odessa but against the forts at the mouth of the Dnieper, which were Ochakov and Kinburn. Odessa was considered to be an extremely beautiful city and of no importance militarily; this latter point was as well for it could easily have been shot to pieces. The arrival off Odessa became somewhat of an anti-climax by virtue of the thick fog which suddenly descended on sea and land. It lasted two days. The main attack was on Kinburn where large numbers of Russian guns were put out of action by a landing party. Vieth found himself in the party assigned to Kinburn, the purpose of which was kept secret till they set off. After the fog around Odessa they had a period of rough weather that made landing impossible. However, on 15 October a landing was made in Cherson Bay without any opposition, although the heavy surf did not help matters. There was a spirited race between the boats as to who should land first. Vieth's boat won: 'I was the subaltern that day carrying the Queen's colour, Lacy, my chum, having the regimental one. Scarcely had the boat touched when, grasping the staff, I jumped into the water and wading on shore drove the end of the staff into the sand, letting the colour float on the breeze. It has been said that a boat of the 17th regiment landed first but the fact remains that the Queen's Colour of the 63rd Regiment was the first British flag on the soil of Russia proper.' Placed there, he might have added, by a Canadian.

Kinburn was soon pounded into surrender by the guns of the Allied fleet. When Vieth entered the town he was not surprised to find it had capitulated for the naval guns had done enormous damage.

Having accepted the surrender, the invasion party was not left inactive. There was a rumour that General Liprandi was about to attack with some twenty thousand Russians and in order to forestall this or—what seemed more likely—to disprove the rumour, they set out a reconnaissance. Vieth describes it:

> Our expedition consisted of about 4,500 men and nearly 300 horses. The marching was very heavy, as the sand under our feet gave way at every step. Each man carried besides his knapsack, great coat and rifle, sixty rounds of ball cartridge and his rations for three days in his haversack. Personally I found it hard enough, for in addition to my rations (each officer carried his own) I had my great coat, and the Queen's Colour in heavy oilskin covering—no light weight in itself. We marched only about ten miles that day and then bivouaced for the night.

However, in spite of hearing rumours of Russians and hovering Cossacks they encountered none, and returned to Kinburn. As far as Vieth was concerned it was interesting, fairly arduous, but uneventful. With some delight he records that one of his soldiers managed to get himself dead drunk, although there was apparently no alcohol for miles. This man, however, had contrived to wheedle a bottle of 'raki' from a Russian peasant. He had drunk it all himself and soon lapsed into complete unconsciousness. It was not unusual for an ingenious soldier to acquire a bottle of liquor in an apparent desert and drink himself silly, but what made this situation unusual was that the man was six foot five in height but only eighteen inches across the shoulders. Vieth inquired why it had taken six men to carry him to the guardroom, instead of the usual four. The officer of the picquet had apparently sent six 'as the man was so d–d long he was afraid he would break in two'.

Drunkenness was, however, no joke. Vieth has some chilling comments on this point:

> There were few, if any means out there for our men having any innocent recreation when off duty. While a fair percentage of steady men saved most of their pay by entrusting it to their officers, or the pay-sergeant for safe-keeping, there was always a certain number who cared for nothing but spending it on grog, and though excessive drinking entailed a very severe punishment it failed as a deterrent. The penalty for habitual drinking in those days was flogging (thank heaven it is now a thing of the past). Nothing, I believe, could be devised that would more degrade a man and be more likely to make him a brute than to tie him up to be lashed on the bare back with the cat o' nine tails in the presence of the whole regiment. It was always a revolting sight. Once having undergone corporal punishment the man often became utterly reckless and was seldom out of trouble.
>
> I remember a splendidly made fellow in our Grenadier Company*, considerably over six feet in height, a terrible fellow when in liquor but a good soldier otherwise—that I saw flogged twice within a very short time.
>
> Punishment parade was always held early in the morning and on occasion the air was frosty and a keen wind was blowing as the grenadier was stripped of his shirt, his wrists and ankles tied to the triangle of stretcher poles, and his bare back exposed. A drummer plied the cat o' nine tails and the drum major counted the strokes. The man received fifty lashes, and he took them without a murmur, though the blood came before he had received them all.
>
> After it was all over, and he was released, he pulled down his shirt,

* The right flank Company; it contained men specially selected for their height. The left flank Company had men selected for alertness and activity as they were frequently used as skirmishers.

adjusted his stock, buttoned up his tunic, and saluting the Colonel, who stood by, said, 'That's a warm breakfast you gave me, your honour, this morning,' and again saluting, faced about, and was marched away to hospital.

In the light of earlier days it was lenient. Then a man might get five hundred strokes. But–it is remarkable to note–Wellington never permitted the lash to be used in his armies.

# 9

# Sebastopol—1855—the Main Battle

Although by 1855 the war had been going on for eight months there was still no sign of a decision, and clearly would not be until Sebastopol fell or the Allies were driven into the sea. The Alma, Balaclava and Inkerman had been bloody enough, but they had settled nothing. So far the main victor had been disease, which had inflicted heavy casualties on both sides, but whatever disease had done so far was nothing to what it would do when allied to the rigours of the Crimean winter.

The weakness of the English position now began to make itself felt. The storm had destroyed all chance of a decent issue of warm clothing for the winter, but there were other troubles nearly as bad. The failure to secure the Woronzoff road meant that all British supplies had to be brought up seven miles along a track which could hardly be called a road, and which, after torrential rain, became an extended quagmire. The only pack-animals available turned out to be not horses, which could not survive, but soldiers. As there was constant fear of a sally by the Russians the troops in the line were on duty five nights out of six; on the seventh they would draw rations from Balaclava. Conditions in the trenches were appallingly uncomfortable; men were often up to their knees in water, their clothing soaked through, and unable to get to any hot food or drink as there was no fuel for cooking. Everybody was so dirty and muddy that it was necessary to order officers to wear swords—so that they might be distinguished from the men. Normally of course their uniforms would have made the distinction. This anonymity was an advantage, as they were soon to realize.

In order to understand the next stage of the war it is necessary to have a clear understanding of the layout, disposition and problems involved in Sebastopol in 1854. The most concise yet comprehensive account of the area was written by Captain H. C. Elphinstone, RE, and published in 1859 as the *Journal of the Operations conducted by the Corps of Royal Engineers.* Elphinstone won a V.C. in June 1855 at the Redan.

An extensive inlet of the sea, called the harbour of Sebastopol, which runs inland to a distance of nearly four miles, divides this fortress into two distinct parts, a north and a south side perfectly separated from each other. The only means of communication between either is 'by boat' across this harbour, or else by making on land a circuit of many miles. This separation of the two sides is not limited to the harbour only, but extends to the ground beyond, for several miles to the eastward; where the wide and swampy valley of the Tchernaya, bounded on each side by lofty and precipitous rocks, renders communication from one side to the other extremely difficult at all times and during the rainy seasons quite impracticable, excepting in one or two places where roads and bridges have been established.

The separation of the two sides is so complete that the force investing the one side would find it impossible to render ready assistance to a force besieging the other; and they would be utterly unable to supply each other with provisions and ammunition. Each would have to act independently and trust exclusively to its own resources.

A complete investment was therefore impracticable without the employment of two separate armies, each having its own base of operations, and each of sufficient strength to compete by itself with the total force of the Russians in the Crimea. Again, the capture of either side by no means necessitated the fall of the other; for neither can be said to have any command over the other, on account of the great distance between them; and in the event of either side falling to the possession of the attacking party, the great basin would still form an almost insurmountable barrier to the further advance of the besiegers; so that to obtain entire possession of Sebastopol two independent attacks, one against the south, the other against the north front, would be requisite.

Elphinstone's account makes any attack on the fortress seem a near-impossibility, and ignores the fact that the Russians eventually abandoned their efforts to defend the fortress when only one key point had fallen. It is therefore instructive as showing the rigid orthodoxy which characterized military thought at the time, which drove the enterprising and the adventurous nearly insane and accounted for the loss of countless lives in long drawn-out unnecessary campaigns.

Elphinstone is at great pains to convince his readers that surprise attacks would have been folly, and that detailed conservative preparation was unavoidable. He writes that, 'To assail such a position by a *coup de main* with an army but little superior to the defenders, with nothing but field pieces at its command, and with its flanks and retreats quite insecure, would have been a most desperate undertaking, with every probability of a failure or repulse, the consequences of which would have been most disastrous.'

It is interesting to see that Elphinstone still resolutely adheres to the belief that Allied strategy was right although it must have been obvious by the time he wrote the account that this had hardly been proved correct by subsequent events. However, the factual value of the report should not be overlooked in spite of some of the conclusions he drew from it.

The principal defences faced the sea, and on that front were of permanent character, very extensive, and armed with powerful batteries. At the entrance to the harbour, on the south side, stood the two forts of the quarantine and Alexander, mounting 60 and 90 guns respectively; the former a closed earthen redoubt, with its guns mounted *en barbette**, commanding the Quarantine Harbour; the latter a permanent work of masonry, casemated, and likewise closed at the gorge by a crenellated wall.

There was much more information about the harbour defences, all of which led him to conclude that, 'All these defences towards the sea were of so formidable a character as to nullify one of the great advantages which the possession of a most powerful fleet gave the Allies over the Russians; so much so that the co-operation of the fleet in a joint attack with the land forces could not produce any decisive effect upon works of such strength and magnitude.' This view appears to have been held by others as no attempt to storm Sebastopol through the harbour was ever made.

He continued:

On the land side the works of defence to the south of Sebastopol were at this time comparatively trifling, but they occupied very commanding positions and were placed on ground which nature had strongly fortified.

A single stone wall (about twelve feet high and six feet thick) crenellated, but quite exposed, surrounded part of the town, and extended

* On platforms so that they could fire guns over the top of the walls and not through embrasures.

partly as a 'bastion trace' and partly as an 'indented line' from the Artillery Bay to the Central Bastion. A wide and steep ravine, answering the purpose of a huge ditch, ran in front of the line, from the Quarantine to the Central Bastion, and so completely separated it from the ground beyond that all approaches by trenches on that side were subsequently found to be quite impracticable. The wall, along its whole extent, was lined with numerous pieces of artillery, of which those in the most prominent position were of heavy metal. Exclusive of the 56 guns in the Artillery Fort, about 42 pieces of ordnance of various calibres were then in position in the rear of the crenellated wall.

To the south-east of the Central Bastion, but separated from it by a deep ravine, across which a dry stone wall had been hastily constructed, and armed with about 24 field pieces, was an earthern battery, nearly completed, called the Flagstaff Bastion, occupying a very commanding site, and finished with 12 heavy guns. [Elphinstone appended a note to this and said 'The information respecting the defences has been obtained from Russian official sources'; this was presumably because they would have changed completely by the time the Allies entered the town.]

Such were the works of defence on the west side of Sebastopol. Of these the Flagstaff Bastion formed the key, for it took in reverse all the works to the west of it. But although the possession of this battery might have led to the fall of the town side of the place, it would have been difficult to hold it without at the same time obtaining a footing on the eastern side as the ground and works to the east of the Dockyard Creek in their turn commanded this battery, and took it in reverse.

On the eastern side, which was perfectly separated from the western by deep and precipitous ravines at the head of the dockyard creek were the following works:

1st An earthen battery called from its shape the 'Redan'* which was armed with 17 heavy guns, and at which large working parties were still busily engaged. Immediately in its rear, a dry stone wall, skirting the brow of the hill, branched off in a westerly direction to a place subsequently called the Barrack Battery where at present 10 field pieces were in position to flank the Redan and the ground to the west of it, and in the valley just beneath it, at the head of the Dockyard Creek, about a dozen field pieces, protected by a low stone wall, fully commanded all approaches to the town from the valleys beyond.

2nd The semicircular masonry tower of the Malakoff, mounting five heavy guns *en barbette* around which was a circular entrenchment, with a short flank at each end, nearly completed and armed with 10 heavy guns.

* i.e. tooth from the French word *'dent'*.

3rd A battery called the Little Redan, still incomplete but most probably armed.

4th Adjoining the harbour a considerable-sized stone building in the shape of a cross, which had been converted into a defensible barrack.

Of all these defensive works the Malakoff had the most commanding position, and formed the key of the whole of the south side of the place. It took in reverse all the works on the eastern side, and from its position on an independent high knoll afforded a good site from which to repel assaults at any time. The enemy appeared fully aware of the importance of this site and employed large working parties in strengthening it, and he had even commenced in its rear a dry stone wall, which surrounded part of the Karabelnaja suburb, and answered the purpose of an inner or second line of intrenchment.

Such were the fortifications on the south side, which, although not strong in themselves, were powerfully armed and occupied, a position most favourable for defence. Both flanks were unassailable; the left flank rested on high land abutting on the great harbour, and was protected in front by an extensive wet ditch, in other words, by the Careening Bay, which, with all approaches to it, was under the command of the shipping in the harbour; while the right flank, in front of which was the wide and steep ravine referred to above, was raked by the fire of the guns in the gorge of the Quarantine Fort, and by the men-of-war that could at any time be posted under cover of Fort Alexander. The centre of the position was occupied by the three main batteries, the Flagstaff, Redan and Malakoff, powerfully armed, nearly all equally salient, and on commanding positions at the extremity of three leading spurs, by which alone an enemy could approach, and over which the garrison had full view for a distance of more than 2,000 yards to their front. The ravines between these ridges, although winding, run directly towards the batteries, and were consequently enfiladed throughout, and commanded by the enemy's guns. Men of war likewise were moored in the dockyard and careening creeks, and at the head of the harbour, with their broadsides bearing on such of the lines of approach as might be taken by the storming parties.

This survey of the ground makes it clear that once the initial opportunity for an assault had been missed there was no alternative to a long and tedious siege conducted with every attention to detail. The report went on:

Whether the assailants, therefore, advanced along the ridges or defiled through the ravines, they must be exposed to the fire of the batteries, and to that of the men-of-war and steamers in the harbour. Their attack must have been made from a very extended diverging circumference, over ground quite unknown which was broken by deep, and in parts almost impracticable ravines, rendering mutual support quite impossible, whereas the enemy occupied a central position from which his works were easily accessible, while these works communicated with each other without difficulty. The Allies would have had to advance with forces whose numerical strength could not have been greater than that of the defenders, and with nothing but field pieces at their command, exposed for a distance of upwards of a mile to a galling fire of more than 100 pieces of artillery, exclusive of the guns of the shipping, and without any retreat in case of reverse.

This was no mere academic account. Elphinstone had come to Sebastopol on 17 October 1854 as a trench officer in the Right Attack. He was eventually evacuated after being wounded on 8 September 1855.

It was obvious to those on the ground even if not so obvious to others, both at the time and subsequently, that once the Russians had put their defences in order the task facing the Allies was extremely complicated. However, the terrain was not entirely unfavourable to them for as we have already seen the Inkerman ridge constituted a formidable obstacle to Russian attack. Equally useful were the ravines which enabled the Allies to establish dumps of stones and ammunition very close to their front-line trenches; however they also had the disadvantage of hampering communication between the occupants of the different ridges and distorting the orthodox—but necessary—continuity of the parallels.

As the plateau in front of the town was neatly divided in half by a deep ravine it was very reasonably decided that the best arrangement would be to allot the western side of this to the French for their attack and give the eastern half to the British. One point the report does feel bound to criticize. It states among other recommended dispositions:

The Engineers had further recommended the occupation of the Mamelon, for the double purpose of supporting the posts on the Inkerman Ridge, and to admit of the construction of advances against the Malakoff Tower, which was considered the proper point of attack.

It is much to be regretted that the British force was even at that time considered too weak to take up so extensive a position, as there can be no doubt that had the arrangements recommended been carried out many subsequent disasters would have been avoided, and the fall of the place might have been insured within a comparatively short period. With the reduced state of the army, however, the occupation of so advanced a position was considered impracticable, and although a detachment of about 80 riflemen had been ordered to take up ground on points overhanging the bridge on the Tchernaya River, and the road across the valley of Inkerman, it was thought that even this advanced post could not be properly supported and was liable to be cut off at any moment.

The report becomes increasingly critical, and even bitter as it continues:

In the meantime the French *Corps d'Observation,* anxious to protect itself, was busily engaged on throwing up with all haste intrenchments on the heights facing the plain of Balaclava. On the British right, on the contrary, where advanced works would have been of the greatest importance, men could not be obtained either to construct or occupy them.

The British Army now found itself engaged in an enterprise for which its force was, strictly speaking, very inadequate, but from which it had not the power of withdrawing. No other course was left but to persevere with resolution, to strain every nerve, but as it had not the means of guarding itself equally at all points, it was required to exhibit extraordinary vigilance and activity to face the enemy wherever he might show himself.

Early in the siege operation it was

Thought advisable at once to assume offensive operations and without waiting for the disembarkation of the entire siege 'material' to place in battery the Lancaster guns, whose range was said to exceed 4,000 yards, with great accuracy of aim; and in order not to draw upon these pieces the concentrated fire of the whole of the Russian artillery; they were placed at such a distance as to be barely within reach of the enemy's batteries, while they were still within their own reputed range.

These Lancaster guns were an immensely important asset and were treasured accordingly. It was natural therefore to write that:

Both these Lancaster batteries were, of necessity, established on very rocky ground, and the earth for the parapets had to be collected in baskets and sandbags from a considerable distance. One row of gabions only was used for the revetment of the parapet, owing to the scarcity of material.

Notwithstanding these difficulties, both batteries were completed in a very short space of time, namely—the Left Lancaster on the night of the 9th, and the Right on the night of the 10th.

The gabions which are frequently referred to, and which are much in evidence in photographs of the siege works here and elsewhere, were wicker (or sometimes metal) baskets of earth. The word really meant a cage. They were a most useful device for they could be moved around with comparative ease, and could raise or extend a parapet in a matter of hours. They were ideal for protecting gun emplacements. Fascines were bundles of sticks, used for plugging gaps, strengthening walls and so on.

According to Elphinstone:

> The officers of Engineers had reconnoitred the ground on previous nights and had selected such sites as were best suited for batteries, without special reference to their appropriateness for first parallels, because at that time there was no intention to throw up a systematic system of trenches, which would only have delayed the operation of the assault. Regular siege operations were not then contemplated by the Allies, and such operations were in fact impossible and diametrically opposed to first principles, so long as the investment of the south side remained incomplete.
>
> The Allies had but one object in view and that was to establish batteries which it was hoped would soon damage and silence the enemy's works sufficiently to render them open to assault, and this object alone guided the selection of the sites for the first line of trenches of the 'Right' and 'Left' attacks.

This may have been true in the very early stages of the attack but was not true for long. It was of course an established military maxim that a siege should never be attempted if it could be avoided, either by blockade or swift attack, because it was slow and costly. Nevertheless—as we have seen above—it was impossible for Raglan and Canrobert to see their task in any other but siege terms. The idea of making a sudden attack, of using deception or diversion—these were completely outside their concept.

Conditions for digging trenches were extremely bad, partly because of the rocky ground which made drainage very difficult, partly because of the weather:

> The rain poured down in torrents for days together, almost without a moment's intermission, converting the soil into mud so deep as to render the roads almost impassable. Portions of the trenches were inundated, and many of the floors of the tents, which had been sunk below the surface of the ground for the sake of obtaining greater warmth and more space, were frequently flooded.

Constant exposure, heavy fatigue duties and broken rest, rapidly thinned the number of effective men, and the strength of the working parties was in consequence greatly diminished.

Even as early as the end of November 1854 there were eleven thousand sick in the army. Ironically some of the fitter men belonged to what was called the 'Provisional Battalion': they were a mixed force who had been sent to Balaclava to recover their health, so the army thoughtfully employed them on building wharves of stone and rubble at Balaclava.

As the winter wore on, the track from Balaclava to the front grew longer and longer. This was because the worst places had to be avoided by a detour and the accumulation of detours soon added a further mile and a half to the journey. A siege gun needed a day to make the journey, but it could only be done if some forty horses were available. Although 'General January' and 'General February' were reckoned as the Allies' most formidable opponents the Russians were not inactive either; their sharpshooters took a steady toll and sometimes raiding parties broke into the Allied front-line trenches, particularly of the French. Typical reports are those for 4 and 5 January 1855:

4 Jan, Day, 32 men, under Lieut Pratt and Lieut Wolseley, finished laying two platforms, and relaid sleepers of a third.

Cleared out drains in third parallel.

4 Jan, Night, 100 Turks. The inclement weather prevented any work being done and the Turks were sent back to camp.

5 Jan, Day, 92 men under Lieut Crofton and 60 men under Lieut Murray. Cleared out drains. Laid one gun platform and part of a mortar platform in Gordon's battery.

Materials carried down from the park. Pte Jarret, 2nd company R.E. was particularly mentioned for his energy and zeal.

5 Jan, Night. The thick drifts of snow and the cold prevented any work being done; the Turks were sent home accordingly.

Under these conditions the concept of Sebastopol being under siege became somewhat unrealistic. By the end of January only eleven thousand men were fit for duty and were thus hopelessly outnumbered by the men they were attempting to besiege. Fortunately the Russians were either unaware, or too lethargic to take advantage of this fact. The Allies appear to have been oblivious of the fact that

Sebastopol, as a fortress, might contain a vast number of guns. It proved to be so, and even in the closing days of the siege there were still hundreds of brand new guns available. Ammunition was never short for, of course, the line of communication with Russia was always open.

Curiously enough the British force should not have been on the right–which proved to be the more difficult position–but on the left. As the first to arrive in Balaclava the British were entitled to the more honourable position in the attack, which was right. Before, as we have seen at the Alma, this position was taken by the French; now out of courtesy the French deferred to the British and themselves moved to the left. Subsequently both sides suffered appallingly but the British had a harder time than the French by virtue of the difficulties of the supply line from Balaclava. But Allied friendship was in no way impaired, as will be seen later.

Before going into details of the last nine months, as seen by contemporary accounts, it will be an advantage to look at the main events. When Russell's reports, and a number of private accounts of conditions in the Crimea, were read in England, there was a wave of public indignation and horror. Although some part of the wretchedness of the troops could be put down to inexperience combined with bad weather conditions (normal enough for the Crimea though apparently unsuspected by the Allies) a large part of it was found to be due to indifference, greed and incompetence by the administration at home. Hunts for politicians blood brought the resignation of Lord Aberdeen, the prime minister, and the Duke of Newcastle, who was Secretary of State for War. Aberdeen was replaced by Lord Palmerston and Newcastle by Panmure. Men, supplies and efforts were poured into the Crimea. Not least was the reorganization of the medical services under the supervision of Florence Nightingale. One of the most effective moves was the building of a light railway from Balaclava to the front.

As the winter passed, supplies built up and the Allied situation looked more favourable; it seemed to many that the end was in sight. They were to be cruelly disappointed. Although the warlike Tsar Nicholas died on 2 March and was succeeded by the mild, peaceful, Alexander II, it was too much for the Russians to accept a humiliating peace from the strong position they were in. British and French diplomats had been active during the winter hoping to bring in more allies with their valuable manpower, and in consequence a conference began at Vienna in March 1855. It dragged on till May. The Allies had hoped to enlist Austria but she proved more sympathetic to the Russians than to themselves. Curiously enough, a useful ally came from an unexpected quarter; this was Italy or rather that part of it which was known as the Kingdom of Sardinia. The aim of the minister for Sardinia, Cavour, was to gain foreign support for a united Italy, and he realized that at comparatively small cost he could give his country a place at the eventual conference table. Recognition as a power was to his mind the first and most suitable step towards making Italy a united country. Cavour produced fifteen thousand men who were added to the forty thousand British and hundred thousand French.

In spite of the tide of war turning against them the Russians, apart from their killing of some of the wounded, behaved extremely well during the war. They earned praise for their dogged resistance and they earned admiration in other, though scarcely less influential, areas by continuing to pay interest on debts or bonds to the Allies all through the period of the hostilities. However fervently Alexander II wished to bring the war to an end it was scarcely practicable to expect him to accept severe peace terms when Todleben was apparently a match for the Allies on his own, and the combined forces of France and England had been unable to do more than capture a few minor outposts of the Sebastopol defences.

In the spring matters became somewhat easier for the British. As the French greatly outnumbered them it was suggested that they should share some of the British trench duty. The French did not find this entirely to their liking and preferred to take over a sector of the line; this was eventually decided upon as the extreme right. As it happened this put them on the former battleground of Inkerman and confronted them with the Malakoff. It was, in the event, a fortunate disposition; not only did it release fifteen hundred British troops from the part of the line and enable them to concentrate more effectively elsewhere but it also presented the French with a challenge which they met, and which decided the result of the war.

But six months were to elapse before the fighting stopped, and a further six months before peace was signed.

In a war of missed opportunities, few were as great as that of 8 April 1855. It was the greatest offensive to be launched so far in the war. It lasted ten days and silenced many of the opposing Russian batteries. There were many unexpected successes; the Malakoff was silenced, as was one face of the Redan, the Mamelon was put out of action and the Central Bastion was breached. The Russians expected an immediate attack, and in order to counter it kept large numbers of men close behind the batteries; the slaughter among these was immense and was said to total close on six thousand. There were, of course, considerable Allied casualties in the counter-bombardment but these amounted to less than one third of the Russian. The most extraordinary feature of this event was that it led to precisely nothing. Had the Allies launched an assault, Sebastopol might have been theirs, but the opportunity faded away and the Russians displayed their usual alacrity in repairing the damage. Canrobert was blamed–nobody apparently expected Raglan to exercise any further initiative–but whether Canrobert or Napoleon III was to blame for this undue conservation of French resources it is impossible to ascertain.

In May 1855 Canrobert resigned and Pélissier was appointed in his place; nevertheless the former French commander-in-chief still continued to serve, though under the command of his successor. Pélissier, who had risen from the ranks, was a man of great determination and purpose. He had no hesitation in rejecting the advice of Napoleon III, and had his own ideas as to how the war should be won. With those ideas to the front of his mind he applied himself with great vigour to his task. At first it seemed that complete success was well within his grasp. He reduced a Russian redoubt forward of the Central Bastion and he sent a successful expedition to Kertsch; this last was to interrupt Russian communications severely. It seemed that everything was now in the Allies' favour, particularly as the Sardinians, very smart and warlike, appeared and took up their positions in May.

In June it was decided that the time was now ripe for another immense artillery barrage followed by entry into the town. The bombardment began on 6 June and, using 544 Allied guns, achieved as much as could have been expected. The Mamelon was put out of action and the Malakoff severely damaged, the area known as the 'White Works' was so battered that French troops were able to occupy it prior to making it a part of their own offensive position: on the 7th a determined French assault took the Mamelon, was expelled, reocuppied it, and finally after intense struggles held it. As this was going on the 2nd and Light Divisions attacked the Quarries and after desperate struggles in hand-to-hand fighting, retained this also. Pélissier's efforts were not, however, appreciated by Napoleon who constantly sent him telegrams suggesting an alternative plan; Pélissier ignored them. Nevertheless, the combined effect of his difficult operation, and his lack of support, interspersed with occasional obstruction from his emperor, appears to have worried him; at all events he seems to have faltered in his judgement and made up his mind to launch an attack which, when it occurred, was found to have been insufficiently prepared. By nightfall of 16 June most of the Russian guns, including those in the Malakoff and Redan, were out of action, and the time seemed ripe for a final clinching assault. Raglan agreed that this was so and it was accordingly planned for the night of the 17th. By that time the 600 Allied guns would, he thought, have accounted for most of the 550 Russian guns opposite and a good quantity of the Russian defence system as well. Unfortunately, and quite unpredictably, Pélissier changed this plan at the last minute and decided instead to launch the assault on the following day. Raglan was virtually presented with a French ultimatum, with which he felt unable to disagree in view of the disparity in numbers of the two forces involved, but of which he had considerable apprehension; he knew that the assault would go in over some four hundred yards of open ground.

The plan went wrong for the Allies from the start. The Russians were alerted just as the attack was preparing and as a result they were in position and ready to fire point-blank at the advancing infantry. The French assault party was in three different columns of six thousand men each but the synchronization of these was badly at fault. Not only was their advance blocked by the troops on the ground but owing to a mistake the right-hand column went in too soon and was caught in Allied fire. Its commander General Mayran was twice wounded, then killed outright. He was outstandingly brave and the errors were in no way his. Meanwhile, the centre column was delayed; when it eventually came forward half an hour late its commander General Brunet was also killed and the column failed to get into the Malakoff. The third column, under General D'Autemare, was caught in heavy Russian fire and pinned down.

Not knowing precisely what had happened to the other French

columns, but seeing D'Autemare's in difficulty before him, Raglan gave the order for a British advance to get the attack moving again. Unfortunately the confusion in the British advance matched the French. An attack had been planned in which each face of the Redan would be assaulted separately and independently. But the smoke and general confusion was so great; and the Russian counter-fire so close and intense, that the original plan went by the board, and each group tried to get in where it felt there might be an opportunity. The assault plan was somewhat optimistically conceived, for the aim was for a mere hundred skirmishers to precede and protect eight hundred men carrying eighteen foot ladders, and wool bags. On arrival the ladder men would hoist their burdens against the wall and enter the Redan, the Russians permitting. The Russians were not, however, prepared to facilitate this operation and in the words of Raglan's subsequent dispatch, 'assailed with a most murderous fire of grape and musketry'. Those in advance were either killed or wounded, and the remainder found it impossible to proceed. 'I never before witnessed such a heavy fire of grape combined with musketry from the enemy's works, which appeared to be fully manned.'

As may be imagined the assault party was cut down like grass. By the time the party had reached a point that was still thirty yards from the Redan there was only one ladder, although, by a near miracle, this ladder survived and was placed against the outer defences. The entire assault force was now down to approximately a hundred men and with one ladder was about to attempt to scale a five-foot outwork, cross a ditch fifteen feet wide and eleven feet deep, and struggle up a huge earth rampart. Behind that were the Russians. Nevertheless the effort continued. Among those killed at this stage was the redoubtable Colonel Yea, who had fought with distinction at the Battle of the Alma. He was one of the bravest, though perhaps one of the least popular, officers in the army at that time. There were numerous examples of individual heroism and great presence of mind but they did not suffice to save a situation which seems to have been both badly planned and badly directed. The only success was achieved by the 18th Brigade, mainly made up from the 18th Royal Irish, who at great cost captured a portion of the Russian main line near Dockyard Creek. The cost of that operation was 360 casualties (30 officers) out of 2,000 which seemed a high price. During the day the British lost 1,554 including 100 officers, and the French 3,550. The Russians, who had been exposed to heavy fire over a long period, acknowledged losing 5,400.

The inquiry produced the following conclusions. It was a mistake for Pélissier to have taken the command of the French assault troops from Bosquet and given it to General d'Angely who had arrived recently and did not know the ground. It was felt that Bosquet's close knowledge of the ground would have been invaluable. For some unaccountable reason the French went in with an insufficient preliminary bombardment; it was said that this was because Pélissier had set his heart on attacking on the day of the anniversary of Waterloo, which is possible, but it does not explain why in that case the bombardment was not begun earlier. As it was the French troops attacked the Malakoff with inadequate artillery preparation; what should have been done before the attack was shown to be perfectly possible after it was over. Because the French had gone in the British felt in duty bound to support them so they went in also, although here again only the most inadequate preparation had been made.

It is usually said that grievous disappointment caused the death of Lord Raglan, on 26 June, but it would seem that the more immediate cause was cholera. He was succeeded in his post by General Sir James Simpson. Simpson was apparently unwilling to accept the post as he did not feel capable of solving the Sebastopol problem. Meanwhile the artillery barrages grew in frequency and intensity; the Russians in a more confined space suffered appallingly and were said to be losing over a thousand men a day during heavy periods. Their high casualty rate from gunfire, and the fact that their previous efforts at initiative had come within measurable distance of success, caused them to stake everything on one final throw which might disrupt the Allies completely. This was the Battle of the Tchernaya (Tractir Bridge) on 15 August.

The point of attack was the French right flank and the newly arrived Sardinian force. It was launched with some sixty thousand Russians, although half of these were in support or in reserve. It was one of the bloodiest though least-publicized battles of the war. To everyone's surprise the Italians distinguished themselves, but the main cause of the Russian defeat was an insufficiently prepared attack on a very strong French position.

To all intents and purposes the war was over, apart from the fact that the Russians still held Sebastopol, as before, and would take a lot of dislodging unless they evacuated it voluntarily. Soon it was obvious to Allied observers that they had that in mind for barricades began to appear in the streets and a bridge of boats was built across the river.

By the beginning of September the French forward trenches had crept to within twenty-five yards of the Malakoff. On 5 September the Allies began a tremendous bombardment that did not slacken for three days. The Malakoff was clearly the vital point but—this was the first hint of deception in the entire campaign—it was apparently to be subsidiary to other assaults; the British would attack the Redan, the Sardinians the Central Bastion, and the Flagstaff Bastion would be assailed by other French forces.

In the event the subsidiary attacks were less successful than the one on the Malakoff, though there were times when the success of that also hung in the balance. The British force reached the Redan, but, having entered it, badly needed reinforcement. The commander of the British force, General Windham, was criticized for himself going back to gather further support; it was no reflection on his personal courage which was above criticism. It seems that Windham felt that he was more likely to produce the urgent effect he wanted if he appeared personally; unfortunately his disappearance from the front caused morale to sag and the effort to be uncoordinated. The Russians evacuated the city—under a ferocious Allied bombardment—but the final stages left a bitter taste in British mouths for they felt that after all the effort, suffering and achievements of the previous eighteen months that their story had ended in failure, and the French had snatched the prize of victory.

# 10
# The Fighting Men

What of the men who fought in these armies, who endured hunger, thirst, cholera, heat, cold and intense periods of slaughter? How did they do it? Why did they do it?

They were worthy opponents of each other. Courage breeds courage, just as fear breeds fear. Russians, French, British and Sardinians (the latter including the renowned Berseglieri) stood the rigours of the campaign, stood the endless artillery barrages, and fought like tigers at close quarters. The British who saw the French fight could not understand how such magnificent fighters had been vanquished in the Napoleonic wars; the French, who saw the British on many other occasions than the Charge of the Light Brigade, considered them the bravest troops in the world; and both thought the Russian soldier a man of the highest quality, as indeed he was.

It is usually assumed that discipline was by the lash, and the soldier faced death because he was more afraid of what might happen if he flinched. This is obviously not true, as was shown in all the battles, in the trenches, and at Redan. It is also assumed that the relationship between officers and men was based on fear—on both sides.

Hedley Vicars was with the 97th Regiment. He was a cheerful extrovert person who had enjoyed his military service since he had been commissioned in 1843. He was killed leading an attack on Sebastopol, in the spring of 1855. Possibly he was more sensitive than some of his fellow officers—and a better leader. 'I have had very little trouble with the men—less so than others complain of. Indeed (though I say it that should not) I know they like me and would do anything for me; and all officers who treat men with the same feelings as their own, and take an interest in their welfare, find they do not see much insubordination nor want many courts-martial. Yet I am very strict with my men, but they soon get accustomed to this.'

In the trenches in December 1854 he wrote: 'I think more of the pouring rain and standing in thick mud all the time than of Russian grape or bullets.' He himself was religious and deplored the lack of chaplains to minister to the spiritual wants of the army but he did not let it prevent him from relishing some of the more vigorous moments of the conflict. 'The British bayonet settled the business; they fight well though; in that battle it was a regular hand-to-hand encounter. A sergeant of the Scots Fusilier Guards told me that he saw a Guardsman and a Russian both dead, with each other's bayonets transfixed in their bodies.'

After Vicars' death, a private in the 97th (John Cotterall), mentioned him in a letter to his wife. 'Several of our regiment got killed, and amongst them was our gallant captain, poor Mr Vicars, who was so deeply loved by all the regiment. Even the officers almost all cried the morning after the affair.'

His servant, R. Young, wrote, 'I believe there is not a man in the regiment but would have run any risk to save his life.' Possibly Vicars was somewhat of an exception because he was much liked even when adjutant—a post that does not usually give occasion for much popularity.

The ranks of the armies contained a wide variety of people. This was the first war that the British had fought for nearly half a century and most of the people who rushed to join the colours had no idea of danger or discomfort but only of plunder and military glory. For many it was an adventure, a chance to see a foreign country, and rather a joke. There were some who hoped to redeem themselves for some misdemeanour. These latter were doubtless good-hearted spirited youngsters who had offended against the strict laws of their parents, and left home accordingly. The following letter from Sam Brooks, about whose subsequent fate nothing is known, is a good example.

BALACLAVA
—December 1854

My dearest Father,

How shall I address myself to you after my late disgraceful conduct at home* but duty and love now prompt me to do that which I ought to

* Possibly seducing one of the maids.

have done before. My dear Father, tomorrow we march to Sebastopol, when my life will not be safe a minute, and I cannot bear the thought of descending to my grave with my sins to you unforgiven. I have been very much to blame, but I hope in the position of life I have chosen I may retrieve my character in some measure; be sure I will never disgrace it on the field of battle, either in Victory or Defeat. I owe you some explanation of my conduct since I left Newport. I had as you know only a few shillings with which I went to Liverpool and enlisted into the 90 Regiment of foot, in a week I was sent to Chatham, and was there till about 3 weeks ago when I volunteered to the 90 Light Infantry to come out to Turkey. I wanted most earnestly to write all the time but I could not summon courage enough. We were about 15 days coming from Kingstown, Ireland, to Balaclava, we have been here a week yesterday, living in tents on the hills, we have a good many sick now, and in a fortnight, as we get to Sebastopol tomorrow, it will be impossible to tell the number we have missing but it will be very large. I hope I may be preserved to see the shores of England again. We are pretty well off here considering we get Grog twice a day and salt Beef and Biscuit, poor rations indeed but sufficient to satisfy the cravings of hunger, but I am afraid it will be much worse at Sebastopol. What a change from the comfort and luxuries at home. I have no time to say more. I will write again on the first opportunity. We get no pay here. If we did we could buy many little things. They are come for the letters. Farewell.

A remarkable feature of the Crimean War was the number of non-combatants who were able to wander around with no other interference except from a stray shot or shell. They included a number of wives. Many of them left no record, which is a pity, for women have a sharp eye for the details that would be appreciated by posterity. But among them was Mrs Henry Duberly, the wife of an officer in the 8th Hussars, who left a journal of her experiences. She seems to have been unbelievably tough and enduring. 'Was awoke by the *reveillée* at half-past two; rose, packed our bedding and tent, got a stale egg and a mouthful of brandy, and was in my saddle by half-past five.

'I never shall forget that march! It occupied nearly eight hours. The heat intense, the fatigue overwhelming but the country—anything more beautiful I never saw.' (This was when they were still at Varna.) A few days later she records:

'Marched to Gottuby and encamped on cholera-stricken ground just vacated by the Heavies. We had appalling evidence of their deaths. Here and there a heap of loose earth, with a protruding hand or foot, showed where the inhabitants had desecrated the dead, and dug them up to possess themselves of the blankets in which they were buried.'

Mrs Duberly had to disguise herself to get on to the boat to the Crimea, an enterprise in which several people abetted her. She had to stay in her cabin for seven days before they left Varna. The death rate was mounting.

> Since I have been here death has been amongst us. Poor Captain Longmore, who on Friday helped me up the ship's side, was dead on Sunday morning. Death with such inexorable gripe appears in his most appalling shape. He was seized but on Friday with diarrhoea, which turned to cholera on Saturday, and on Sunday the body was left in its silent and solemn desolation. During his death struggle the party dined in the saloon, separated from the ghastly wrangle only by a screen. With few exceptions the dinner was a silent one; but presently the champagne corks flew and—but I grow sick, I cannot draw so vivid a picture of life and death. God save my dear husband and me from dying in the midst of the din of life. The very angels must stand aloof.

They might well.

The diaries are particularly vivid for they record all the little items of rumour and gossip which float around all units. In the twentieth century this farrago of hope, rumour, misinformation and occasional fact is known as 'the griff'. Mrs Duberly heard the 'griff' that the Russians had retaken Eupatoria, then had not, that Sebastopol would be stormed the next day, then that it would not. She was, however, usually shrewd enough to recognize a rumour when she heard one and enjoyed much of it:

> We left at dusk and rode slowly down to Balaclava, our hearts and ears filled with the magnificent din of war. Our casualties have been very few. Poor Captain Rowley and the assistant-surgeon of the 68th are dead. The gathering twilight prevented our seeing much of the damage done to the town. We fancied it greater than it proved. One of our Lancaster guns burst today; the other is doing good work. The shot rushes with such vehement noise through the air that it has been surnamed the 'Express Train'. We fired 170 rounds a gun yesterday (so they say). I was not sorry to find rest on board ship.

She mentioned the confidence of the Allies: 'We thought Sebastopol was to stand, perhaps, a three day's siege—more likely a single day; while some, more arrogant still, allowed it eight hours to resist the fury of the Allies.' In fact, Sebastopol was thought to be such an easy prey that gunners were told not to fire into the town for fear that it would make its occupation less pleasant.

Mrs Duberly, not unnaturally, was deeply concerned at the fate of the horses—referred to frequently as 'cattle'; 'the din and noise of the quay, the flagging, jaded and dying horses, and the voices of the soldiers, cursing with every imaginable oath their exhausted cattle.'

The grey horse 'Job' died this evening of sheer starvation; his tail had been gnawed to a stump by hungry neighbours at picquet. Poor 'Job', he earned his name from his exhaustless patience under innumerable afflictions; he was an enormous, powerful and hungry horse and he sold his life by inches. There was no help for it; had it been myself instead of him, I must have died.

The Turks were not so highly esteemed: 'The place stinks already with the number of sick Turks, who have turned it into a half-putrid hospital. I never saw people die with such dreary perseverance as these Turks. Two hundred of them were buried in one day a short time since.'

Not that the wounded after the Alma were faring much better.

I hear the sick are dying at an average of eighty per diem. With some horror (not much) and a great deal of curiosity, I watched from over the taffrail of the *Star of the South* the embarkation of some Russian prisoners and English soldiers (all wounded) for Scutari. The dignified indifference of the medical officer, who stood with hands in his pockets, gossiping in the hospital doorway—the rough, indecent way in which the poor howling wretches were hauled along the quay, and bundled, some with one, and others with both legs amputated, into the bottom of the boat, without a symptom of a stretcher or bed, was truly an edifying exemplification of the golden rule 'Do to others as you would be done by.'

She gave a graphic account of Balaclava.

Take a village of ruined houses and hovels in the extreme state of all imaginable dirt, catch about 1000 sick Turks with the plague and cram them into the houses indiscriminately, kill about 100 a day and bury them so as to be scarcely covered with earth, leaving them to rot at leisure, taking care to keep up the supply. Drive all the exhausted ponies, dying bullocks and worn-out camels and leave them to die of starvation . . . when they will soon begin to rot and smell accordingly.

She went on to describe the contents of the water, which can be imagined, and said 'If this is not *piquante* enough let some men be instructed to sit and smoke on the powder barrels landing on the quay; which I myself saw two men doing today, on the ordnance wharf.' She mentioned that in the early days a party of Russians did attempt to get into Balaclava but were intercepted; this, of course, had been Codman's nightmare.

Some of her information is quite astonishing: 'There are Russian residents permitted in Balaclava; amongst them a Mr Upton, son of the engineer who constructed the forts of Sebastopol, and who was taken prisoner when we first marched down upon that place.' Whether the man was half-English is not disclosed. There were, of course English residents in the area.

'One Englishman interested us all; a Mr Willis, who had been for five and thirty years head caulker in the harbour of Sebastopol. He grumbled sorely at the advent of his countrymen, who, as he said, had pulled down his house, and loopholed it, and had destroyed his vineyard—his 999 trees.' A little later she writes: 'The cold to-night is *intense* and as we have no fire on board this ship our sufferings are very great. But "there is in every depth a lower still" and we should be worse off in the trenches. It is when suffering from these minor evils of cold and hunger (for our table is very much neglected) that I feel most how much my patience, endurance, and fortitude, are tried. The want of fire, of a carpet, or even a chair, makes itself terribly felt just now.' However, even when she records 'Day cruelly cold, but very bright', she says 'Henry and I walked to the Genoese Fort, and watched the ships sailing harbourwards on the calm and shining sea.'

Even when the ship, loaded with a thousand tons of powder, was found to be on fire she displayed commendable calm. The fire was in the lower hold and burning within six feet of the magazine: 'At such a time there was no thought of fear. It had been raining; and Henry and I, unwilling to add to the crowd forward, after getting some galoshes, went on deck.'

This attention to galoshes recalls similar attention to detail of the commanding officer of the King's Liverpool Regiment in the trenches in the First World War. Whenever an attack was pending he drew his adjutant's attention to the need to make sure that his toast rack was transported to the regiment's new position. 'Because,' as he would always explain, 'you must put toast in a toast rack. If you don't it falls on its side and goes flat. Absolutely essential, a toast rack.' His contempt for shell fire, German machine-guns, dirt, discomfort and danger were, however, a great inspiration to the regiment.*

Aid gradually began to trickle in during the January of 1855. 'A cargo of navvies arrived today in the *Lady Alice Labton*. Their arrival makes a great sensation. Some of them immediately went ashore, and set out for a walk "to see if they could see e'er a — Rooshian".'

So too did eight nurses under the direction of a 'Lady Eldress' and Miss Shaw Stewart. Their comments were doubtless as interesting as those of the navvies but less forceful.

The fate of the camp followers, the women, married and unmarried, who kept up with the armies, washed for them, cooked for them, nursed them and even fought for them, was hard in the Crimea.

> Lunched in camp with Colonel Doherty, and afterwards went to see one of the women of our regiment, who is suffering from fever. I found her lying on a bed on the wet ground; she had lain there in cold and rain, wind and snow, for twelve days. By her side, in the wet mud, was a piece of ration biscuit, a piece of salt pork, some cheese, and a tin pot with some rum. Nice fever diet. She, having failed to make herself popular among the women during her health, was left by them when she was sick; and not a soul had offered to assist the poor helpless, half-delirious creature, except her husband and a former mate of his when he was a sailor.

And, they were nothing if not resilient. A few days later we hear that:

> Started on horseback at one o'clock to attend the 'First Spring Meeting', the first race of the season. Wonderful that men who had been starved with cold and hunger, drowned in rain and mud, wounded in action, and torn with sickness, should on the third warm, balmy day start into fresh life like butterflies, and be as eager and fresh for the rare old

* A story recounted by the late Lt-Col R. H. O'Brien, who served as a subaltern in the regiment.

English sport, as if they were in the ring at Newmarket, or watching the colours coming round the corner.

There were four races: the first I was not in time to see. Just as the riders were going to the starting post for the second race, somebody called out, 'The picquets are coming; the Russians must be advancing.'

However, it was a false alarm, caused by five Russian deserters. They were soon back on the race ground. Two pony races were won by sheer good riding, by Captain Thomas, RHA, and after the 'Consolation Stakes', as the sun was still high, the meeting dispersed for a dog-hunt. I rode with them as far as Karani and then turned back. I could not join in or countenance in any way a sport that appears to me so unsportsmanlike, so cruel, so contrary to all good feeling, as hunting a *dog*.

She notes that the French attack and fail nightly in their attempts at taking the rifle pits of the Russians. 'The French can beat us in their commisariat and general management, but the Englishman retains his wondrous power of fighting that nothing can rob him of but death.'

As the weather improved diversions multiplied. There were a number of race meetings. These, of course, were essentially officer/cavalry diversions but undoubtedly were good entertainment for any soldiers who happened to be able to watch. The men had other activities arranged for them—ceremonies which were good for their immortal souls—church parades. On one Sunday it was so hot that 'the men fell out in all directions from church parade'. It is, of course, a well-known military phenomenon that men who are as solid as teak and can witness the most appalling sights unflinchingly will go down like ninepins on a hot parade ground—and not least on church parades.

Omar Pasha, the Turkish commander-in-chief, whom she met on a social occasion 'impressed me as being shrewd, decided, energetic, as well as an amusing companion, and man capable of appreciating more of the refinements of life than I would have thought he would have found among the Turks.' She mentioned that in May Captain Christie died while still awaiting a court-martial for the loss of the ships which were left outside the harbour in the hurricane of the previous November. His funeral was attended by a large sympathetic congregation. It would appear that as there was no room for most of the ships inside the harbour he can have had little option but to leave them outside.

She watched the departure of the Kertsch expedition, 7,000 French, 2,600 English, on 3 May—'we all hope much from this expedition'—but was astonished to see the entire fleet back in harbour three days later. If she ever learnt the reason she did not record it although three weeks later she recorded that the expedition to Kertsch was very successful, 'Kertsch was taken, without difficulty, the moment the Allies appeared before it, as the Russians blew up their forts and retired.'

When the 10th Hussars arrived with their 'finest Arabs in the world' they were the admiration of all, perfect in shape, so purely bred that each horse might have been a crowned king—their small heads never resting, and their eyes like outlets for the burning fire within.' Approximately a month later, when it had rained almost incessantly she went to have another look at them.

> Poor little brilliant Arab horses, they looked like rats that had been drawn through wet mud and hung up in the sun to dry. They were living cakes of mud, their long tails reminded us of ropes of sea sand. Poor little gay creatures, all draggled and besmirched. Vicious to a degree beyond words are these fairy horses; and if they once get loose, they fly at, fasten on to, and tear each other with tenacity and venom that I should have supposed only to have existed among women.

She rode happily around, occasionally, if allowed, joining in a reconnaissance. But even without a reconnaissance her riding party needed always to be ready to take evasive action, for sometimes Cossacks would appear on the skyline and take an interest in them. At the end of May she rode along the North valley, scene of the famous charge.

> The ground lay gaudy with flowers, and warm and golden in the rays of the setting sun.
>
> Here and there we passed the carcass of a horse—we saw five with 8.H. on the hoof. Six-point shot lay strewn about thickly enough, and pieces of shell. I did not see it but was told that a skull had been found quite blanched and clean, with most wonderfully beautiful and regular teeth. We saw today no traces of unburied human bodies—the horses had all been lightly covered over, but many of them were half-exposed.

In the same entry she writes—with rather more compassion—'We hear most distressing reports of the sickness among the Russians.

Fifteen thousand are supposed to have been sent from Sebastopol to Kertsch, Yenicali, etc.'

Just as there had been a party of Russian wives and friends at the Alma to watch the battle so did Mrs Duberly and her particular circle do likewise at Sebastopol: 'Lady George Paget was sitting on the rock-work of the quarry, vainly endeavouring, as were many more, to trace the operations through the fog. We, who came up at so much cost to ourselves, were determined to see if possible. . . .' The next day she got up at three in order to be present at the start at four am. However, it became rather hot and boring, in spite of nearly being caught by a stray Russian cannon ball, so at ten o'clock they set off home. But: 'On our way home we were met by a French officer who told us on no account to omit being at the front at four o'clock this afternoon.'

Although matters would have doubtless been better arranged with the Quorn—or even at a bull-fight—the spectacle when they arrived was worth it:

> Under what a storm of fire they advance, supported by that impenetrable red line, which marks our own Infantry. The fire from the Malakoff is tremendous—terrible; but all admit that the steadiness of the French under it is magnificent. Presently the twilight deepens, and the light of rocket, mortar, and shell falls over the beleaguered town.
>
> We cannot hope to hear any accurate report of what has been done tonight; and as it is near ten o'clock and too dark to see anything, we catch our horses and ride slowly away.

On 8 June she wrote: 'Was again at the front, though the fire had considerably slackened, and there was nothing doing. But who could keep away from a place where so many interests were at stake? Not I.'

She was not without her troubles however—one of which was 'the cause of very great annoyance and inconvenience'. Her box, which had been dispatched from England in February 'in consequence of a stupid mistake on the address of the box had been left at Scutari on 7 May. It contains all my summer clothing.'

On 18 June 'we were a few minutes late for the opening fire, but in time for such a storm of shot, grape, shell and musketry as had never before annoyed the ears of heaven.' The attack was, as we have seen, a failure, but Mrs Duberly takes it phlegmatically: 'We too turn away—blind with watching and stupefied with the intense heat of the sun. We meet countless wounded coming down. Sir John Campbell is dead, Colonel Yea is dead and Colonel Shadforth; while many others that we know are cruelly wounded. Many soldiers, shot through arms and legs, walked up from trenches, self-supported and alone; nor would any one have perceived their wounds but for the small hole in coat and trousers.'

On 24 June General J. B. Estcourt died of cholera, and on 29th Lord Raglan. Of the latter she says 'I can hardly imagine a greater misfortune to the army than his death at such a moment as the present. We are almost tempted to lose sight of the inefficient general in the recollection of the kind-hearted, gentlemanly man, who had so hard a task, which he fulfilled so well, of keeping together and in check the heads of so many armies.'

Kinglake expressed it even more strongly: 'Many know, and some envy, the blissful look of content that lights on the face of a soldier when slain by a gunshot-wound; but the toils of a commander are toils of the mind, of the heart.

'The expression that fastened on Lord Raglan's countenance in the moment of death seemed to tell of—not pain—but care.' However, had Kinglake taken the trouble to look he might have found other cholera victims with careworn expressions, and they might perhaps have outnumbered the soldiers who were blissfully happy to have their inside spilt on to the ground in front of them.

Cholera never ceased entirely. In July it killed off Mr Calvert, who at headquarters filled the office of chief of the Secret Intelligence Department. It would have been interesting to have had an account of his functions; security cannot have been among them, and it seems inconceivable that any moves by either side would not have been widely spoken of before they had even been planned.

Although some of Mrs Duberly's comments seem a little naive, and her attitude to war as a spectacle somewhat callous, there is no doubt that she was more humane and sensitive than many of her contemporaries. There is, of course, no doubt in her mind about her right to privilege and social position but at least she sees that responsibility should be accepted with rank, and human beings, as well as animals, should be treated with kindness. But, she noted:

At a little distance from us were riding three officers belonging to the

English cavalry, when we suddenly heard shouts and cries, and saw a Tartar running with all speed towards the three, holding up his hands, and apparently appealing for protection. The three rode on, until at last the Tartar, by dint of running, overtook them and tried to speak. With frantic gestures he endeavoured to induce them to listen, and with what success? Two endeavoured to ride over him, and I believe I am right in saying that one of the two struck him with his hunting whip; at any rate the arm was raised. As we rode homewards, I reflected on the vast superiority that exists in the civilized over the uncivilized part of the world; the latter true to the old world instincts implanted by nature, appeals from the weak to the strong for protection—from ignorance to education and Christianity; civilization (perhaps because he has not been introduced) rides over the man who is defenceless and wronged, or rids himself of him with the thong of his hunting whip. Let us sing *Te Deum* for civilization, Christianity, and the Golden Rule.

However, as she well knew, because she probably recognized them or at least realized their regiment, those three officers probably took excellent care for their horses, and reasonable care for their troopers, and would ride on another charge of the Light Brigade without considering it anything but their simple duty.

A more heartening story came from one of the divisional hospitals.

Lord Rokeby . . . going the rounds of the hospitals of his division to see the men wanted for nothing, recognized a man who had distinguished himself for steadiness in the camp and gallantry in the trenches. On being asked what was the matter, the poor fellow said: 'I've lost a leg, my Lord. I and my two brothers came out with the old regiment: the first one died at the battle of the Alma, the second one had both his feet frozen off when we were up at the front, soon after Inkerman, and died in hospital; and now I've lost my leg. 'Tis not much to boast of—six legs came out, and only one goes home again.

She continued to be fascinated by the battle although having certain setbacks:

9 September—Last night I was overcome with the shock of poor Buckley's death and felt so unhinged that I did not start for the front until eleven this morning. After some difficulty in 'dodging' the sentries which General Simpson, with his most unpopular and unnecessary policy, insists on placing everywhere, we reached the Fourth Division . . . but we were advancing on batteries, so we turned our horses heads

across the ravine, and rode up to the front of Cathcart's Hill, where we found the cavalry at their usual ungracious work of special constables, to prevent amateurs from getting within shot. Now, in the first place, amateurs have no business within range; and in the next place, their heads are their own, and if they like to get them shot off it is clearly nobody's business but theirs.

Yet she seems to be the only person to have grasped why the attack on the Redan failed. It was not, according to her, through using newly arrived unseasoned troops, but through the use of veterans.

Men who had been fighting behind batteries and gabions for nearly a twelvemonth, could not be made to march steadily under fire from which they could get no cover. As Colonel Windham said, in speaking of the assault, 'The men, the moment they saw a gabion ran to it as they would to their wives, and would not leave its shelter.' Why not have taken all this into consideration and ordered the newly arrived regiments to lead the assault?—the 13th Light Infantry and the 56th.

Why not, indeed? There were dozens of reasons. One of them was that the troops who were in the first line were not much less raw. Nobody, apparently, realized that once men become accustomed to using cover they look for it. The troops needed for the Redan were the infantry who had marched up the slopes of the Alma. But those who were left from those days—and there were not many—were now 'veterans'. A 'veteran' is an old soldier. He has survived, and knows that he has had a great deal of luck. He takes no unnecessary risks. After a time he endeavours to take no risks at all. He is a difficult man to lead because—without actually disobeying an order to come on—he is proceeding with caution, using every available bit of cover. He has seen it all before. The 'veteran' can be superb—or a disaster.

Mrs Duberly—as may be guessed—was soon into the Redan, the Malakoff and the rest of the town. Although 'of absorbing interest . . . I cannot wonder at my fatigue of last night, or my headache of today'. She 'stood by Mr Wright, on Sunday morning, when he read the funeral service over 700 at once.'

Her discerning eye was quick to appreciate the cunning of the Russian defences:

What wonderful engineering! What ingenuity in the thick rope-work, which is woven before the guns, leaving only a little hole, through which the man laying the gun can take his aim, and which is thoroughly impervious to rifle shot. The Redan is a succession of little batteries, each containing two or three guns, with traverses behind each division; and hidden away under gabions, sandbags, and earth, are little huts in which the officers and men used to live.

She observed a wounded English officer of the 90th Regiment who had been taken prisoner. With no food and no treatment he had gone mad, 'yelling and naked. I think the impression made upon me by the foul heap of green and black, glazed and shrivelled flesh, I shall never be able to throw entirely away—once perhaps the life and world of some loving woman's heart.'

It must have been an impressive sight, for she goes on: 'We turned quickly back from this terrible sight, and soon after left the town. Riding up towards the Little Redan, we saw where the slaughter of the Russians had principally been. The ground was covered with patches and half-dried pools of blood, caps soaked in blood and brains, broken bayonets, and shot and shell; four or five dead horses, shot as they brought up ammunition from the last defence of the Malakoff.'

The Malakoff was also 'a wonderful example of engineering'. 'It is so constructed that unless a shot fell precisely on the right spot it could do no harm. What with gabions, sandbags, traverses, counter-traverses, and various other means of defence it seemed to me that a residence in the Malakoff was far and away more desirable than a residence in the town.'

By now Balaclava too has changed. It is now 'fresh, healthy and even pretty . . . rows of trees are planted and down the centre street the railway runs, giving dignity and importance to the place. . . . I think the thanks of the army, or a handsome national testimonial, ought to be presented to Mr Russell, the eloquent and truthful correspondent of *The Times* as being the mainspring of this happy change.' With *The Times*, she also gave credit to other newspapers. 'Our best general, our most unflinching leader has been the Press.'

But, as she very well knew, the war was not yet over.

Many of those who fought in the Crimea subsequently put their memories, and opinions, on paper. Among them was Lord George Paget*. He too was greatly troubled about the Charge of the Light

* He had led the second line of the charge with the 4th Dragoons.

Brigade, although if he had realized that it would go down in history as a magnificent tribute to British courage rather than—as he saw it—a symbol of staggering idiocy, he might have been less concerned. Having delicately introduced this view with the words: 'While I am desirous of avoiding, as far as possible, all matters of controversy in this short sketch of the Light Cavalry Charge, my reluctance to tread on such forbidden ground would amount to an absurdity were I to omit all reference to what has, alas, been so notorious.' From this disarming beginning he proceeds to analyse what was said—or what he thought was said—and went on to explain what should have been said, so that the entire disaster might have been avoided. He considered that Airey was mistaken in choosing Nolan to take the order—a brave cavalry officer, doubtless, but reckless, unconciliatory and headstrong—ill-suited for so grave a mission. Nolan delivered the message 'to Lord Lucan in a tone and with gestures which could only have been expected by those who knew Captain Nolan's character (among whom should have been Sir Richard Airey).

'It were perhaps asking of human nature more than one is warranted in doing, or rather expecting, to censure Lord Lucan for not keeping his temper at such a momentous crisis, and under circumstances to trying to human passions but nevertheless I venture to think he might better have "risen" to the occasion.' He then gently turns so the supreme idiocy of placing Lords Lucan and Cardigan in the relative posts to which they were appointed, for the disadvantage to the service of this arrangement (however good an officer in himself each may have been) is apparent from the well-known relationship in which they stood to each other.'

This, of course, is a delicate way of saying they loathed each other most heartily.

Paget had considerable doubts whether Cardigan really knew what was going on in the charge, though Cardigan claimed he did. Paget clearly did not like Cardigan and went on to say: 'Lord Cardigan was a vain as well as an ambitious man, and his vanity led him astray when he came in contact with the admiring mob of London.'

On the other hand he felt that Lucan knew what he was doing: 'No cavalry man was ever heard to say anything against Lord

Lucan; all had respect for his military character, and all sympathized with him on his recall.'

At the end of his journal he gives a number of dispatches, messages and brigade orders. One of the latter shows that armies change little in their ingenuity:

> Eupatoria 22 November 1855
> 1. It appears that several casks belonging to the Government have been used by officers of the brigade for building stables, etc. This practice is for the future strictly forbidden. Those casks now in use must be returned to the commissariat, and if any are damaged or missing, they will be charged to the regiments.
>
> Officers commanding corps will be responsible that this order is carried out.

Nowadays the word would go around 'No more casks to be "liberated". It's up on orders. They mean it.'

Lt-Colonel Anthony Sterling, who served in the Crimean War, subsequently produced a book of letters entitled *The Story of the Highland Brigade in the Crimea.* They are extraordinarily vivid and interesting, partly because he has a lively and humorous style, and partly because he expresses a number of forthright views. Many of his opinions may have been widely held but few would have expressed them so frankly. His two principal targets were the Press and the Regiments of Guards. Of the former he wrote:

> The newspaper Press of England was required by the nation to supply perpetual information about military movements, and perpetual gossip about the routine in the camp. The gentlemen sent for the purpose did supply all this, to the best of their ability; but unfortunately the British people could not receive this information and this gossip without providing it also for the use of the enemy and for the astonishment and ridicule of our Continental neighbours.
>
> If the British nation chooses to have its army governed by the newspapers, the result must be that by degrees all the officers who reflect will, as it becomes possible, get out of the service. No army can succeed with such spies in its camp. No general can command when his character and conduct is canvassed openly by editors and while their remarks on both are soon broadcast among the soldiers. I do not believe that the outcry in the papers did any good. There is no doubt in my mind that the evils complained of would have been remedied as soon as possible whether the newspapers had taken up the question or not.

But, it seems, the greatest crime of the newspapers was that they did not campaign for the appointment of Sir Colin Campbell to be commander-in-chief when Lord Raglan died. At certain periods in every army's history it is felt that all the best appointments go to members of one or two regiments. This is not surprising; talent is not spread evenly throughout the army and it may be that one brigade has a better selection than another. Also, of course, it is inevitable that a senior officer will pick out and prefer someone he knows and can trust. Whatever may be said about these appointments—and plenty is—there is seldom criticism on grounds of efficiency, or if there is it is no greater than the general criticism which is levelled at all and sundry—that they are absolutely useless. It is an astonishing fact that a man can command a unit, small or large, with great dash, verve and skill, show outstanding courage and endurance, yet have the whole performance dismissed by his contemporaries as, at the best, 'It was about the only thing he could do.'

Sterling seems to have had a valid point in that the 'double rank' system of the Guards 'frequently put them in charge of older and more experienced officers. . . . But three of the captains are Guardsmen, consequently lieutenant-colonels in the Army, so that this command will not fall to the senior captain in the service, but to a young gentleman probably years his junior in age and experience, but who is only nominally a captain being in fact a lieut-colonel.'

A little later he is provoked by seeing Highlanders made to carry up shot for the Artillery and develops his point more forcefully:

> These *corps d'élite* will be much improved by a thorough reform; all the good things at Woolwich are monopolized by a family clique, who look upon the establishments there as belonging to their sons and nephews, so that it seems almost more provoking than the Guards' arrangements whereby the aristocracy have such a pull over the rest of the nation. That is part of the constitution. In the army here, there are thirty-nine battalions, each commanded by a lieutenant-colonel. There are here, likewise, three battalions of Guards, all the captains of which are lieutenant-colonels, and which battalions, including their commanding officers and majors, produce about thirty-three lieutenant-colonels, all of whom have the right to compete, and do compete successfully, with the thirty-nine Line men for employments in the highest Staff situations. As the Guards gain, by their privileges, a more rapid promotion to the rank of lieutenant-colonel than usually falls to the lot of us poor working soldiers, the in-

equality is the more felt. If there is to be a privileged corps it should be composed of officers and men picked out; the first, not for being of good families, but for distinguished service; and the latter not merely for being six feet high.

Sterling was an extraordinary mixture of indignation and compassion, humour and obtuseness. He laments the death of his friend Eliot 'his poor wife, now twenty-two years old, will be confined in December. All his money lost with his commission, and the most she can hope for is a pension of £80 a year.'

But there are certain features of the war for which neither the Guards nor the Gunners can be blamed.

The mistake that has been made has been a very common one in our country, viz, not keeping up certain military establishments in peace, because people took it into their heads that war would never come. In France there is a permanent waggon-train always organized, a permanent commissariat, and also a permanent ambulance; these three departments hang very much upon one another. The English people having destroyed these above-named departments, which existed during the Spanish War, or which rather were then formed, its Government, on deciding upon war, should have instantly begun to organize them again. This is a matter of time as well as money; there has now been time enough allowed to slip away; but nothing is really organized yet.

And this when our army belongs, not only to the richest country in the world, but to the country richest in horses and ships. Many of the Staff and general officers were appointed from interest. It seemed either that Lord Raglan did not expect war, and so gave places to anyone who had influence, or if he did expect war, he intended to do all the work himself. . . . Estcourt was pitch-forked into the important office of adjutant-general, with high pay and powers; but his business is discipline, which he endeavours to combine with amiability; a most charming man in private life, but quite out of place here.

About the achievements of the Highlanders he is becomingly modest. At the Alma: 'The men never looked back and took no notice of the wounded. They ascended in perfect silence and without firing a shot. On crowning the hill we found a large body of Russians, who vainly tried to stand.'

Of the 93rd at Balaclava he wrote, 'The little 93rd stood fast and fired away. The cavalry could not bear the fire, and swept off to their left, trying to get round our right flank, and cut in on the Turks. But

C. wheeled up the Grenadier Company to the right, and peppered them again, and sent them away with a flea in their ears.'

In view of the appalling condition under which men lived—or died—it may seem astonishing that morale should be high. But it was:

All our poor soldiers out here, however, are in the highest spirits, and ready to knock their heads against any wall behind which they can find Russians. They are the true England; stars whose brillance will be historical when aristocratical names are forgotten, or covered with immortal shame. I believe they would fight and die to the last man in this wild Tauris, rather than give in and give up. Beaten they never can be. Remember they are not chosen; a great majority entered from poverty or misconduct. What an army would conscription give us.

Possibly morale was high throughout the army because conditions were seen to be the same for all. These are the situations when true leadership tells, when the leader has no privileges additional to his men, other than having more work and responsibility. Russell said:

The oldest soldiers never witnessed nor heard of a campaign in which general officers were obliged to live out in tents on the open field, for the want of a roof to cover them, and generals who passed their youth in the Peninsular War, and who had witnessed a good deal of fighting since that time in various parts of the world, were unanimous in declaring that they never knew or read of a war in which officers were exposed to such hardships. They landed without anything but what they could carry, and they marched beside their men, slept by them, fought by them, and died by them, undistinguished from them in any respect, except by the deadly epaulet and swordbelt, which have cost so many lives to this country. The survivors were often unable to get their things from on board ship. They laid down at night in the clothes which they wore during the day; many delicately nurtured youths never changed shirt and shoes for weeks together, and they were deprived of the use of water for ablution, except to a very limited extent.

'Rank and fashion' under such circumstances, fell a prey to parasitical invasion—an evil to which other incidents of roughing it are of little moment. The officers were in rags. Guardsmen, who were 'the best style of men' in the Parks, turned out in coats and trousers and boots all seams and patches, torn in all directions and mended with more vigour than neatness, and our smartest cavalry and line men were models of ingenious sewing and stitching. The men could not grumble at old coats, boots, or shoes, when they saw their officers no better off than themselves. We had 'soldiering with the gilding off', and many a young gentleman would be for ever cured of his love of arms if he could but have seen one day's fighting and have had one day's parade of the men who did it. Fortunate it was for us that we had youth on whom to rely, and that there were in old England men 'who delight in war' and who would be ever ready to incur privation, danger and death at her summons.

That was in November, but the effects of the comradeship in mutual dependence sustained the Army till the end of the campaign. But by the spring the whole supply situation had changed:

> From hunger, unwholesome food, and comparative nakedness, the camp was plunged into a sea of abundance, filled with sheep and sheepskins, wooden huts, furs, comforters, mufflers, flannel shirts, tracts, soups, preserved meats, potted game and spirits. Nay, it was even true that a store of Dalby's Carminative, of respirators, and of jujubes had been sent out to the troops. The two former articles were issued under the sanction of Dr Hall, who gave instructions that the doctors should report on the effects. Where the jujubes came from I know not; but had things gone on at this rate we might soon have heard complaints that our Grenadiers had been left for several days without their Godfrey's Cordial and Soothing Syrup and that the Dragoons had been shamefully ill-supplied with Daffy's Elixir.

While the British were being supplied with jujubes however the Russians were being supplied with reinforcements, as soon became apparent.

Sterling had considerable foresight, although his predictions were not always entirely correct:

> Patience in tax-paying cannot endure for ever; you will all be tired of the war. Russia will quietly slip back to Sebastopol, build new ships, scheme new schemes, and some fine morning, when we are all republican, a sudden pounce will place her at Stamboul. I cannot believe that any amount of calamity will break up Russia. It is a great nationality—not to your taste no doubt but such is the fact. No enemy will dare invade her territory, beyond such small nibbles as we are making.

Florence Nightingale, who was so widely and justly praised, incurs his annoyance for her ability at obtaining combat-fit soldiers to use as nursing orderlies at Scutari.

> It is really too bad. Why do they not form a corps expressly for this duty. We are now obliged to take our finest men, just as if they were

going on guard, and we are forbidden to relieve them. The same men are compelled to remain until they become sick, then we are ordered to replace them. But our chiefs are so pusillanimous that they submit, for fear of being attacked in the papers.

He returns to the subject of morale. Referring to the Malakoff he says:

The Russians had a mine, which it only required two days' work to complete, when they would have blown up the whole of the French advanced trenches. The French were driven back three times. Vinoy's strength of character kept his men to their work. He planted his sword in the ground near the flag which was hoisted at the gorge of Malakoff, and, with revolver in hand, threatened to shoot at any one who retired behind the sword.

Of the Russians he said: 'Their officers behaved admirably; their men showed great endurance; but they want the intelligence of the French. All that teaching can give, they have, but they are only serfs after all, and cannot in the long run stand against free men.'

He believed that stocks of courage could be exhausted but then built up again:

A wise general will never employ troops in a ticklish operation who have been much punished previously. Place them in reserve; their self-respect is preserved, and they gradually come to again. The greatest, and also the rarest, valour is shown by troops which can bear to be beaten day after day, and yet come again. To do this you should have old soldiers, and not mere boys. Some martinets, who have seen nothing but parades in England, imagine that a boy put into a red coat becomes wood and iron. There is as much art in maintaining the courage of soldiers as in preserving their health; in both arts, Campbell, from long experience, as well as natural aptitude, is a master. The bravest have always most compassion, and make the most allowance for youthful nervousness.

This account has been concerned with the front-line war, and is an attempt to present it as the author believes it to be—that is, an achievement, not a disgrace, of the British Army. It also reflects great credit on the French and Russian armies, as will have been realized. It was a great triumph for the British Army for it was not its own fault that it had been run down, shorn of its vital ancillaries, and dumped in a disease-stricken port, but it was by its own efforts that it won battles in spite of the most impossible handicaps. As a saga of human endurance the Crimea has few equals. All those concerned were fighting at a vast distance from their homes, in a climate which suddenly went from one extreme to another, crammed into a confined space, with no lofty ideals to inspire them. These were the great achievements of the war, not the devotion of Florence Nightingale, nor the gallant Charge of the Light Brigade, nor the brave stand of the 93rd; of those three the last was the only one which could have had any real effect on the outcome. Unfortunately, many people have been given the impression—though not from the books listed in the bibliography—that most of the British Army perished in the Charge of the Light Brigade, and the remnants were nursed back to health personally by Florence Nightingale.

The war was a great tribute to the skill, improvisation and tenacious courage of all the armies concerned, British, French, Russian, Sardinian and Turkish—even the last, as the account of Kars should testify. In one sense everyone was a victor, for all triumphed over the ravages of weather and disease, and also over their own handicaps. It was man against weather, man against disease and man against man. It ranks with the trench warfare of the First World War, with the Somme and Passchendaele, and the desperate struggles of the Second World War such as Alamein, Stalingrad and Imphal. There are times when men stand and fight, defying heat, cold, disease and despair, and carry on fighting. It is unlikely that they are sustained by war aims, by thoughts of a higher standard of living, a balanced budget, a democratic constitution, or—in the Crimea—the keys to a church in Jerusalem which none of them would ever visit, if they survived. They are there to fight, and that is what they will do. Afraid to die, but more afraid to show it, unaggressive and unproud, they will kill and be killed, suffer and endure, and win or lose because that is all, at that time, they are employed to do. This is what they did in the Crimea, and did superbly well, but, sad to say, the achievement of the ordinary soldier has been obscured by more glamorous though less important events, by scandals of mismanagement and corruption, and by stories of medical horror which took place hundreds of miles from the battlefields.

But the Crimean War produced many real and lasting results, even if the curbing of Russian ambition was only temporary. It led to widespread reforms in the Administration of the British Army. A new organization called the War Office was created (cynics may say this was worse than the horrors of Scutari!) and it comprised the old War Department, the Artillery, Engineers and Ordnance (from the old Civil Board) and Supplies and Commissariat, which had been a Treasury responsibility. There was an end to the ancient system of colonels organizing the supply of clothing to the men under their command and instead it would be provided centrally from an Army Clothing Factory. Small arms would be produced from Enfield, which had already given its name to the rifle that had begun to replace the Minié, and which in its time would produce millions of highly accurate and reliable weapons for the soldiers of two world wars, as well as for countless peacetime marksmen. Training camps were established at the Curragh, Colchester and Aldershot; this last has for long proclaimed on notice boards at the entrance to the town 'Home of the British Army' but recently has begun to replace these notices by the bleaker statement, 'Aldershot Military Town'. For those who returned from the Crimea it was indeed home, for that was where they first went into camp.

Three important training establishments were created. The most important was the Staff College, at which officers who had had some years of experience of regimental soldiering could train for three-year appointments on the Staff. The lack of adequately trained staff officers had been particularly felt in the Crimea. The other establishments which would make a valuable contribution to army efficiency were the School of Musketry at Hythe and the Gunnery School at Sheerness. From these modest beginnings numerous other 'arms schools' would be inspired.

The medical services saw the greatest and most far-reaching changes. At the outbreak of the war the Army Medical Department consisted of a director-general and 163 officer surgeons; this was expected to cope with the world-wide commitments of the British Army. As it was scarcely managing to do that in peacetime it is hardly surprising that it ran into considerable difficulties from the very beginning of the Crimean expeditions. Casualties were meant to be carried from battlefields by the Hospital Conveyance Corps, but this consisted of such feeble members that they were hardly able to get themselves from one place to another, and, in consequence, bandsmen or even the doctors themselves did most of the work. Florence Nightingale achieved wonders of reform, not because she worked twenty hours a day at Scutari during the winter of 1854–

magnificent achievement as that was—but because she brought pressure to bear in places where reforms could be made. In a profession whose previous members had been thought to be the social equivalent of whores she was something of a phenomenon. She was a personal friend of Lord Herbert of Lea, the Secretary at War, and gave him no peace till he did what she wanted. In 1857 she was put in charge of an inquiry into the health of the Army, and was soon deep into such matters as food, clothing, and housing. Her recommendations were the basis of subsequent reforms, long though some of them were in taking effect. Two that were implemented earlier than the others were the establishment of the Army Medical Board at Netley, near Southampton, and the establishment of the Nightingale Training School for Nurses, which she opened at St Thomas's Hospital in 1860.

Our knowledge of events in Sebastopol is all the greater for the presence of William Simpson whose sketches made the scene familiar to many, and Roger Fenton, the first really effective war-time photographer. Fenton arrived in February 1853 and concentrated on photographs of everyday life. Being aware that his admirers at home might be upset very easily he avoided horrifying scenes. James Robertson, who arrived in the Crimea the following autumn, was an enthusiastic amateur photographer, who took a number of pictures after the fall of Sebastopol. Some rather inferior photographs were also taken at the time by G. S. Lefevre.

Approximately twenty-five years after the event it celebrated, there was formed the Balaclava Commemoration Society. It came into being, as Rule 2 states, 'for the Purpose of Assembling Annually the Survivors of the Charge of the Light Brigade at Balaclava 1854, including 1 Troop Royal Horse Artillery'. Nobody could become a member unless he was actually present on the field of action. Rule 5 said 'That a Dinner of a private character shall be held on the 25th October annually', and Rule 7 'That each member shall pay the sum of Five shillings to meet the expenses of the Dinner.'

The survivors and their ranks are listed. Of the 4th Dragoons 118 set out and 39 returned from the Charge. Of those lost, some were wounded and taken prisoner, although the majority were killed. They had 53 members. The 8th Hussars were 104 strong, of whom 38 returned; there were only 32 surviving in 1877. The 11th Hussars set off with 110, of which 23 came out, but many of their wounded survived, and they managed 69 members. The 13th Light Dragoons, who were in the 1st line, set out with 130, of which 61 returned. They could only find 36 members in 1877. The 17th Lancers were 145 when they set out, and only 35 returned. However some were wounded and taken prisoner and as a result they mustered 63. 'I' troop was not listed. The printed lists contain occasional notes, such as that next to Major R. de Salis, of the 8th Hussars. It runs 'Retreated on foot, leading his horse with a wounded trooper', and a note at the bottom of the 17th Hussars lists–'Sgt Talbot, K. rode on headless.'

The booklet contains a number of poems: Tennyson's 'Charge of the Light Brigade', three by Lydia Melland, of Edinburgh, one being 'To the Memory of our Noble Leader Lord Cardigan'.

> And still he chafed to lead us on
> Until the fatal day
> When down that Northern Vale we rode,
> Fought death and tore away
> And showed the world what soldiers mean
> By that short word 'obey'.

Whether the authors, if male, of any of the other poems were present on the original battlefield is not disclosed. One poem concludes with the words:

> Long may our Navy be supreme
> Nothing our Army e'er degrade
> And 'The Six Hundred' be the theme
> To cheer some future 'Light Brigade'.

In these appalling poems lies much of the reason why the Crimean War has been so badly distorted. The 'Charge' and the 'Thin Red Line' were an open invitation to every heroic ballad-monger. This book was written in order to put the record straight and to set out in proportion the glamour and the squalor, the incompetence and the skilled management, the loss and the gain, of one of the most extraordinary wars ever fought by the British Army.

# 11

# The War Elsewhere

The Crimea was only one part of the Allies' war with Russia, although admittedly the major theatre. There were other theatres which will now be examined.

War, like any other event, is a reality in many different ways. The reality of the results of the Crimea in political terms has been fully discussed elsewhere, and is therefore only lightly touched on in this book. The reality of the war in medical terms was—as often happens in wars—to give tremendous impetus to medical science and discovery. Of this more later. The reality of the war in terms of human experience is much more difficult to assess, and this book makes no attempt to do so, merely presenting situations and leaving the reader to judge. It has been said that no one can understand the mind of the medieval knight. It may not be impossible, but is certainly difficult. It is however probably no less difficult to understand the mind of the Crimean cavalryman, even when displayed by the sensitive and discerning letters of Temple Godman. This book neither condemns nor excuses, and although any process of selection of letters or papers might well be considered to be an attempt to influence, the purpose here is to give the reader an opportunity to make his own assessment.

### *The Baltic*

First then to see the Crimean War in its entirety. Although Sebastopol was an important Russian naval base it was not the only one—there was also a considerable fleet in the Baltic. At the start of the war it was clearly important that this Russian shipping should not be allowed to add its contribution to that in the Black Sea. The task of preventing this was given to Admiral Sir Charles Napier, who, coincidentally, was the same age as Lord Raglan. It may seem strange that, in a period when the expectation of life for the unmoneyed was nineteen years, and for the moneyed only thirty-five, these two should even have been alive at all, let alone in command of powerful armed forces. British naval resources were, as may be expected, in little better shape than the land forces, but this did not prevent Napier from trying to blockade the Baltic outlets; it did however prevent him from trying to attack Kronstadt, which at one time he was rumoured to be about to do. He was well aware of the strength and complexity of the Kronstadt defences.

He concentrated on three main areas; the Gulf of Finland, which was the most important, the Gulf of Riga and the Gulf of Danzig. In the early stages a few minor raids were mounted which did little damage to either side. In the summer of 1854, before the land battles of the Crimea occupied the public's mind, there was considerable interest in what the fleet, now joined by eleven thousand Frenchmen, could manage. Napier was a highly experienced officer and did not underrate his task (he had ample courage but it was tempered with commonsense). He therefore directed his efforts at the more suitable, but not by any means inconsiderable, port of Bomarsund in the Ahvenanmaa Islands at the mouth of the Gulf of Bothnia. It was not a particularly glittering prize, and it was well defended by guns and masonry. A preliminary bombardment was made in June 1854 but not followed up; it was in the nature of a trial run but served for little but to alert the Russians of Allied intentions. A second attack was made in August, during which two parties were landed. Casualties were high but the attack was successful and the town surrendered. Although a success, it achieved nothing of any real value. When the winter settled down there was, of course, no opportunity for further conflict.

The following summer saw naval hostilities renewed—but not with Napier. He had been replaced, not for incompetence, but because of what was thought to be an indisciplined attitude to his lords and masters in the Admiralty. He had complained bitterly about such matters as Minié rifles being supplied without ammunition. Somewhat oddly, in the opinion of many, his command was given to Admiral Dundas, who had not exactly proved himself a spectacular success in the Black Sea. Nevertheless Dundas was a better man than many thought, and he had enough experience of bombarding from the sea to realize how remarkably unsatisfactory that process was. Although he was quite firm about the impossibility of attacking Kronstadt (which had sunken ships around it like Sebastopol) he was persuaded that it would be reasonable to launch an attack on Sweaborg. Sweaborg was a complex of fortified islands surrounding the main fortress of Vargon. An Allied fleet moved into position and poured every shot it could manage on to every fortification men could see. This went on for three days, by which time all ammunition, guns and personnel were exhausted. There was no question of a landing; the operation merely served to show that the Allies were in force in the Baltic and Russian ships would venture forth at their peril. Neither this, nor a short blockade of Archangel, nor an abortive attempt to land in Kamchatka, had the slightest effect on the war.

There were many suggestions as to how the Russians might be impeded in their northern ports; one was that in the winter trenches should be made by breaking up the ice, thereby effectively locking the Russians in. The ingenuity of this suggestion was matched by one in the First World War to throw a black searchlight beam on to the moon, and thereby hinder the Zeppelins.

### *The Kars Campaign*

One of the most successful naval operations, though it had no effect on the war, was the raid on Kertsch and the Sea of Azov. Here there was a ready-made target of numerous dockyard installations. The joint Anglo-French expedition had a bad start because just before it was due to attack the French portion was recalled by Canrobert (4 May 1855). Twelve days later he resigned and handed over to Pélissier: the Allies set off again and after a successful landing burnt large quantities of Russian stores (25 May to 14 June 1855).

Considerable activity–and writing about it–occurred at Kars, at the eastern end of the Black Sea where Turkey and Russia had a common frontier. Indeterminate battles took place between Russian and Turkish forces in the summer of 1854 and although the Turks had by no means the worst of the encounters they deemed it prudent to fall back on Kars, which was an ancient fortified city. In September 1854 Colonel Frederick Williams, RA, was sent with a small staff to act as liaison officer but at the same time to exert as much control as he could tactfully do, if he deemed it necessary.

It did not take Williams long to decide that the most appropriate action was to take over the entire force and to reorganize both the Army and the defences of Kars. Neither of these tasks was easy, both of them were impeded by the inherent corruption, inefficiency and apathy of the Turkish Army. Soon, however, he found that the potential was good and that if the Turks were properly organized and led they became very useful soldiers. His progress in reorganizing the defence was, however, much facilitated by the arrival of Colonel Attwell Lake, an experienced engineer from the Indian Army. These and other officers, notably Major Teesdale, General Guyon and Captain Thompson, achieved great success though in view of the size of the task in front of them they could hardly feel confident.

Eventually, after some preliminary skirmishing, Kars came under siege in June 1855. Although well aware that the best course for a besieged force normally is to harass the attacker, Williams decided that the morale and quality of his force did not justify the inherent risks of such an action. Fortunately the Russians did not seem disposed to try their luck in all-out attack and the months dragged on with very little action. The Russians had vast superiority in numbers, and appeared to have decided that there was little point in fighting for what starvation would soon put into their hands. As cholera broke out among the garrison it seemed that this must happen at the end of the summer. However, it did not, and at the end of September, when Sebastopol had fallen and the beleaguered garrison had hopes of a relieving force, the Russians attacked. With a vast superiority in numbers it seemed inevitable that the Russians must win but they were disconcerted by the number of casualties they sustained—a figure given as six thousand—and broke off the engagement. The siege of Kars continued, with both sides so weak that no further action could be taken. Unfortunately the garrison had been so weakened by starvation that they were incapable of a break-out, and Williams, not wishing to see the entire population of Kars die around him in the coming winter, surrendered the town. He and his companions were agreeably surprised to find how well they were treated.

Lake considered that Kars was an important post as it was 'the key to Asia Minor'. In his book *Kars and Our Captivity in Russia* he gave his observations in an amusing but astringent style. Speaking of Williams he said:

He had to inspire courage and confidence in men who had been in the previous year signally defeated by the Russians in the battle of Kurukderi, and who had encountered such disasters and been so cruelly plundered of their pay by those in command of them, that desertion had become an everyday occurrence, and who were disorganized and demoralized to the last degree. Twenty-four months pay was due to them and their uniform was in rags.

It is so painful to reflect on the obstacles which we encountered in the corruption and bigotry of the Turks in command that I prefer not dwelling unnecessarily on the subject. Of the several branches of the Army the only one in a satisfactory condition was the artillery. Ibrahim Bey was an officer who thoroughly understood his duties, and was at the same time not too self-opinionated to adopt the suggestions of others.

Anything more lamentably wretched than the state of the cavalry cannot be conceived. Their swords were too short, their lances too heavy, their uniform torn and tattered, and their horses old, worn out, and therefore useless, and the men themselves such indifferent horsemen that they could scarcely keep their seats. So little had they been drilled that they could as easily have written an epic poem as perform an adroit manoeuvre.

He blamed this on the higher command saying 'some of their officers were ignorant even of the words of command. Such is the result of a system in which men are raised to high posts in the army through nepotism and favouritism.'

But he went on:

The Turkish soldier, I must again repeat, is a brave, loyal, long-suffering, hardy fellow, and if well-led, is inferior to no soldier in the world. The national decay occasioned by the venality, the rapacity, and intrigue combined with the indolence and the sensualism of the higher orders of Turkish officials, has scarcely yet reached the overworked, ill-paid and maltreated commonalty, who are often preserved by their very poverty and sufferings from the crimes, vices and abominations, which degrade their social superiors.

However, Lake, Williams and others, managed to pound the Turks into military shape, and when the Russians attacked and 'nothing could be more perfect than the handling of the enemy's army as it advanced upon the front of our entrenchments', it must have been a pleasure to see that 'The spirit of the Turkish troops was excellent, evincing as they did, as much readiness in the defence as they had shown in the construction of their epaulements. If the enemy had attempted to carry his original intention into execution he would, I confidently believe, have met with signal disaster.'

The Turks continued to improve and, in the final battle, drew high praise. Williams wrote: 'If only we had possessed a few hundred cavalry we should have utterly destroyed their [the Russian] army; their losses in officers had been enormous, and they behaved splendidly; three were killed on the platform of the gun in Tachmasb Tabia, which at that time was worked by Major Teesdale, who then sprung out and led two charges with the bayonet; the Turks fought like heroes.'

Williams, who did not give praise lightly added that 'The mist and imperfect light of the dawning day induced the enemy to believe that he was about to surprise us; he advanced with his usual steadiness and intrepidity, but in getting within range he was saluted with a crushing fire of artillery from all points of the line; this unexpected reception, however, only drew forth loud hurrahs from the Russian infantry as it rushed up the hill on the redoubts and breastworks.'

These opinions of the Russian and Turkish fighting qualities were not long-distance guesswork; the British officers earned the respect and devotion of their men not only by showing them how to drill, shoot and manoeuvre but also by fighting alongside them with rifle and bayonet:

. . . these battalions, joined to those directed by Lieut-Colonel Lake, gallantly attacked and drove the Russians out of the redoubts at the point of the bayonet after the artillery of the enemy had been driven from their lines by the cross-fire directed from Fort Lake, and from Arak-Tabia and Karadagh, by Captain Thompson. This officer deserves my best thanks for having seized a favourable moment to remove a heavy gun from the eastern to the western extremity of Karadagh and with it inflicted severe losses on the enemy. During this combat, which lasted nearly seven hours, the Turkish infantry, as well as artillery, fought with the most determined courage; and when it is recollected that they had worked on their entrenchments, and guarded them by night throughout a period extending to nearly four months; when it is borne in mind that they were ill-clothed, and received less than half a ration of bread, that they have remained without pay for twenty-nine months, I think your Lordship will admit that they have proved themselves worthy of the admiration of Europe, and established an undoubted claim to be placed among the most distinguished of its troops.

The fighting qualities of the Turks are, of course, well known. Just before the British party arrived morale, efficiency and organization were probably worse than they had ever been previously. Lake, Williams, Thompson, Teesdale and others organized and led them with that peculiar paternal brand of leadership that achieved so much success for British arms in the nineteenth century. Sheer professional efficiency and courage were part of the magic but these alone would not have aroused the devotion that existed in many units. (The Indian Mutiny is always held as an example of the falsity of this belief but as any close examination of the Mutiny shows it proves the exact opposite; the Mutiny occurred when the system was altered and agitators were able to exploit the omissions.) The secret was something which appears to be noticeably absent from present-day discussion on man-management. It was an acceptance of responsibility, and a genuine liking for the people a man led. In these days of independence and false values of self-importance, it would be very hard to re-create the same feeling—although crisis and hardship—as in the London blitz—might do so. This peculiar feeling of interdependence and liking existed, of course, throughout the entire army—even though punishment was excessively harsh and distinctions of rank and privilege were very marked. It existed within the cavalry but not usually between the cavalry and other units. Even Cardigan was part of it—otherwise his men would not have followed him. It is quite credible that he did say, as he was alleged to at the end of the ride, 'It was a stupid thing to do', and equally probable that his men replied 'Never mind, my lord, we would do it again.'

Captain Thompson's letters from Kars show a tolerant sense of humour:

I am getting very tired of water as a beverage and begin to be of Mr H's opinion that a bottle of it *well-corked* ought to last a lifetime.

We have a capital cook who compounds messes for us, which I look at with aversion, and eat with considerable awe. I never venture to inquire of what animal or vegetable they are manufactured; I live principally on tobacco. I am much interrupted by the children here, who will knock at my window, and consume my substance in the way of pennies or piastres. Two of them have taken a great fancy to me and bring me fresh eggs daily for breakfast.

Thompson threw some light on the peculiar problems of expatriate wives:

What do you think of *this*. We have a real European *lady* in Kars. She is the wife of one of the Hungarian officers here. She only arrived yesterday, and I hastened to throw myself at her feet, and commence immediate worship. Poor creature, she must find it dreadfully dull here. She does not smoke or drink grog, so I don't know what she is to do. She can't drill troops, can't talk English, and hasn't got a piano. She is rather pretty, but as she is already married we poor wretches have no chance. I think we must ask the General to send her back to Constantinople.

In June 1855 Thompson was reasonably confident about the outcome of the siege: 'I am convinced that the Russians can never take Kars, as long as our ammunition lasts, and I think it will last longer than their provisions.'

Thompson thought that the fall of Sebastopol was imminent and the Russians would therefore give up the attempt to take Kars. What he referred to as 'a good skirmish' had taken place the previous week. The Russians put in a sizeable attack 'large masses of troops' preceded by Cossacks. The Cossacks drove all before them, then 'came right under my guns and began throwing rockets into our cavalry. But their fun was of very short duration for, under the General's direction, I opened upon them, at about 800 yards, with several large guns. They must have lost more than 150 men. Our loss was 14 killed and 24 wounded. We sent them to the right about directly and they retreated to their camp. They had very few wounded, as cannon balls at that distance generally kill if they hit at all.'

The neglect of this theatre by both sides is one of the most extraordinary aspects of the war. Had the Russians really applied themselves they could have turned Sebastopol into a secondary theatre, causing unbelievable confusion to the Allies. Thompson summed it up:

If the English do land troops at Anapa or Batoum we shall winter at Tiflis. This is certain but there is such a painful forgetfulness of our existence on the part of both the Turkish authorities and those of the Allies, that one would imagine there was no army here, and that Kars was not the key of Anatolia. If the Russians take Kars there is not a *single regiment* between them and Constantinople, and hardly the means of procuring troops, except from the Crimea, so you imagine what a fight we must make of it.

But, although the hardships were glossed over, it was a strenuous time:

7 pm 20 June. This is most harassing work. I have not had a good night's rest for a long time. We are obliged to get up to visit our outposts and pickets, and as there are only two to do the duty, we have to be out four hours, and sometimes more, every night of our lives, and to make it more agreeable it rains here continually. It is raining dreadfully at the present moment, and in three hours I shall have to mount my horse and ride in the dark over hills that few men would like to face in broad daylight. My interpreter, a young Hungarian, told me the other day, that it was his belief that *Der Herr Gott* had rained stones here at some previous period, for the whole country is one mass of them, large and small.

It was an extraordinary war, tough and brutal but at the same time chivalrous. For Thompson and his friends it was very frustrating:

We are placed here in a very tenable position, but with a lamentable lack of all necessaries of war. We are very badly off for ammunition, food, and clothing, and our army is in a sad state of discipline. The Russians are encamped on the other side of the valley in our front, about two miles and a half at most, and are only I think prevented from attacking us by the heavy ground in the valley, caused by the almost incessant rain we have had for the last ten days. Our communications with our rear are almost entirely cut off, and our last English post was captured by the Russians. General Mouravieff very politely sent us in our private letters; but all newspapers and dispatches he has kept, bad luck to him!

(A modern general would probably be more suspicious of private than official correspondence—and with good cause.)

We have here, of all arms, some 18,500 men, many of whom are irregular troops utterly innocent of all drill and discipline. The Russians have 24,000 but have even more irregulars than we, and theirs are mostly slaves from the Mussulman population of Georgia, who will desert to our side the moment we attack. I have the command of one of the largest forts here, with 3,500 men and seventeen guns, and I mean, please God, to hold it. We are very anxious to hear some further news of Sebastopol, as our fate depends very much upon that.

Then, as he has emphasized before, he repeats:

There is not a single soldier now between Kars and Constantinople, and we must hold the place until the Russians walk into it over our bodies, or the alternative is that we leave an open road to Constantinople and endanger all the Black Sea forts. However, I hope to come home and show you another medal in addition to my Burmah one, and that will repay me for the hard work of Kars. I have not had a dry thread on me for nearly a fortnight.

By the end of June Thompson was still cheerful, though under strain. 'Mouravieff [the Russian General] won't fight us, and won't go away, and is making himself altogether obnoxious and unpleasant.'

There is an odd aside in this letter. Some lady friend must have criticized the condition under which he received a wound in the Burmah war for he says: 'Tell S— that if my wound was not received in battle I am anxious to know what she considers a battle; as on that occasion we lost two officers, and twenty-seven men killed and wounded. On receiving her answer I will try to get up a battle according to her definition, and then perhaps she will be satisfied.'

By July the situation was getting worse:

It is a most melancholy state of things; the Seraskier and authorities at Constantinople appear to care nothing for General Williams's requisitions; we have not got siege ammunition for a week. The poor soldiers never get their full rations, and many of them are twenty-eight months in arrears of pay. While such things are going on, it is a wonder to me that the soldiers don't lay down their arms, or desert by thousands; but strange to say desertions are rare, and the men are in the best spirits. I think they are the finest soldiers (or stuff to make soldiers of) that the world can produce. Nothing comes amiss to them; they are literally in rags, and yet they never complain, although they are nearly always wet through. It would astonish you to see a regiment of them on parade. You could hardly pick out a worse lot from all the beggars in England.

Unless we get *English or French* reinforcements in a month or two, you may give up all chance of seeing my beloved countenance again, for there will not be a man of this army left alive. If the Russians don't kill us we shall die of starvation, which is not by any means a pleasing alternative.

Our communications are almost entirely cut off and the country swarms with Cossacks and Armenians (who are all hostile to us). Write me a long letter soon, with nothing but *nonsense* in it and believe me ever yours . . .

In mid-July he is still hoping that the Russians will come to the attack, when the fortress guns might inflict a defeat on them. But the Russians manoeuvre without attacking. Clearly their objective is to decoy the defenders out of their citadel; equally clearly the starving garrison is not going to be lured out. But there are lighter moments: 'I have just received, as a guest, a small and very emaciated cat, which suddenly appeared from some unknown region, and took up its quarters on my table. I fear it must shortly have its nose dipped in the ink, if it does not leave off making these insane darts at my pen, to the great detriment of my handwriting, as you may see.'

Cats in beleaguered fortresses have varying fortunes. Some disappear into cooking-pots, others are petted and cherished. In the National Army Museum they have stuffed an enormous cat which was found in the ruins of Sebastopol. It was quite tame and survived the siege by some two years. It is like a miniature tiger.

Thompson was nothing if not a realist:

They say that 17,000 men are on the march to our relief from Batoum, and 12,000 more from Trebizond, but these are all Bashi-Bazooks, and we are much better off without them, as they will only consume our provender, and run away on the first opportunity.

You may imagine what a state this army is in from the following circumstance. Yesterday I ordered my horse to go into the town and forage for some barley, when my interpreter, who is a lieutenant in the Turkish Army, begged to be allowed to remain behind. On my inquiring the reason the poor fellow told me he had received no pay for eighteen months, and that he owed 400 piastres in the town, and consequently his creditors insulted him on every occasion. Can you imagine such a state of things. I have given him the money, about £3 4s od, and he can now hold up his head.

Thompson was liked by the Turkish command, although he himself had little respect for them. However he realized there was nothing to be gained by showing it:

The Musir Pasha has just been up to my battery. He always takes hold of my beard and calls me baba (son) which makes me highly indignant but as the old man is very fond of me, and that is his way of expressing it, I am unable to resent it by taking a good pull at his, which I am often inclined to do. He says he will make whoever tried to turn me out of the command of these batteries eat an unlimited quantity of dirt, and that their parents' graves shall be defiled, which is, of course, highly gratifying to me.

During August when the flies were so plentiful they clogged up the ink-bottle he mentions he had acquired a young bear as a pet. Although short of food he had various medicaments that had been sent to him, to ward off coughs and colds. As he was at the time suffering from neither, he decided to eat the pills and drink the liquids as a preventative. He had mixed the camphor infusion and was preparing to drink it when he found that the young bear had upset the tumbler, and was enjoying himself very much licking up the remains on the floor. 'The poor bear was very sick but I have not felt any of those symptoms of giddiness to which you allude.'

On 27 August there was a faint hope that the coming of winter—with snow—would cause the Russians to lift the siege: 'We have now been fourteen weeks invested, and the Russians are not nearly so sure of taking Kars as they were at first. We have plenty to eat till help arrives, and if the snow will only come down a little earlier than last year we may laugh at the beards of the Russians.' The food may have still been plentiful but it was clearly not to his taste: 'I made a glorious salad yesterday out of an old cabbage, which was eaten with much relish. That little cookery-book which E— gave me has been of much service.* My breakfast has been just sent away untouched, being of too disgusting a description for even a hungry man to eat. The rice was intermingled with small stones about as big as swan-shot, and the meat and eggs were so highly oleaginous and dusty that they had been cooked I suppose upon the kitchen floor.'

Part of the strength of British influence was their reputation for integrity. He wrote:

We have received intelligence today that Omar Pasha, at the head of a large army, is about to land at Batoum. When I see him and his army I

* Soldiers on active service are addicted to carrying around cookery books; even if they do not use them they enjoy reading them—and dreaming.

will believe it. The Turks say, 'It must be true because an Englishman has written it' which I take to be a great compliment to the veracity of our countrymen. They say the French and the Russians are the fathers of lies, but that an English private soldier will always speak the truth although he gets drunk and abusive at times. While I was at Constantinople I do not think I saw more than three English soldiers tipsy, whilst I saw hundreds of 'foreigners' rolling about the streets.

On 29 September the Russians attacked. Thompson saw five battalions of Russian infantry, sixteen guns and three regiments of dragoons move in to attack the English batteries, which they did successfully. They were then well within artillery range, however, and were eventually driven out:

Some seven or eight hundred Russian fell here, and I lost some twenty or thirty killed and wounded. They had nothing but small field pieces with them and I had large guns, or the event might have been different, but my thirty-two pounder carried more than double the distance that their guns did.

It has been a most bloody affair. They say we shall be attacked again but I cannot believe it. However, we are all on the alert, in case such a thing should occur, and the Russians will get a worse drubbing than they did before, if they try it on again, for our fellows are in such spirits now that they will fight like so many tigers. The fight lasted for seven hours and a half, and the roar of artillery and musketry was terrific. . . .

I went over the field as soon as I could leave my post, and found the ground completely covered with dead bodies. In some places they were actually lying in mounds, heaped one over the other, mostly smashed to pieces by our guns.

This battle was considerably bloodier than many other better-known encounters. In his letter from Kars, Thompson gave the figures: 'I suppose you have heard of our attack and likewise of the way we whipped the Russians. Up to this morning we have buried 6,250 bodies and more still remain. This is no exaggeration, but sad and solemn truth. Our killed and wounded amount to about [illegible],200, all told.' (This was, of course, over twice the casualty rate of the Charge of the Light Brigade.)

Thompson's last letter was dated 30 October. What happened to him is not easy to discover, although Lake refers to him as 'my late lamented friend' in 1856. Apparently he survived captivity in Russia.

Letters from Colonel Lake and General Williams tell much the same story. Teesdale continued the account after Kars fell. His letter on 29 November was headed 'Russian Camp, near Kars' and ran:

> The game has been played out and we are prisoners. . . . Still, even in our degradation, I cannot help feeling that the disgrace lies with those whose duty it was to help us; and not with us, who, I believe in my heart, have done what men could do. The Russians have gained half a province, and would have had the greater part of Armenia, without a struggle, had not our resistance been sufficiently prolonged to let the winter be far enough advanced to prevent any more operations.

Teesdale, like many others, was deeply incensed at the lack of Allied help and appreciation for their efforts:

> Have the Allies ever thought, I wonder, how much it would have cost them to redeem all this ground, or what they will have to pay, even for what we have lost. The whole business passes my comprehension, and I can scarcely yet believe that all our trials have ended thus; that six months of endless toil, misery, privation, and, at last, moral agony, should have such a termination.

In the context of the Crimean War, with its peculiar strategy, the neglect of Kars is, of course, perfectly understandable. Unfortunately, or perhaps fortunately, the defenders of Kars were unaware of the strategy and tactics elsewhere. Perhaps it was just as well that they did not realize that Sebastopol could very well have fallen in the late autumn of the previous year, and their painful experiences been avoided completely. However, once the opportunities of 1854 had been missed and Sebastopol settled down to its long siege, the defence of Kars was of great importance. That it was not recognized as such at the time, and has hardly been noted since, does not make it any less significant.

It was important not only strategically but also in terms of mutual understanding. Lake wrote:

> On 28 November 1855, the Turks laid down their arms. It was with the greatest difficulty that they could be persuaded to do so. The brave fellows wished to die at their posts, although worn out by famine, privations, and hardships. Indeed it required no little tact to prevent a serious disturbance, which might have thwarted the favourable intentions of our generous enemy; for the Pashas and superior-officers of the Turks were

far from being contented with the conditions granted by the Russian commander-in-chief.

However, as prisoners-of-war they fared well. There are several references to 'a plentiful supply of wine' and on one occasion Lake remarks: 'at the next day's dinner we were superbly treated—their champagne sparkled in our glasses, and claret gurgled forth from the decanter with that gushing music so peculiar to the best of wines.'

Conditions were not always so pleasant but rarely became harsh. Their journey into Russia provided some interesting experiences, such as arriving at Karshowar on New Year's Day. '. . . the whole village was drunk. Every man was distinctly and unmistakeably intoxicated, and it is to be hoped, and is indeed strongly suspected, that the men had not been so ungallant and selfish as to exclude the women and children from their share in the excitement. There were no teetotallers in Karshowar.'

# 12

# The Aftermath

The Crimean War was not limited to the Crimean area, or the attack of Sebastopol. Undoubtedly Sebastopol was important, but there were other theatres elsewhere, where the war could have been lost by the Allies. Kars was clearly one of them as was seen in Chapter 11 and it is worth considering–though not here–what might have happened had the Russians decided to renew their attacks through Moldavia and Wallachia.

In assessing the Crimean War and the armies that fought there, the public mind has been greatly influenced by the highly dramatized accounts of the sufferings that took place. Much of the criticism has been focused on the medical services, which were quite unable to cope with the strain put on them. Even without cholera and other epidemics the medical service would have been hard put to cope. The 'hospital' in Scutari, an old Turkish barracks, was of course appalling. Whether the smell there was worse than from the Thames at the same time might be debatable. Whatever sewers there were in London all discharged into the river and it was said that it was impossible to work in the Houses of Parliament in summer because of the smell from the Thames, even though the windows were kept closed. Although bad smells–with the exception of that from farmyard manure–were thought to be unhealthy there was no understanding why this might be so. Only after the Crimean War was over did Pasteur and Lister prove that microbes and bacteria existed; viruses were a discovery for the distant future. However, even if they had been known and understood it is unlikely that the knowledge would have made much difference to the Crimean War.

Surgery, as far as the battlefield was concerned, consisted mainly of amputation. The nearest approach to Crimean War surgery that has occurred in this century would be the operations carried out in the Thailand jungles on prisoners-of-war working on the Bangkok-Moulmein railway. Jungle ulcers, mainly caused by bamboo cuts, were widely prevalent and would frequently rot away the flesh down to the bone. Sometimes maggots would obligingly eat out the rotting flesh; at other times the few hard-pressed doctors would try amputating. There were, of course, no facilities for anything, no proper anaesthetics, antiseptics, dressings, bandages, nor any means even for sharpening the few and inadequate instruments. Nevertheless, many of the patients recovered, and this in spite of the fact that they probably also suffered from malaria, diarrhoea, beri-beri and general emaciation. In order to reduce the shock of the operation the surgeons worked with tremendous speed. Chloroform had, of course, been invented ten years before the Crimean War broke out but was not used very much; there was a suspicion—well founded—that some patients who might otherwise have recovered died because of the anaesthetic. 'Yell and get well' was considered to be preferable to 'Sleep, and have your relations weep.'

It seems likely that most people were much less sensitive to pain and of course discomfort, than they are today. They were perhaps a little nearer to animals, which can sustain deep and jagged wounds and yet soon appear to sleep reasonably comfortably. Civilized living undoubtedly weakens a person's capacity to endure pain but after a certain time, in conditions which prevailed in the trenches in the First World War, and in certain theatres, for example Burma, and Italy in the Second World War, people began to recover a certain immunity to pain and discomfort—although it might not actually stop them complaining. However, even though you may not complain about conditions of wet, cold, undernourishment and disease, it does not mean that they will not kill you—as the Crimea showed.

Surgeon-General Longmore, who conducted an inquiry into the medical service in the Crimea, produced some surprising information. His, and other reports, showed that many of the deaths could have been prevented had the administration been better. The total number of British deaths in the Crimea was 18,058. Of these 1,761 died from enemy action, the remaining 16,297 from disease. Of those who died of disease 13,150 died in the first nine months. The figure of 1,863, for those who died in the second nine months of the war, was only three-fifths of the number of those who died in barracks in England. This latter figure may be partly explained by the fact that those left in England would naturally include the sick and the infirm but it still is a surprising statistic. As the average strength of the British forces in the first nine months was thirty one thousand the mortality rate in the Crimea during this period was therefore sixty per cent. This was greater than the mortality rate had been in England during the great plagues. The mortality rate in the Crimea in the second half of the war was lower on average than it was at home.

The explanation is not difficult. When the initial shock of the news of Crimean mismanagement reached England public indignation was enormous, and took a practical form. Reforms were instituted and the conditions of the Army were improved by both governmental and private means. The Army was soon well accommodated, well clothed, and well fed.

The French Army, by contrast, had almost an exactly opposite experience. During the first nine months the French health record —although they too had cholera—was far better than the British. This seems to be accounted for by the fact that they were better cooks, and more skilled at improvising—when there was anything to improvise with. In the second winter, when the British sickness rate fell away to a negligible figure the French soared. This was explained subsequently by the following facts. Whereas the British were well housed and hutted during the second half of the war the French were still under canvas; the French Government was by this time losing interest in the war and was cutting back its expenditure; the wretched French troops therefore saw their situation becoming worse rather than better. Secondly, French field hygiene was well below the British standard. There is only one standard for field hygiene of course, and that is that it must be perfect. Nothing else will suffice. Latrines, drains, grease-traps, camp discipline must all be regarded with meticulous care. Obviously British standards also fell a considerable way short of perfection but there was enough stored-up knowledge gained in fighting across the globe from Canada to China, from the bitterness of the Arctic to the fever-laden swamps of the Tropics to have given the British Army a knowledge of the requirements of field hygiene that was second to none—as the pamphlets and booklets which it has produced over the last hundred years will amply testify. It was not always implemented at the start of campaigns but after a few sharp lessons all necessary steps were taken. The French however were unfortunate in that they had typhus to contend with in the second winter, and this took a devastating toll. Nevertheless, with all these factors taken into account it still remains somewhat of a mystery that the sickness rates for the two armies should have varied so greatly under such similar conditions.

There were of course many visitors to the battleground after the last shots had been fired. Codman, whose *American Transport in the Crimean War* was quoted earlier, could hardly believe his eyes as he travelled up the road from Balaclava and on to the Woronzoff Road. 'For the last two miles the ground was literally covered with balls and shells which had been fired from the Malakoff and Redan.' The situation inside Sebastopol was of course much worse; there the shot and shell fragments lay so thick that the entire road surface was made up of them. Looking at the Mamelon Codman said of the final rush—when 'the English were exposed to such a storm of shot as had seldom before been faced by an army':

Standing there now it was difficult to imagine the possibility of its accomplishment even if the thousands of dead, who had been thrown into the ravine, had already been there to lessen its depth. We first entered the Redan, and there, as afterwards at the Malakoff all preconceived notions were dissipated. Instead of granite walls of masonry there were barricades of sand-bags, more formidable and more easily repaired than fortifications of stone.

The estimate of the plunder found in the city has been much exaggerated, the inhabitants having long before removed their money and valuables to places of safety in the country. The prey that remained was distributed in a ratio of two-thirds to the French and one-third to the English, each of whom made the Sardinians a small allowance. The Turks got nothing, it being supposed that they owed the whole of their share in gratitude.

Ascending a quarter of a mile we stood upon the Malakoff, the key of Sebastopol. From its summit was the most comprehensive view, and the whole field of operations could be taken in at a glance. The tower of the Malakoff, of which so much has been said, was nothing but a small stone battlement, whose foundation only remained. The earthworks were like those of the Redan, excepting that they consisted of baskets of dirt and of the rigging of dismantled ships instead of bags of sand. The position far exceeded that of the Redan in size, strength, and ability for desperate resistance. In both forts, as well as everywhere else in the vicinity, the ground had been ploughed up by shells, which must have cost the lives of thousands of the brave defenders.

Turning around and looking beneath we could see the long zig-zag lines of attack, those of the French reaching to the base of the Malakoff.

At the right and facing the Redan were the English works uncompleted in their length. By Pélissier's order the English were obliged to storm the Redan under a disadvantage not shared by the French; for they were forced to run down a hill into the ravine, and thence to attempt an ascent which proved to be impossible. Nearly all were mowed down by the Russian guns and fell into this valley of the shadow of death, which became a vale of mortality made almost level with the bodies of the slain. The English were compelled to retreat. But the Redan was evacuated in the night, and they entered it unmolested in the morning.

Yet unbelievably in this maelstrom of human sacrifice there were conventions:

By a tacit understanding, the dinner hour had been respected during the siege, and both parties were allowed to dine quietly, and after a suitable allowance of time for pipes and cigars, fighting was resumed. It was therefore justly considered an affront by the Russians when this conventional truce was broken by the other side, and the French commenced the scaling of the Malakoff, just as they were sitting down at their noonday meal.

Codman had a few shrewd comments to make on the closing stages of the war, of which he said:

The English were opposed to a speedy termination of hostilities, while the French were anxious to bring them to a close. The élan with which they had gone into the war had long since subsided. On the other hand, the mistakes the English had made, and their suffering in consequence of them, had taught them some salutory lessons. In short it may be said at this period that the French had become tired and demoralized, whereas the English, with bull-dog pertinacity, had got themselves into good fighting trim. The French were ready to leave off; the English were ready to begin afresh. The news was therefore hailed with joy by the French, and received by the English as a bitter pill that Napoleon obliged them to swallow.

Codman considered that Napoleon III was well aware that his forces were spent and any further victories would be won by the English. He added this somewhat surprising statement about Napoleon III:

> From first to last his army had not only been fighting the Russians, but it had been engaged in humiliating the English, and this process was as much a source of satisfaction to him as were his victories over the common enemy.
>
> The land forces of the French being the most numerous, their generals naturally exercised a greater control. This was made manifest in things both great and small. It was a luxury for the French to supply the deficient commissariat of the English, and it was their policy to place them at a disadvantage in battle, as they did in the culminating event of the war, when, as has been already related, the English were repulsed at the Redan while the French triumphantly scaled the Malakoff. French and English alike held the Turks in derision. All three of them had a greater respect for the Russians than for each other.

These anti-French views appear to have been written when Codman's contract with the French had been terminated, and he was employed by the Turks. Nevertheless—as with his earlier remarks which were not particularly favourable to the British—they represent a widely held view. But he claimed no authority for his conclusions. As he put it: 'They may not be those of the historian, the statesman, or the politician. They claim no such authority. They simply emanate from the quarter-deck of an American transport steamer.'

But this particular onlooker saw enough of the game to see who was winning and why. He noted that the English Navy was infinitely superior to the French in seamanship: "It was a study to see an English and French line-of-battle ship or frigate coming to anchor together. On board the former, silently and as if by magic, every sail was furled at once before the Frenchmen could man their yards and gather up the bunts, chattering all the while like a lot of magpies, and all apparently giving orders to each other.'

Although '1855 was still the era of sailing ships in the navies as well as in the mercantile marines of the world—a surviving era of a now almost forgotten seamanship . . .' the English made a 'rude beginning' [to the introduction of iron-clads] in the war:

> Two iron-clads were sent out from England in tow, although they had limited steam-power of their own. They were wooden vessels plated over with iron sheets not more than an inch thick, with open bulwarks, and

decks rounded up so that a shell might roll into the water in case it did not immediately explode. They floated almost as low as rafts. At the reduction of Kinbourn the masts were taken out of them, and they were towed as far as it was prudent for the tugs to accompany them, and then they propelled themselves under batteries which they successfully silenced.

The Navy made a small but very important contribution to the war in the Black Sea.

Almost its only use was to prevent the exit of the Russian fleet from Sebastopol, which would have been disastrous to the seaports in its neighbourhood occupied by the Allies, and to the transports that brought their supplies of men, munitions, and provisions.

As for the Russian fleet, it had accomplished its purpose of annihilating that of the Turks at Sinope before the Allies made their appearance in the Black Sea. After that, it retired to the harbor of Sebastopol to await the course of events. When the fortune of war at last went against the Russians, as we have seen, their ships were scuttled and sunk.

Sebastopol had fallen, the Russians had been ready for peace talks for some time, yet the war dragged on for a further six months. The campaign had virtually petered out but the problems that had caused it were still unsolved. The Russian Army had evacuated Sebastopol but this was by no means synonymous with its being annihilated; on the contrary it had merely withdrawn to those areas north of the town about which there had been so much controversy, but which were no longer in their former weak state. At one point it looked as if the campaign might begin all over again—with certain modifications. The Allies could land again at Eupatoria and move south, there could be a second Battle of the Alma, and the flank march would take place as before but this time it would be from south to north instead of the other way.

None of these possibilities occurred. Although the French had put in a major effort they had little real interest in the war, and having achieved the distinction of capturing the key point in the defences (the Malakoff) they were happy to think about peace terms. Unfortunately for their army these were long in coming into being, and having suffered nearly as badly as the British Army during the previous winter they suffered even more in the one that followed. By this time the British Army was properly fed, organized and employed. It was in many ways a vastly different army from the one that had borne the brunt of the war, and superior in every way except that of courage which we have already seen to be unsurpassable.

By 1856 there were many developments that few would have envisaged at the beginning of the previous year. In order to make up what was thought to be the required numbers, a volunteer force of soldiers of fortune was raised from overseas. Germans, Italians, Swiss and even Americans joined this force, which eventually totalled ten thousand although less than half ever went to the Crimea. Ultimately the British expeditionary force numbered close on a hundred thousand and was an efficient, balanced, well-supported command. In the public mind to this day the Crimean War was a futile struggle of a disease-ridden army, dying like flies, whose only redeeming feature was the gallant charge of the Light Brigade. The truth was of course, very different: the Charge of the Light Brigade was of no importance whatever except perhaps as a symbol of the courage which made the British Army face impossible odds and usually win through. The great achievement of the war was the rapid and miraculous transformation of an obsolete system, which had not been used for forty years, into a highly efficient up-to-date force, while at the same time not losing any battles, as the Alma, Balaclava and Inkerman showed. It demonstrated the vital importance of marksmanship, first with the Minié but later with the Enfield which replaced it—that would be used with deadly certainty in 1914. There would of course be other mistakes; there would be set-backs in India, in Zululand and South Africa, but the Crimean War served a vital purpose in that it checked the decay which might have ruined the British Army and made it quite unfit for its future tasks.

The same was not true of the French Army. It is difficult to judge whether the cause was that the French Army was less affected by the Crimean experience than the British Army had been, or whether the benefit it gained was dissipated by the follies of Napoleon III. Whatever the reason, it needed the stinging defeat and humiliation of 1871 to bring French military thought back into focus.

But although the war did much for the British and little for the French it had—as it was bound to have—much wider effects. One of them was to involve Britain in a war with Persia. While Britain was engaged in the Crimean War—and apparently by no means having matters her own way—the Shah of Persia had decided that now was the time to increase his own prestige at the expense of Britain, and improve his standing as a world power by a successful war. The former he decided to do by being offhand to the British Minister; the latter by invading Afghanistan and capturing Herat. As soon as the Crimean War was over Palmerston lost no time in teaching the Shah what he felt to be a suitable lesson. The ensuing brisk little war in which the Shah's army was soundly beaten at the Battle of Kooshauh came to an end in March 1857, but this too had repercussions, for the army which had beaten the Persians was drawn from India. Had India not been so drained of British troops the Mutiny might not have occurred. Without following this chain reaction any further it will be appreciated that any war has far-reaching effects; some good, some bad.

An interesting side-effect of the Crimean War was that it facilitated the union of Italy. Cavour's contingent of Italian soldiers did sufficiently well at the Battle of the Tchernaya to enable Sardinia to take a justified place at the ensuing conference table. The Peace of Paris which ended the Crimean War in March 1856 gave little apparent support to the unification of Italy and its freedom from Austrian domination, but Cavour was satisfied enough, for he realized that Napoleon III was in sympathy with his aims. Three years later Sardinian and French armies were once more fighting side by side but this time against Austria, and with Italian independence the ultimate goal.

The interests which the war was mainly meant to further were less affected than they might have been. The terms of the final treaty were that the Black Sea would become neutral, it would be open to merchant ships of every nation, but not warships, and the Danube would be open to all countries. Neither Turkey nor Russia would be permitted to build fortifications on the shores of the Black Sea. Russia was forced to give up her protectorate over the members of the Greek Orthodox Church in Turkish territory. Russia also had to hand over to Turkey a strip of territory at the mouth of the Danube (Southern Bessarabia) which effectively pushed the Russian frontier back from that area. To make the humiliation of Russia more complete the other powers agreed collectively to guarantee the independence and integrity of the Ottoman Empire, that is to support the Turks against Russia no matter how badly the Sultan behaved. The effects were not precisely as envisaged by the peace-makers. Russia was indeed humiliated but her reaction to that was to bide her time and to expand to the east until a further opportunity came along by which she could once more turn her attention to the west. She used the time well, and when in 1871 Napoleon III was crushed by Prussia, the Tsar had no hesitation in repudiating the Treaty, re-fortifying Sebastopol*, and rebuilding the Black Sea fleet. However, to have kept Russian expansionist aims in check for fifteen years was no slight achievement. There were other far-reaching effects—or perhaps at this stage it would be fairer to call them influences; they were the unification and rise of Germany and the disintegration of the Austrian Empire.

Yet in the general denunciation of the follies and incompetence of the Crimean War, which has been fairly consistent over the years, one vital fact appears to have been overlooked. Russian expansion was contained. Not until over a hundred years later did her ships appear in the Mediterranean; had the Crimean War not been fought and won by the Allies they might have appeared half a century earlier.

* The wrecks in the harbour had been cleared by an American engineer, and the task took six years.

# Maps

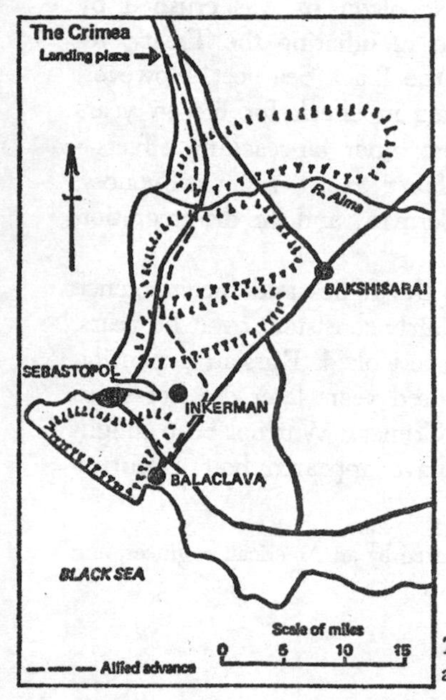


*The Crimea* Sites of the main battles and the line of the Allies' advance

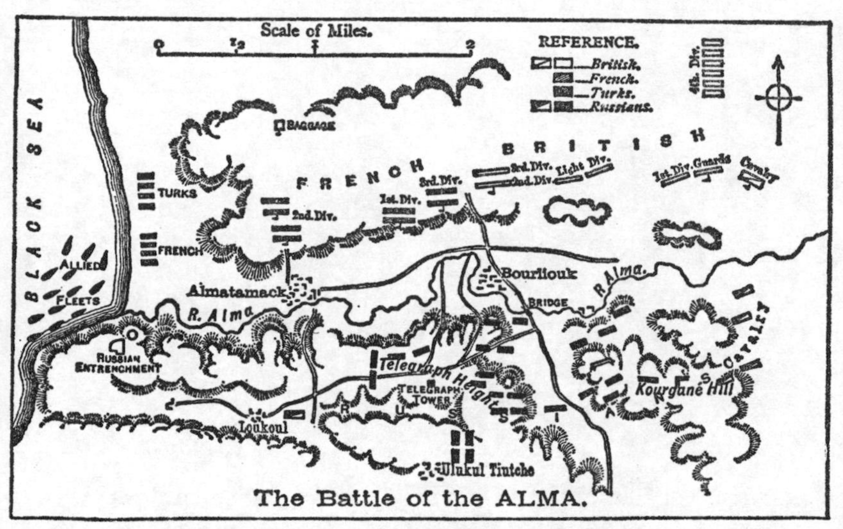


Plan of the Battle of the Alma, 20 September 1854

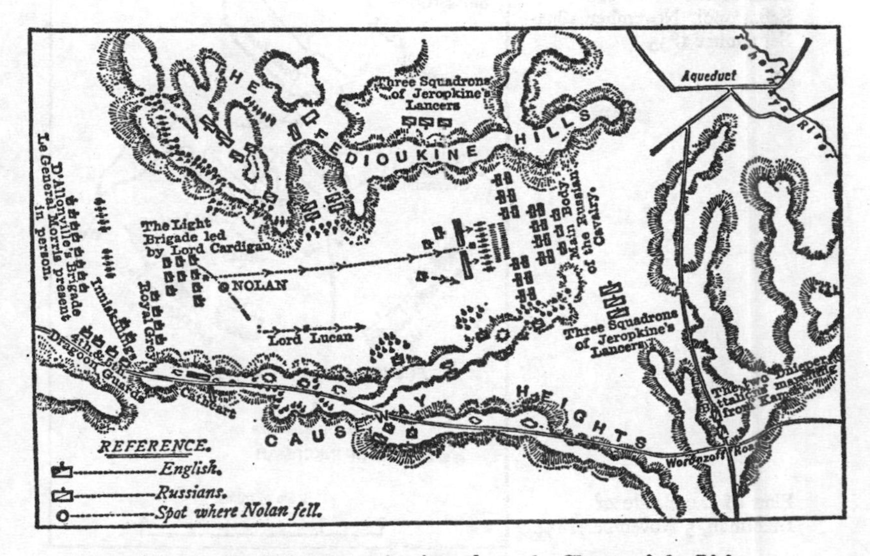


Plan of the Battle of Balaclava, showing, *above*, the Charge of the Light Brigade, and, *below*, the Charge of the Heavy Brigade, 25 October 1854

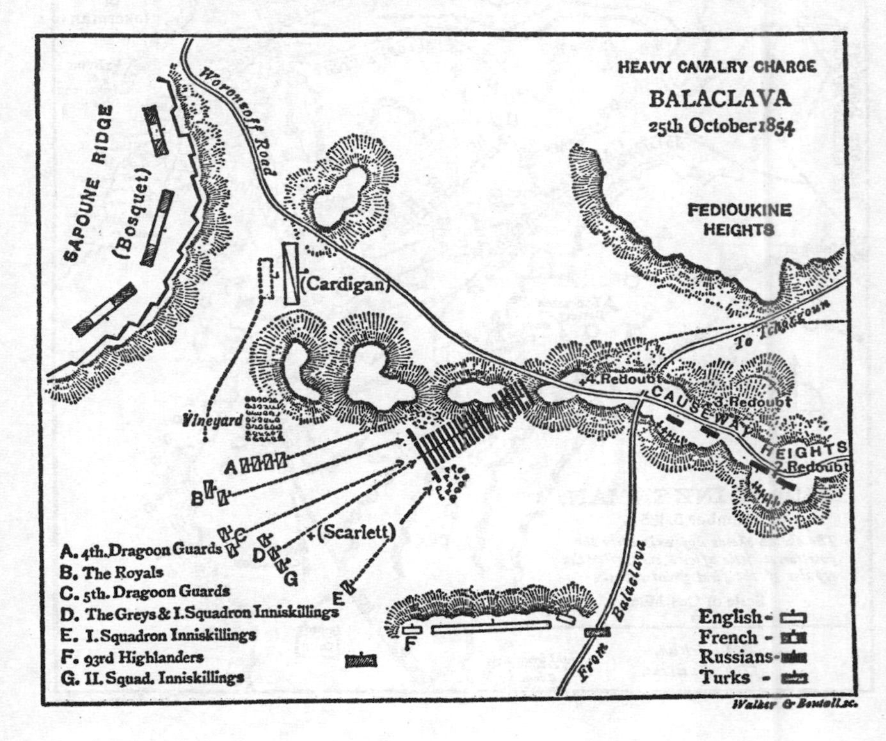

Plan of the Siege of Sebastopol, November 1854–September 1855

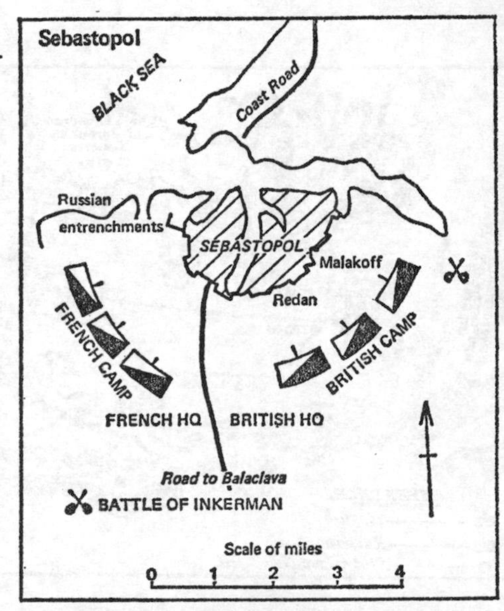


Plan of the Battle of Inkerman, 5 November 1854

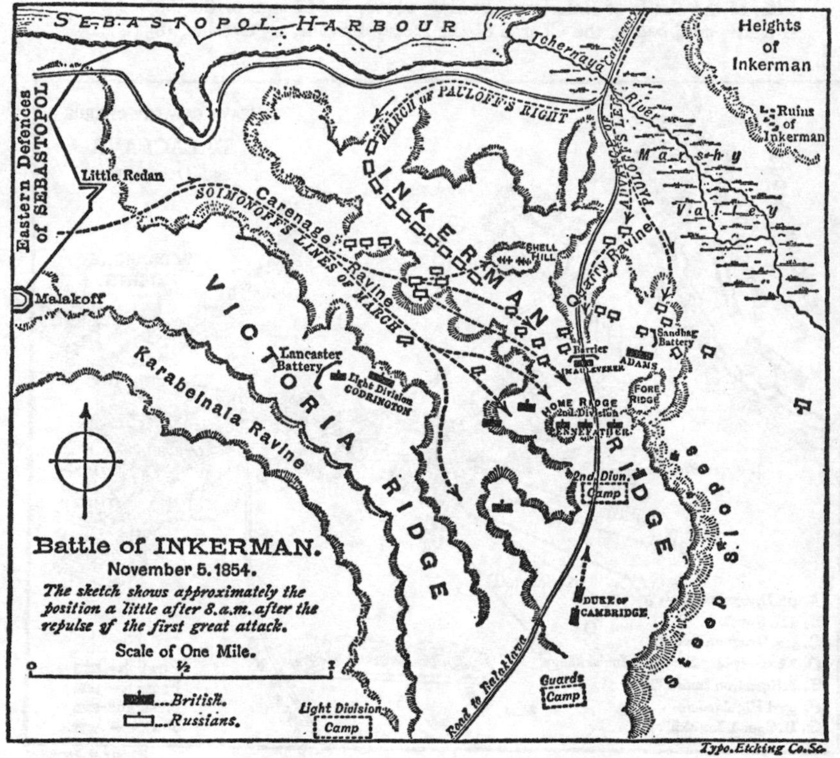

# Select Bibliography

ADYE, Lt-Col J. *A Review of the Crimean War* (London 1860)
ANON. *Memorials of Capt. Hedley Vicars (97th Regiment)* (London 1865)

BARKER, A. J. *The Vainglorious War 1854–6* (London 1970)
BONHAM-CARTER, V. (ed). *Surgeon in the Crimea: The experiences of George Lawson recorded in letters to his family 1854-1855* (London 1970)
BRACKENBURY, G. *The Campaign in the Crimea* (2 vols) (London 1856)

CALTHORPE, S. G. J. *Letters from Headquarters; or the Realities of War in the Crimea* (London 1856)
CHESNEY, K. *Crimean War Reader* (London 1960)
CLIFFORD, Sir H. H. *Henry Clifford, V. C.* (London 1956)
CODMAN, J. *An American Transport in the Crimean War* (New York 1896)
COOK, R. W. *Inside Sebastopol* (London 1856)

DUBERLY, MRS H. *Journal Kept During the Russian War* (London 1855)

FALLS, CAPT. CYRIL (ed.) *A Diary of the Crimea by George Palmer Evelyn* (London 1934)
FENWICK, K. (ed.) *Voice from the Ranks* (London 1954)

GIBBS, P. *Crimean Blunder* (London 1960)
— *The Battle of the Alma* (London 1963)

HAMLEY, GENERAL SIR E. *The War in the Crimea* (London 1892)
HIBBERT, C. *The Destruction of Lord Raglan* (London 1961)
HODASEVICH, CAPT. R. *A Voice from Within the Walls of Sebastopol* (London 1856)
HUME, MAJOR-GENERAL J. R. *Reminiscences of the Crimean Campaign* (London 1894)

KINGLAKE, A. W. *The Invasion of the Crimea. Its Origin and Account of its Progress down to the Death of Lord Raglan* (8 vols) (London 1887)

LAKE, COLONEL A. *Kars and Our Captivity in Russia* (London 1856)

MCMUNN, LIEUT-GEN SIR G. *The Crimea in Perspective* (London 1935)

PAGET, GENERAL LORD G. *The Light Cavalry Brigade in the Crimea* (London 1881)

*Bibliography*

PEARSE, MAJOR H. *Redan Windham, The Crimean Diary and Letters of Lt-General Sir C. A. Windham* (London 1897)

RUSSELL, W. H. *The British Expedition to the Crimea* (London 1858)

SELBY, J. M. *The Thin Red Line* (London 1970)

STERLING, LT-COL A. *The Story of the Highland Brigade in the Crimea* (London 1895)

TOLSTOI, COUNT L. N. *Sevastopol* (trans. from the Russian by I. F. Hapgood) (London)

VIETH, F. H. D. *Recollections of the Crimea Campaign & the Expedition to Kinburn* (Montreal 1907)

WARD, S. G. P. *The Hawley Letters* (London 1970)

WOODHAM-SMITH, MRS C. *The Reason Why* (London 1953)

YOUNG, BRIG. P. *Diary: Sir John Burgoyne of Sutton 1854* (London 1951)

# Index